This book is dedicated to the memory of
Henry Dietrich Fernandez
1950–2009
and
Kari Jormakka
1959–2013

THE FOUNDING MYTHS OF ARCHITECTURE

KONRAD BUHAGIAR
GUILLAUME DREYFUSS
JENS BRUENSLOW

Artifice

CONTENTS

PREFACE

Konrad Buhagiar, Guillaume Dreyfuss and Jens Bruenslow

In the opening scene of Pier Paolo Pasolini's *Medea* the centaur confronts Jason with the crisis that inevitably awaits him, a crisis embodied in the timeless question: how can man reconcile the two vital forms of perception, the mythical and the rational?

It is precisely an interest in this dichotomy, and particularly in the intersection of mythological and modern, or more explicitly rational, consciousness,[1] that initiated a symposium in Malta on the theme that inspired this book.[2] With this as a beginning, *The Founding Myths of Architecture* has become a collection of writings which explore the overlap between these two visions and their relation with architecture by analysing several of the multifarious reconstructed or imagined origins of architecture throughout time. In doing so, the essays trace startling trajectories, drifting through geographical, historical and anthropological fields, and criss-crossing one another's paths with many unpredictable points of contact and overlap. In spite of this, they represent only an infinitesimal fraction of the ideas, thoughts and theories which lie in the bottomless well that the subject calls to mind.

Formal and technical controls have today come to form the foundation of the architect's discipline, the relentless progress of architectural technology and practice having become an irresistible seduction to architects everywhere. As a result of this distraction, the profession has maybe unconsciously, but surely regrettably, relegated the authentic values of architecture to a subsidiary role, and has concentrated its unequivocal attention on the pragmatic or diagrammatic science of building.

Marc-Antoine Laugier's *Essai sur l'Architecture*, 1753, was instrumental in steering architecture away from the notion of a theory reduced solely to an *ars fabricandi*.[3] In his preface, he distanced himself from the rational architectural principles of Vitruvius and his followers and strongly advocated the need to penetrate the mysteries of architecture. He argued that this could be achieved by providing a theory of architecture which is grounded in a philosophical discourse derived from the dialectic between science, nature, art and society.

This was a timely reminder that there can be no moving forward without a re-evaluation of the origins of architecture and its role as a bearer of symbols. Architectural history, theory, creativity and criticism cannot exist in Laugier's view without an understanding of the founding myths of architecture, those that recount the origins of man and his relationship with the environment.

Indeed, in spite of the unremitting erosion of the deeper meanings of architecture, the need to stand back and rediscover its roots has consistently re-emerged from time to time. Laugier's primitive hut as a symbol of the architecture of man in an idyllic and natural state became, in this context, the most significant representation of the quest for the true meaning of architecture that took hold of the imagination of architects and philosophers at different times.

Paradoxically, however, the only certain conclusion that emerges from this research is the ineffable quality of the origins of architecture. This deduction reinforces Derrida's questioning of the assumption that beginning has a simple unity. Origins have complex and articulated structures whose genesis is the result of a destabilisation process admitting and encouraging reinterpretation.[4]

In this reversal of the classical authority of essence over accident, Derrida, like Nietzsche before him, stresses the Dionysian aspect of the Dionysian/Apollonian dualism in art.[5] His theory opposes the Platonic principle of an original essence and essential forms, thus preparing the way for a more complex and inclusive understanding of the origins of architecture.

One of the aims of this book is to unearth a sense of the anthropomorphic mysticism which permeated architectural theory in different periods and which can provide a much needed anchor to a profession steadily challenged by commercial pressures and advancing building technologies. It intends to induce this consciousness by offering a few insightful studies on the survival of ancient myths, and the creation of modern ones, that have been a source of inspiration throughout the ages.

Myths, as Barthes attempted to prove, are invented for a reason, sometimes political, often social and cultural, exploiting the inexorable link between origins and the modern-day to reinforce argument and give force and meaning to choice.[6] In architecture, these myths resurface from time to time in a spontaneous, but nevertheless consistent way. They are present in theories and buildings of protagonists as distant in time as Vitruvius, Alberti, Sullivan or Le Corbusier.

To some degree, this is proof that the freedom gained from the birth of reason has not fully substituted a spiritual vision of reality embedded in myth consciousness. On the contrary, this freedom provides hope that the mythical and the rational can coexist and contribute both to depth and meaning in today's architecture and architectural discourse.

As with all things in life and, more so, mythology, no account ends with a hopeful and optimistic glimpse into the future were it not for all those characters and spirits seen and unseen who stand by our heroes, assisting them to confront and overcome all the obstacles and challenges that appear on their path. It has not been any different with this book. It is in this spirit, albeit without the ambition of completeness, that the editors wish to thank Vannessa Eggert and Claire Maurel in Arles and Kristine Eggert in London for their admirable translations of a number of the essays presented in this book from French. We are grateful to Alain Blondy for his helpful and encouraging review. Krystle Farrugia helped us greatly by compiling the index. Claude Calleja was instrumental in securing the funding for this project and we would have been lost without the constant support and organisational help of Simone Vella Lenicker and Ann Dingli. Last but not least, this book would have never been possible without the contagious spirit, passion and dedication of all the staff of AP Valletta who, through the generosity they bring to their everyday work, allow AP as a laboratory for ideas to reach out for its vision. Thank you!

/ **1.** See Stephen Snyder, *Pier Paolo Pasolini*, Boston: Twayne Publishers, 1980.

/ **2.** The Founding Myths of Architecture, conference organised by Architecture Project (AP) at the Archeological Museum, Auberge de Provence, Valletta, Malta, 7–9 October 2005.

/ **3.** Laugier, Marc-Antoine, *Essai sur l'Architecture*, Paris: Chez Duchesne, 1753.

/ **4.** See Jacques Derrida, "'Genesis and Structure' and Phenomenology", and "Structure Sign and Play in the Discourse of the Human Sciences", in *Writing and Difference*, London: Routledge, 1978, pp. 143–155 and 247–260 respectively.

/ **5.** Nietzsche, Friedrich, *The Birth of Tragedy & The Genealogy of Morals*, New York: Doubleday, 1990.

/ **6.** Barthes, Roland, *Mythologies*, Paris: Seuil, 1957.

ARCHITECTURE AND THE PRIMORDIAL WATERS

GODS OF ARCHITECTURE IN THE WEST

Pedro Azara

Earth, the solid surface beneath our feet, is necessary for our survival. Someone going through a difficult time, who is confronted with insurmountable difficulties, is said to be losing his grip. To lose one's footing, as if the ground were slipping away under one's feet, means, metaphorically, to fall into a void, to disappear, to cease to exist. The surface of the earth, therefore, structures our life. It constitutes a reference point on the basis of which we orientate ourselves, position ourselves with respect to our surroundings, and exist as part of creation's rich tapestry. To lose one's point of reference, to go astray in this world: these expressions refer to someone who has no direction, someone who lets go, gives up and falls.

On the other hand, those who are down-to-earth and who have their feet firmly on the ground, have a clear mind. They are aware about the need to organise their life. They follow their course firmly and consistently. Nothing is coincidental.

Given these current linguistic uses, it is understandable why, in ancient Greece, banishment (which in Spanish is called *destierro*, literally meaning expulsion from the earth) was the worst of punishments, received by those who had committed a serious offence. Man needs this surface: steady, stable, regular, looking towards and linked to the sky.

In the light of these interpretations, one can only be surprised to learn that the great work of the Mesopotamian god of architecture was built not on earth, but on water. This civilisation gave the very symbol of movement and lack of stability the role of foundation for the prototype of architecture. Furthermore, this characteristic choice of the Mesopotamian 'architect god' also exists in varying degrees in other cultures. How can this be interpreted, and which image of architecture emerges from this strange relationship between architecture and water?

In order to build, today as in the past, it is necessary to go through a series of obligatory preliminary stages. The land must be flat (or composed of a series of horizontal terraces). Even in the case where a slope is retained, trenches are dug into the earth in order to build the foundations that must necessarily stand perpendicular to the ground, thus opening up a geometric volume with perpendicular walls. The land has to be cleared; the trees, weeds and litter must be removed. It is preferable to have solid, compact ground. Layers of different consistencies should be avoided; where this is inevitable, the foundations have to penetrate deep into the earth until they reach a hard, rocky layer, which is a costly operation. It is nevertheless a fact that a ground that is too compact makes the construction of the foundations difficult, at times nearly impossible. Furthermore, an excessively hard ground is not flexible. That is why Pliny recommended marshy land, like the land on which the temple of Artemis in Ephesus was built, as, thanks to the flexibility of its foundations, the building is more resistant to earthquakes (that are so frequent in Ionia). Nonetheless, the foundations rested on a first layer of compacted coal and a second layer made from sheep skins to stop the humidity from eroding the base of the columns.[1]

The ground is therefore the 'base' of architecture, even if lakeside constructions are not rare (from the traditional houses along the Mekong River, for example, to the oil rigs in mid-ocean, far from the coast). These bases and buildings, however, have to be supported on piles sunk into the river and sea beds, and the floors of the houses have to be placed high enough to avoid all contact with the water which could otherwise threaten not only the fabric of the house but also the comfort or even the lives of the inhabitants. The marine gods, on the other hand, lived in dark and silent abyssal palaces. As for underwater cities—laid out in any case on the ocean floor as if they were on land exposed to the sun—they exist only in our wildest dreams and in myths, now and perhaps forever.

Water is necessary for life, and therefore also for towns. The latter were nearly always founded next to a watering place, a spring or a river. Numerous Greek foundation myths describe how the founding hero had to fight against the guardian of a watering place, often a snake. Its body, cold and undulating, covered with shiny scales that glistened in the sun, evoked the waterway slithering its way through the grassy fields. Cadmos, for example, confronted a gigantic serpent before taking possession of the spring and, in so doing, founding the town of Thebes. Apollo, on the other hand, had been involved in a titanic fight against Python—or his mother Delphyne—who watched over the Castalia fountain next to the site of Delphi, a struggle which culminated in the god founding his main sanctuary there. Water was indeed the source of the life that the newly-built town was going to protect.[2]

Water could however also be destructive. The numerous myths about the Flood (in Mesopotamia, Palestine and Greece for example) are clear evidence of its potentially negative force. Life depended on the goodwill of the waters, that is, of the god who controlled its course and flow. In the light of this, the question that springs to mind is, precisely: why build on water? What was the relation between water or the waters and architecture?

The Sumerian god Enki (*Ea* in Akkadian) was the Mesopotamian god traditionally associated with architecture.[3] He was thought to have invented construction techniques, as well as the teaching of them, and to have given them as a gift to man. Furthermore, Enki/*Ea* was also a divine master builder as he built towns, temples and palaces. Enki himself built the E-engurra, his palace in Eridu.[4] Finally he created a series of minor gods dedicated to watching over the different techniques required for the art of building, from the lighting of the fire and the firing of the bricks to the covering of the walls, from the first preparatory works on the land to the final decorative touches. Enki conceived and even made all of the necessary tools from the simple brick mould to the plow which traced the furrows into which the foundations were laid.

The long poem *Enki and the World Order* enumerates some of these gods of building techniques: Enkimdu, the "patron of canals and levees" (v. 323), Kulla

(v. 338) in charge of brick production, Musdama (v. 346) laid the bricks to build the walls, the goddess Ninmug (vv. 405–408), sister of the great Inanna, became "the Artist of wood and metals" thanks to the "golden chisel, silver hammer and large flint knife" that Enki offered her, "holy Nisaba" (vv. 411–413) to whom the Great Architect gave "the measuring rod and the lapis lazuli measuring tape" and the goddess Uttu (vv. 383–384), "the loyal and silent" to whom he entrusted "the decoration of the palaces".[5] The "*me*", the divine Powers that were divine prerogatives, were in effect a set of techniques allowing fields to be plowed, lands to be farmed and towns to be founded and built. Many of the "*me*" were therefore related to the organisation of land. It seems that even the plowing and delimitation of land (in order to farm and build) were part of the same series of activities that placed the world at the disposal of man so that he could live there. Marduk was the first to divide fields into squares, to dig furrows, to draw plow lines and to create and plan space for man.[6]

Cylinder Seal: Enki (god of water and architecture), Ur, Paris, Musée du Louvre, AO38845, © AISA.

Both project and construction depended on Enki:[7] the design of the plans (like those of Babylon);[8] the creation of the land register; the choice of site and its delimitation; the plotting of the perimeter of the building directly on the ground, using a line, in order to reproduce its plan; the invention of the plow; the digging of the furrows with a hoe into which the "rectilinear foundations" were to be inserted; the construction of the brick mould; the production of the first brick (the preparation of the mixture, the molding and the removal from the mold) and its laying; the planning of the necessary brickwork, sometimes for an entire town; then the construction and completion of all the main buildings, from the basic structures to the sumptuous wall-coverings "of silver and lazulite [...] enhanced with gold" on the outer walls.[9] "I will control their work, / And the 'architects' of the country will restore the solid foundations. [...] Enki [...] had the brickwork of the cities built, each in their holy place. / After having given each one a name, He assigned them to be successive capitals."[10]

More importantly, Enki was also the god of earth and water, both terrestrial and celestial waters. He was an architect because the waters belonged to him and obeyed him. These Waters were both beneficial and fertile, and without them life on earth could not go on. Thanks to them, the earth and men could be purified.[11]

Enki also controlled the subtle mixture of water and earth and therefore was responsible for and mastered the construction processes. Mud, so valuable in cultivating fields, was also necessary to mold or model statuettes, examples of the prototype of human beings. Was Enki not given various epithets, such as Nudimmud (the skilled god, the creator of images) or Mummu (form, mold, archetype)?[12] He created men, and, like most gods at the birth of architecture, he gave them a protected space (fortified town, house), which provided cover and was defended and where men could find refuge and live in peace. As creator of life, it was his duty to defend it by preparing a place where life could settle.

Enki controlled fresh water, the water coming from the sky ("I am a great storm" he claimed),[13] the water that calmly flowed on the surface of the earth (springs and rivers) and the water that remained underground (groundwater, wells and, above all, the water table with its prime life-giving waters: the Apsu).[14] The two rivers, the Tigris and the Euphrates, their murky waters carrying silt that was slowly deposited in their meanders, were filled with the semen of the god who had masturbated. Enki's son, Marduk, opened up the gates of the rivers when he blinded Tiamat, the dragon of saltwater, against whom he fought for the supremacy and permanent dominion of the world.

Rain, essential for agriculture, depended on the goodwill of Enki who always took man's side. This explains why, when Anu and Enlil, the gods of the sky and the air, worried about the ever-growing number of humans and tired of the deafening noise of humanity that prevented them from sleeping, decided to eliminate them with torrential rains that were supposed to wash everything away, Enki secretly contacted a human being, Utnapishti or Ziusura, defying the orders of Anu and warning him of the gods' plan. He explained how it was possible to survive the flood, by building a waterproof ark whose plans were drawn directly on the ground by Enki himself.[15] In this ark, the Sumerian Noah and the animals of the earth would find refuge before repopulating the earth once again after the anger of the gods had ceased and the water level had started to subside.

All of Enki's power over the waters came down to the Apsu, the true aquatic realm that was in his charge. The Apsu (which was both a place and a god) was the mass of primordial water from which all life (from the natural formations to the celestial powers) had sprung, and that supplied the rivers, lakes, marshes, springs, wells and underground streams. In a Babylonian hymn, the Apsu was described as "Divine River, creator of everything".[16] The famous opening of the Babylonian *Poem of Creation* describes how at the beginning of time "When on high the heaven had not been named, / Firm ground below had not been called by name" only Apsu the First and his wife, Tiamat, goddess of saltwater existed; "When no gods whatever had been brought into being, / Uncalled by name, their destinies undetermined, / Then it was that the gods were formed within Apsu-Tiamat."[17] Controlling the vast and deep domain of Apsu meant obtaining the keys of life. In a sense, the fate of man, his creation and his very existence depended on Enki.[18]

The Apsu depended to such an extent on Enki (who one could say was interchangeable with the Waters) that the latter built his temple or palace either on[19] or in the Apsu: "It is in your depth that Ea/Enki, king of the Apsu, has built his dwelling."[20] The great sanctuary of Enki was known as E-apsu or E-engurra that is "the House of Underground Waters".[21] Enki's first act, the founding act of architecture, was accomplished on the surface of, or within, the primordial waters. The fertile, invigorating waters of the Apsu were indeed the model for the divine construction (the celestial palace of Enki). So this palace was only a second model, a representation of the original model, the Apsu, the Waters of the Life; the palace built on earth was a third image. Yet, in order to turn it into a habitable place, Enki had to reduce it. The Babylonian *Poem of Creation* (*Ee*, I, vv. 65–84) says that it was only after having defeated the Apsu (by putting it to sleep, striking it and killing it), and after having taken full possession of the waters, that Ea/Enki could sink the foundations of his palace and thereby transform it into a place to settle down and live in. It is in the Nuptial Chamber of this palace that Marduk was conceived and born.[22] The Esagil, the multi-tiered tower of the temple of Enki's son Marduk (the "Tower of Babel"), was then built in the image of the Apsu (*Ee*, VI, vv. 62–64) and converted into the terrestrial abode of the gods of the sky, Anu, Enlil and Ea/Enki. In the same way, the ark which had allowed humankind to survive the Great Flood was planned and built following the model of all architecture, the Apsu.

The construction of the palace in the Apsu turned the world into a habitable place and became a symbol of this conversion. A Babylonian prayer for the foundation of a temple (i.e. for the renewal of the spatial organisation pioneered by Ea/Enki or his son Marduk), evokes moments and phases of the Creation. When the holy edifice was built on the Apsu, earth could at last be inhabited: "A holy House, a Temple, had not yet been built in its holy place (...) / All the lands were sea! / The spring in the midst of the sea was only a channel, / Then Eridu [Enki's holy city] was made, then Esagil was built, Esagil that Lugaldukuga erected in the heart of Apsu. / Then Babylon was made and Esagil completed."[23] That Apsu had become the symbol of habitable space thanks to the creative authority of Enki becomes clear in a Hurrian poem, where Apsu, under the barely changed name of Abzuwa, is presented as a city, the city of Ea/Enki, where men could live together in peace and security.[24]

There is nothing surprising about the fact that Enki was the king of the waters, creator of mankind and architect of living space. This trinity exists in other cultures. Some authors compare, probably quite rightly, the Mesopotamian Apsu to the Egyptian Nun. The god Nun was, or symbolised, the primordial waters from which all the natural and divine elements of the world sprang. The subterranean waters, which rose to the surface of the Nile and of all pools, whether natural or manmade (those, for example, built close to temples), equally belonged to Nun. The Nile itself sprang from a cave that plunged into the Nun.

Considering that life originated from him, the god Ptah—whose name *pth* meant to model, to fashion—watched over the Nun who belonged to him.[25] Following a hymn dedicated to him, "He gave birth to the gods, created the towns, founded the provinces and placed the gods as well as their places of worship. He defined the offerings and founded the sanctuaries."[26] Both gods and humans were fashioned by Ptah, a task that Khnum, the other great deity associated with spatial organisation, was also in charge of and who, in Dendera at least, worked together with Ptah.[27] While Nun modeled human beings, Ptah preferred to sculpt them.[28] At times, Ptah was even confused with Nun.[29] Ptah therefore incarnated the primordial active waters. Elsewhere, the fertile and dark soil of early times, slowly appearing like a huge sea monster from the silt-laden waters of the Nun, was named Ptah.[30] Ptah incarnated the waters and the lands, and was the creator, using the water and earth from which he had sprung and which were part of him. Creativity sprung from his very being. That is why, as he and the invigorating waters were one and the same thing (they were his own inseminating body), Ptah was also the god of vegetation. The rare rains that came from the waters of Nun depended on him, and rose to the sky always with the approval of Ptah, before descending down upon the mountains and joining the Nile where the lands would reappear once the waters had subsided. The sources of life were under the protection of Ptah, as were the places that watched over them.

This is how the town of Memphis became the "first" city to originate from Ptah. According to Apollodorus the mythographer (*Ap.* I, 4), Memphis was one of the very first deities present at the beginning of the world (one of Memphis' daughters was Libya, the name given to the whole African continent and not just the northern coast opposite Greece). Ptah was depicted surrounded by attributes composed of architectonic shapes: chapels, stepped podiums and columns,[31] especially the djeb column that—as the tree of life—supported, structured and protected the world.[32] This column could equally symbolise the god who, in this way, became an architectonic element, the element necessary for the support and order of the world. Ptah himself also placed the cornerstones that marked the limits of a building, "prerogative that is not surprising on behalf of the master of builders, stone-carvers, masons and sculptors".[33] He was himself known as "the divine angle" that structured the universe.[34] In this way, the cosmos—thanks to the presence of Ptah, standing upright, vigilant and supporting with his arms the vault of heaven that he had first separated from Mother Earth—was considered to be an immense construction, a temple of cosmic proportions. The world was transforming itself into the dwelling place of mankind.

Ptah was the Great Architect thanks to whom life had settled forever on earth. He was the creator and at the same time creation itself, the architect and the edifice. The base, the ground, the foundations, as well as the pillars that supported the vault (of heaven) were Ptah. By his presence and his acts, he introduced into space, up to then undifferentiated (the confused and liquid magma of Nun), the notion of spatial coordinates, the horizontal dimension of the ground emerging from the waters and the vertical line that his body, conceived like a cosmic pillar, represented. Space organised itself around Ptah, standing in the centre, materialised by the town of Memphis that he had founded.[35]

In ancient Greece, there were several gods and heroes who were founders and builders (Poseidon, Athena, Prometheus who taught the building techniques to the men he had just modeled, Hephaestus, creator of the bronze palace, the hero Daedalus, patron of architects, who was respected even in the Middle Ages), but none had the importance of Apollo, who, according to Cicero, was akin to Ptah.[36] Callimachus (*Ap.* vv. 55–58) expressed this clearly in one of his hymns: "And Phoebus it is that men follow when they map out cities"; their "bases" (*themelia*), their "founding" (*ktisis*, foundation, creation) are accomplished under the inspiration of Apollo, in imitation of his founding act.

The *Homeric Hymn to Apollo* relates the misadventures of Apollo's birth at length. His mother Leto, secretly carrying Zeus' child, could not give birth on Mount Olympus as Hera, Zeus' wife, would not allow it. However no land on earth dared offer Leto a place to give birth as it would provoke the anger of the matron goddess. When the time to give birth came, Leto traveled across the earth looking for a place to rest that would be hidden and secret. The island of Delos agreed to receive the mother of Apollo who could not bear to wander any longer. But it was far from being a renowned place: "wind-swept and stern" (Call. *Del.*, 11), rocky, stony, nothing could grow from its scorched soil. The island was so insignificant that it was impossible to locate. It was a great rock that drifted in the wake of the waves that lashed it every day. In his *Hymn to Delos*, Callimachus says that the moment Apollo was born, the island that had been at the mercy of winds and waves, "planted the roots of [its] feet amid the waves of the Aegean sea" (v. 54). The image recalls the one described by Hesiod in the *Theogony* (v. 728) at the creation of the world: the Earth became a fertile and habitable place because it plunged its roots into the depths of the Tartarus. These roots (*ridzai*) resembled the foundations of Okeanos (v. 816), the great freshwater river that encircled the earth, penetrating into the primordial Chaos (the Greek Apsu or Nun).[37]

Delos became rooted. The island ceased to drift like a frail boat in a storm. Furthermore, offerings flooded in from every corner of the world. The entire universe started to turn around the island "around and about thee the isles have made a circle and set themselves about thee as a choir" (Call. *Del.*, vv. 300–301). This choir or "round dance" probably very closely resembled the dance performed a couple of years later on the same island of Delos by Theseus and the young survivors who, full of joy, came out alive from the "crooked labyrinth" (vv. 311–313) where the bloodthirsty Minotaur reigned. Ascanius, son of Aeneas, and his companions on horseback, re-enacted this dance when Alba Longa was founded and encircled with walls, shortly before the foundation of Rome, in order to divert and confuse the evil spirits (Vir. *Aen.* V, 595–599).[38]

We are here right at the heart of the term "foundation": the creation of habitable space. Apollo acted as a master-builder, a true architect. He organised and transformed space. Indeed, rocky, barren and drifting Delos was uninhabitable; the island did not exist, was nothing, "*adêlos*" (Call. *Del.*, v. 53), obscure, impenetrable and invisible, denying its own existence. Delos constantly avoided the advances of Zeus and, groping its way down, hid at the bottom of a deep abyss (*taphron*, v. 37), at the very base of a well. "But when thou gavest thy soil to be birthplace of Apollo" (v. 51), the island metamorphosed. Thanks to the presence and the acts of the god, who established the roots and foundations of the earth, the land and the territory, Delos became a "happy hearth of islands" or more precisely "a hearth, an island where it is pleasant to live and dwell" (Call. *Del.*, v. 325), welcoming and open to all. Thus, Apollo made Delos a habitable place. The island became the centre of the world.

Then Apollo left and his journey took him across Greece.[39] Until then, Greece had been virgin territory, unexplored land, uninhabited or populated solely by Chthonian monsters, like the gigantic serpents Python and Delphyne that Apollo confronted during the foundation of Delphi. What Apollo did was to organise, during his ascension to Delphi and his journey through the air to the Land of the Hyperboreans, and to delimit and structure the space that he traveled across. He did this in all directions, horizontally and vertically. After he had defined a centre —and because he had marked it—Apollo could then draw the broad lines that would thereafter allow urbanisation and construction to take place. In fact Apollo was not only an architect, he also personified architecture. His presence structured and delimited space.

Callimachus (*Del.* 22–27) explains this clearly: Delos was built differently. Its foundations and walls were eternal: they were incarnated by Apollo. The islands "are strong by reason of their sheltering towers, but Delos is strong by aid of Apollo. What defense is there more steadfast? Walls and stones may fall before the blast of Strymonian Boreas; but a god is unshaken for ever."[40] The resources were henceforth well established: a centre and spatial coordinates. Men could then organise themselves and arrange the undifferentiated space into protected and habitable places. According to Macrobius, (Mac. *Sat.*, I, 9, 6–7), this always took place under the guidance of Apollo, Apollo Tireus (the protector of the door) or Apollo Agieus (the guardian of the streets).

Apollo's feat was to succeed in overpowering the waters that unrelentingly fought against poor Delos. The waters had succumbed to him. Yet Macrobius reminds us that Apollo was known under the name of *theis ombrous*, that is to say he who commands the rain. Apollo was the god of the waters and of organised living space.[41] It is therefore not surprising to note that Plutarch described Apollo as "friend of mankind", "father (*patroios*)", "creator (*genesios*)" of human beings.[42]

The Roman equivalent of Apollo was Janus who was both Apollo and Diana (Mac. *Sat.*, I, 9, 8; 5). Macrobius added that the epithet Tireus, which Apollo carried, also applied to Janus (*Sat.* I, 7, 9), since he, too, protected doors and watched over pathways. Janus was a very ancient Italic god: Saint Augustine (*Civ.*, VI, 9) says that, according to Varro, Janus was at the top of the list of gods that had participated in the conception of human beings, from birth to death. Macrobius (*Sat.*, I, 9, 16) states that the Romans called him "'Pater', as the god of gods" and he was credited with the creation of the world and the benefits of civilisation, such as architecture. Janus was in fact an architect himself: the foundation and construction of several towns were attributed to him, as was the first settlement around which Rome was founded, the Janiculum.

Janus was also associated with Chaos. The two comprised the original substance that would feed the world. The *Carmen Saliare*, quoted by Varro (*L.*, VII, 26) declared it: "O Sowing God [...], The One who opens [...], the Guardian of passages, the Creator, the God of Beginnings."[43] So life, in particular springs and living spaces, depended on Janus. Springs were in fact the children of Janus. Carmenta (that some call Themis—the protecting goddess of the *themelia*, foundations), the goddess of birth, to whom the education of the Latin people was attributed, was associated with Janus. Her feast day coincided with Juturna's, the wife of Janus and the mother of Fons/Fontus, the god of fountains.[44] The temple of Janus, on the Forum, was built on water: a hot thermal spring flowed under its foundations. According to Cicero (*Nat.*, II, 27, and it seems that the etymology was correct), the name Janus is derived from the Latin verb "*ire*" (to walk). The pathways and passages that help to go beyond barriers or frontiers, like the marks or interruptions that divide up lines, fell under the ascendancy of the god. He watched over the roads and doors that guide and lead, that structure the surface and prevent one from going astray.

Like Apollo, Janus was the god of the centre and therefore of spatial organisation. Plowing, that according to Macrobius (*Sat.*, I, 7, 21) Janus learnt from Saturn, and planning were his doing. Before sowing the fields, a sacrifice in his honor had to be made (Cat. *Agr.*, 134). Janus' steps opened, outlined and defined the furrows and the paths that covered the land. That is how, thanks to his acts, man could find refuge behind walls and doors and venture into domesticated nature, familiar and plowed, without fear of getting lost or of being unable to return.

The major gods of architecture in the West were also creators of the world and of mankind. They exercised their power over the realm of fresh water, as well as of the primordial waters from which life had sprung. The flow, be it beneficial or destructive, of the terrestrial (rivers) and celestial (rain) waters, was regulated by these deities. They taught men how to prepare the soils to plow and to build, by opening deep furrows where seeds and foundations could be planted, horizontally and vertically, in order to prepare a place to live, to find shelter and to socialise. These gods also built themselves: their creations were sometimes erected on the primordial waters, which they encircled in order to stop them from overflowing and destroying life, but also so that these waters, sources of life, could eternally provide sustenance for the home, the land where men would live. In this world-view, an architect is not only a builder, but also a creator who organises the world so that its inhabitants do not feel lost or abandoned. He disposes of the elements necessary for life, a life that can only develop in a limited and protected area, the hearth common to all men.

The architecture of the 'architect gods' was a protective place but also a meeting place, where both the living, from inside or from outside, and the dead, could assemble. This conception of architecture recreated the world, that is, it organised the world into a place where all beings would be able to stay forever, like a timeless source of life. Architecture is indeed the art of inhabiting the world, both visible and invisible, the art of being in the world.

/ **1.** Pliny, *Naturalis Historiæ*, 36.95, see also JJ Pollitt, *The Art of Ancient Greece. Sources and Documents*, Cambridge, New York and Melbourne: Cambridge University Press, 1990, p. 182.

/ **2.** Azara, P, "Por qué la fundación de la ciudad?" in P Azara, R Mar, E Riu, E Subias, eds, *La fundación de la ciudad. Mitos y ritos en el mundo antiguo*, Barcelona: Edicions UPC, 2000, p. 159. The theme of the fight between the founding hero and the water serpent or dragon has been developed, for example, by F Vian, *Les origines de Thèbes. Cadmos et les Spartes*, Études et Commentaires, nr 48, Paris: Librairie C Klincksieck, 1963.

/ **3.** In Babylon, the invention of architecture, as well as the construction of the temples and of the town of Babylon itself, were the work of Marduk, the great Babylonian god, considered to be the son of Ea, and of various other minor gods under his orders. As Marduk could not stay out of the project, he named his father head of works, thanks to which the project conceived by Marduk could be realised. See J Bottero, "L'épopée de la création" in *Mythes et rites de Babylone*, Geneva: Stlatkine Reprints, 1996 (1st ed. 1985), p. 138. ("The authors of the *Enuma Elish—The Epic of Creation*—[...] conceived the latter [Ea], in accordance with his reputation, as a kind of engineer, of *ummâ/-ênu* or *mâr ummâ/êni* [...], in charge of finding and applying technical procedures fit for the creation of the plans of the inventor or the patron."). Marduk built the great mansion of the gods An (father of the gods), Enlil (god of the air) and Ea, the E-sara, on the earth and in the skies. Then he reproduced this celestial model on earth and made it his abode: Babylon. Marduk addressed the assembly of gods and said to them: "As a replica of the E-sara that I personally built for you, / But further down, in a place whose foundation I have consolidated, / I want to build myself a Temple that will be my main dwelling, / In the middle of which I will build my Sanctuary / and I will assign my apartments, in order to establish my reign there [...] / I will call it 'Babylon': 'The Temple of the Great Gods'" (*Enûma Elis*, V, 120–124, 129 in J Bottero, SN Kramer, *Lorsque les dieux faisaient l'homme. Mythologie mésopotamienne*, Paris: Gallimard, 1989, pp. 636–637).

/ **4.** Jacobsen, T, *The Treasures of Darkness. A History of Mesopotamian Religion*, New Haven and London: Yale University Press, 1976, p. 115.

/ **5.** In the long poem *Enki and the World Order*, v. 346, Musdammu or Musdamma, one of the deities created by Enki to participate in the construction of the first buildings, received the title of Architect, "*sitim.gal En.lil.là*"; Jean Bottéro and Samuel Noah Kramer preferred to translate the Sumerian expression as "Great Mason", *Mythes*, p. 177; H Limet, "Le dieu Enki et la prospérité de Sumer" in *Homo Religiosus*, nr 9, 1983, p. 87.

/ **6.** Bottero, J, SN Kramer, *Lorsque les dieux faisaient l'homme*, pp. 646, 648–649, 668.

/ **7.** Vanstiphout, HLJ, "Why did Enki organise the World?" in IL Finkel, MJ Geller, eds,

Sumerian Gods and their Representations, Cuneiform Monographs, nr 7, Groningen: Styx, 1997, p. 121.

/ **8.** Bottero, J, SN Kramer, *Lorsque les dieux faisaient l'homme*, p. 638.

/ **9.** Bottero, J, *La plus vieille religion. En Mésopotamie*, Paris: Gallimard, 1998, p. 279.

/ **10.** The Sumerian Flood Legend, pp. 85–87, 91–92 in J Bottero, SN Kramer., 1989, *Lorsque les dieux faisaient l'homme*, p. 565.

/ **11.** Jacobsen, T, *Treasures*, p. 112.

/ **12.** Jacobsen, T, *Treasures*, p. 111.

/ **13.** *Enki ordonnateur du Monde*, v. 69 in J Bottero, SN Kramer, *Lorsque les dieux faisaient l'homme*, p. 168.

/ **14.** Enki (Ea) was also known as Nagbu, meaning "fountain, water table", thereby evoking the realm of the underground primordial waters of the Apsu, controlled by Enki, and the depth of his knowledge. See J Sanmartin, ed and trans, *Epopeya de Gilgamesh, rey de Uruk*, Madrid and Barcelona: Trotta et Universitat de Barcelona, 2005, p. 109, fn. 1.

/ **15.** Bottero, J, SN Kramer, *Lorsque les dieux faisaient l'homme*, p. 563.

/ **16.** *An Address to the River of Creation*, v. 1 in J Bottero, SN Kramer, *Lorsque les dieux faisaient l'homme*, p. 289.

/ **17.** *Enûma Elish*, I, 1–2, 7–9 in J Bottero, SN Kramer, *Lorsque les dieux faisaient l'homme*, p. 604.

/ **18.** The Hellenistic historian Berosus (4th–3rd c. BC), who lived in Babylon, wrote about a civilising hero, Oannes, in his treatise *Babyloniaca*. The latter, whom the Sumerians already knew under the name of U.an.na, nicknamed Adapa, was a member of a group of very ancient Sumerian gods—much older than the celestial gods—who lived in the dark waters of the Apsu. These figures, called the *apkallu*, were hybrid creatures, half men, half fish. Berosus says that Oannes, being a civilising hero, came out of the waters to teach men artistic techniques, namely the art of founding and building towns. Oannes has been identified with Enki. According to Hallo, Oannes-U.an.na-Adapa may have inspired the figure of Adam (W Hallo, WK Simpson, *The Ancient Near East. A History*, Harcourt Brace College, Orlando, 1998, p. 29. See also G Rachet, *Dictionnaire des civilisations de l'Orient ancien*, Paris: Larousse-Bordas (HER), 1999, p. 304).

/ **19.** *Enki ordonnateur du Monde*, vv. 285–287 (J Bottero, SN Kramer, *Lorsque les dieux faisaient l'homme*, p. 175. See also the commentary of P Azara, *La Fundacíon*, pp. 192–201.

/ **20.** *An Address to the River of Creation*, v. 4 in J Bottero, 1996, *Mythes*, p. 289.

/ **21.** Edzard, DO, "The Names of the Sumerian Temples" in IL Finkel, MJ Geller, eds, *Sumerian Gods*, p. 163.

/ **22.** A probable echo of this fight between the Abyss and the Creator can be found in the Bible. At the time of the Creation and the preparation of the earth for the arrival of various living beings, Yahweh "set a compass upon the face of the depth [...] / [...] he gave to the sea his decree, that the waters should not pass his commandment / [and] he appointed the foundations of the earth" (*Pr.*, 8, 27 and 29. See also *Jb*, 26,10) In the Book of Job, the following is added (*Jb*, 26, 7): "He stretcheth out the north over the empty place [the abyss], and hangeth the earth upon nothing." So "[thou] laid the foundations of the earth, that it should not be removed forever. / Thou coveredst it with the deep [the abyss] as with a garment [...] / Thou hast set a bound that they [the waters of the abyss] may not pass over; that they turn not again to cover the earth." (Ps, 104, 5–6, 9) See J Blockfriedman, "The Architect's Compass in Creation Miniatures of the Later Middle Ages," in *Traditio*, nr 30, 1974, pp. 419–429. It should be specified that the compass is the emblem of the Creator, the symbol of Geometry and the attribute of the architect (as conceiver and head of project). (A Blunt, "Blake's « Ancient of Days ». The Symbolism of the Compasses" in *Journal of the Warburg and Courtauld Institutes*, vol 2, nr 1, July 1938, pp. 53–63).

/ **23.** *Prayer to dedicate a foundation brick of a temple*, vv. 1 and 10–14 in J Bottero, *Mythes*, p. 303.

/ **24.** Guterbock, HG, "The Hittite Version of the Hurrian Kumarbi Myths: Oriental Forerunners of Hesiod" in *American Journal of Archaeology*, vol 52, nr 1, 1948, p. 129.

/ **25.** Van Dijk, J, "Ptah" in *Oxford Encyclopedia of Ancient Egypt*, vol III, , Oxford and New York: Oxford University Press, 2001, p. 75. Later, *pth* would mean to sculpt (M Sandman Holmberg, *The God Ptah*, Hakan Ohlssons Boktryckeri, Lund, 1946, p. 8).

/ **26.** Sandman Holmberg, M, *Ptah*, pp. 22–23.

/ **27.** Khnum was another great Egyptian god associated with the creation and construction of the world and of beings. He was depicted as a hybrid being, half human, half animal, with a ram's head, symbolising his creative powers because of the proverbial fertility attributed to this animal. The source and course of the Nile, that brought life to its banks, were under the responsibility of Khnum who watched over the first flood. His profound knowledge of silt soon made him a divine potter, who fashioned human beings. Following the example of Ptah's work as a master-builder, Khnum modeled the vault of heaven (S Sauneron, J Yoyotte, "La naissance du monde selon l'Egypte ancienne" in *La naissance du monde. Sources Orientales*, nr 1, 1959, pp. 4, 76. Quoted by J Berlandini, "Ptah-Démiurge et l'exaltation du ciel" in *Revue d'Egyptologie*, nr 46, 1995, p. 31, fn. 171.)

/ **28.** Sandman Holmberg, M, *Ptah*, p. 47.

/ **29.** Sandman Holmberg, M, *Ptah*, p. 32.

/ **30.** Sandman Holmberg, M, *Ptah*, pp. 58–59. Ptah was *Ta-tenem*, the Earth that rises up (Yves Koenig, "Ptah" in *Dictionnaire de l'Egypte ancienne*, Encyclopaedia Universalis, Paris: Albin Michel, 1998, p. 313).

/ **31.** Sandman Holmberg, M, *Ptah*, pp. 13–15.

/ **32.** Berlandini, J, *Revue d'Egyptologie*, pp. 13–14.

/ **33.** Berlandini, J, *Revue d'Egyptologie*, p. 15.

/ **34.** Berlandini, J, *Revue d'Egyptologie*, p. 16.

/ **35.** The name of th e great temple of Ptah was extended to the town of Memphis and finally to the whole country: Hwt-kz-Pth (Ptah's Temple of the ka), that became Hikuptah and, finally, in the Hellenistic period, Aigyptos. One of the god's epithets was "He whose walls are to the south of Memphis" (Van Dijk, J, *Ptah*, p. 74). The epithet itself evokes the notions of orientation and space introduced by Ptah.

/ **36.** Vulcan, son of the Sky, was the father of Apollo, whereas a second Vulcan, son of the Nile, was named Ptah, the guardian of Egypt (Marcus Tullius Cicero, *De Natura Deorum*, III, 22).

/ **37.** Azara, P, "L'imaginaire des grottes. Les cavernes et les fondements de l'architecture" in V Fol, ed, *The Rock-Cut Sacred Places of the Thracians and Other Paleo-Balkan and Ancient Anatolian Peoples*, congress proceedings, Institute of Thracology, Sofia: Bulgarian Academy of Sciences (in press).

/ **38.** Frontisi-Ducroux, F, "La danse de Délos" in *Dédale. Mythologie de l'artisan en Grèce ancienne*, Paris: François Maspéro, 1975, pp. 145–150. On the relationship between dances and foundation rites see P Azara, "Dancing in the Streets: la ciudad y el laberinto" in P Azara, R Mar, E Subias, eds, *Mites de fundació de ciutats al món antic (Mesopotàmia, Grècia i Roma)*, conference proceedings from 2000, *Monografies*, nr 2, Barcelona: Museo d'Arqueologia de Catalunya, 2002, pp. 285–290.

/ **39.** Detienne, M, "Un dieu se met en route" in *Apollon le couteau à la main*, Paris: Gallimard, 1998, pp. 21–23. The whole book is useful for the theme of Apollo and the Greek myth of the origins of architecture.

/ **40.** I have followed here the translation of Emile Cahen, in Callimaque, *Hymnes. Épigrammes. Fragments choisis*, Paris: Les Belles Lettres, 1972, pp. 262.

/ **41.** In Ancient Rome, especially in Hispania, the cult of Apollo was associated with that of Bormanicus, the thermal god of boiling waters (MaB Garcia Fernandez-Albalat, "Las llamadas divinidades de las aguas" in MV Garcia Quintela, *Mitología y mitos de la Hispania prerromana*, vol 2, Madrid: Akal, 1986, pp. 141–192). Apollo was equally the protector of fountains (R Guenon, *Symboles de la science sacrée*, Paris: Gallimard, 1962, p. 181, fn. 2).

/ **42.** Plutarch, *De Pythiae oraculis*, XVI, 401f–402a. Quoted by M Detienne, *Apollon le couteau à la main*, p. 218.

/ **43.** On the relation between Janus and Chaos see LM de Padierniga, "Naturaleza de Jano según los 'Fastos' de Ovidio" in *Emérita*, nr 10, 1942, pp. 66–96.

/ **44.** Holland, LA, "Janus and the Living Water" in *Janus and the Bridge. Papers and Monographs of the American Academy of Rome*, vol 21, 1961, pp. 3–76.

UNMASKING THE BEAST

ALBERTI ON THE ORIGINS OF MANKIND AND THE CITY

Caspar Pearson

Alberti, Leone Battista. *Self-Portrait*, Samuel H Kress Collection, c. 1435. Image courtesy of National Gallery of Art, Washington.

Speculation about the origins of cities is perhaps almost as old as cities themselves. Thus, when Leon Battista Alberti turned his mind to the subject in his architectural treatise, *De re aedificatoria*, there was a considerable body of writing to which he could have turned for guidance. Not least amongst the authoritative writers to have discussed the origins of human settlements and societies was Vitruvius, author of the only architectural treatise to survive from Antiquity and one of Alberti's most important sources. Vitruvius had begun the second book of his *De architectura* by explaining how human beings, who previously were "born like animals in forests and caves and woods, and passed their life feeding on foods of the fields" had been brought into communities by the discovery of fire.[1] After this initial breakthrough, the development of human society was swift:

> They added fuel, and thus keeping it [the fire] up, they brought others; and pointing it out by signs they showed what advantages they had from it. In this concourse of mankind, when sounds were variously uttered by the breath, by daily custom they fixed words as they had chanced to come. Then, indicating things more frequently and by habit, they came by chance to speak according to the event, and so they generated conversation with one another. Therefore, because of the discovery of fire, there arose at the beginning, concourse among men, deliberation and a life in common. Many came together in one place, having from nature this boon beyond other animals, that they should walk, not with the head down, but upright, and should look upon the magnificence of the world and of the stars. They also easily handled with their hands and fingers whatever they wished. Hence, after thus meeting together, they began, some to make shelters of leaves, some to dig caves under the hills, some to make of mud and wattles places for shelter, imitating the nests of swallows and their methods of building.[2]

Attracted by the benefits of the new discovery, then, humans found themselves in close contact and developed language. What followed was momentous: concourse, deliberation and a life in common. Having become social, man swiftly became political; once political, he turned his hand to architecture.

There is much that we might expect a fifteenth century humanist to find attractive in Vitruvius' account. Alberti, however, dismisses it out of hand and offers one of his own:

> Some have said that it was fire and water which were initially responsible for bringing men together into communities, but we, considering how useful, even indispensable, a roof and walls are for men, are convinced that it was they that drew and kept men together.[3]

For Alberti, the original impulse towards the formation of communities and the construction of buildings was provided by the need for shelter, an opinion that he elaborates elsewhere in his treatise. Early in the first book, he returns to the theme during his discussion of *lineamenta*. Having found a place to rest in a location that was safe from danger, he surmises, primitive people took possession of the site and divided it into spaces according to function. They then "began to consider how to build a roof, as a shelter from the sun and the rain. For this purpose they built a wall upon which a roof could be laid—for they realised that in this way they would be the better protected from icy storms and frosty winds." No matter who may have overseen this process, and however ornate and diverse buildings may have become, Alberti insists, "I believe that such were the original occasion and the original ordinance of building."[4] Moreover, he adds that "nobody will question our account of their [buildings'] origins".[5] Similarly, he starts the fourth book, on public works, by discussing the origins of architecture, speculating that "if our surmise is correct, man first made himself a shelter to protect himself and his own from the assault of the weather. Men's appetite then grew beyond what was essential for their well-being, to include all that would contribute to their unbridled demand for every comfort."[6]

This disagreement with Vitruvius may seem a trivial matter but it is indicative of a fundamental difference in outlook. Vitruvius' account is an idealistic one. Steeped in Roman tradition, he gives pride of place to political deliberation and social concourse. These, he asserts, are what bound man into a communal life and allowed for the development of useful disciplines; politics, for Vitruvius, is prior to architecture. All of this is lacking in Alberti. Neither politics nor language are said to be prior to architecture and they certainly do not appear as a necessary condition for its development. Instead, the reasons that human beings both formed communities and built structures in the first place were overwhelmingly pragmatic. Settlements and architecture were responses to an essential aspect of man's experience of the world: his confrontation with the forces of Nature. Indeed, the theme of Nature looms large in Alberti's writings and, as recent analysis has demonstrated, stands at the very centre of his speculations.[7] Alberti's concept of Nature is certainly too complex and nuanced to be explored here, but it will simply be observed that throughout his architectural treatise, he continually stresses Nature's destructive qualities.[8] Indeed, the architect's practice derives in large part from the attempt to resist the forces of Nature, or perhaps more properly to diminish their effects. For Nature appears as the ultimate power in the world, one that can never be defeated. Alberti warns time and again of the possible destruction that rain, ice, excessive heat, earthquakes fires, floods, bad air and so forth can—and if not actively prevented from doing so *will*—wreak upon buildings and cities. Anybody wishing to pursue the matter in greater depth is directed by Alberti to his vernacular dialogue *Theogenius*, which he had written some years earlier. Here the character Teogenio enumerates a great litany of natural disasters, some of which are of truly epic proportions, and argues that "it is a constituted law of *fortuna* to pervert every day new things".[9] This frequent characterisation of Nature as containing elements that might be harsh and oppositional to man relates to a strain of Stoic thought, but also to the ideas of some of the great Christian thinkers, many of whom did consider Nature to be hostile to human beings.[10] Such thinkers had argued that this was necessarily so because when man had been expelled from the Garden of Eden he had entered into a different order of Nature; one that was imperfect, at best indifferent and at worst hostile. Indeed, some thinkers believed that when man had fallen, the whole of Nature had fallen with him; man had tainted not only himself but the entire natural world as well.

Alberti does not deal directly with the Fall anywhere in his writings, but he approaches the subject obliquely in his comic masterpiece *Momus*. *Momus* is a novel-like work which tells the story of the god of criticism and mockery and his adventures in heaven and on earth. Momus is a kind of anti-hero, who despises both gods and men and is all but completely lacking in morality. Alberti tells us that he has worked hard in writing the story to make the reader laugh, and the text is laced with a large helping of Lucianic irony. Yet he also hopes that the reader will feel that they are "involved in a thorough inquiry into, and a worthwhile explication of, real life".[11] Alberti thus uses a comic manner to approach serious matters, drawing out moral lessons from the amusing antics he describes. *Momus* is written in four books, the last of which is rather different in tone and involves what is sometimes seen as a lengthy digression. Jupiter has been persuaded by Momus' malicious intrigues that mankind is thoroughly bad and that the only solution is to destroy the world and start again. The gods thus begin to shower humanity with all manner of disasters causing a marked increase in the number of souls arriving at the underworld. Charon, whose duty it is to ferry the dead across the Acheron, learns from these souls that the world is coming to and end, and desires to see it before it does so. Knowing, however, that the journey will be a difficult and dangerous one, he is loath to undertake it without the help of a guide. Finally, he strikes a deal with one of the dead, the philosopher Gelastus, who had been so committed to the ideal of poverty during his life that he turned up at the Acheron without even the money to pay Charon for the crossing. Charon, being a stickler for the rules, had refused to ferry Gelastus across, and the philosopher had thus been forced to wait helplessly on the river bank. Seizing his chance, Charon now offers to take Gelastus over the river, if he will first accompany him on a journey to the world. There thus begins a comic adventure in which Charon is alternately appalled and amazed by the folly of mankind. He and Gelastus make a peculiar and cantankerous couple, who spend much of their time bickering. The common-sense ferryman is often exasperated by Gelastus' elaborate philosophical demonstrations, which he finds absurd and lacking in real wisdom. To this end, he decides he will tell the philosopher a story, one which contains more truth than any amount of philosophising ever could:

> Learn from the ferryman Charon to know thyself. I will tell you what I remember hearing, not from a philosopher—for all your reasoning revolves only around

subtleties and verbal quibbles—but from a certain painter. By himself this man saw more while looking at lines than all you philosophers do when you're measuring the heavens. Pay attention: you'll hear something that is very rare indeed.

> This painter used to say that the artificer of a great work had been selecting and purifying the material from which he was to create man. Some said the material was clay mixed with honey, others said warm wax. Whatever it was, people said that he should mould two bronze seals upon man, one on the chest, face, and the other parts seen from the front, and a second one on the back of the head, the buttocks and the parts seen from behind.[12]

The creator made many different kinds of humans and then took "the defective ones and those marked by flaws" to turn into women. This he did "by taking a little bit from the one and adding it to the other". Using different moulds he made all sorts of other living creatures. However, when his work was finished and he saw that some humans were not pleased with the shape he had given them, he declared that they could take the forms of any other creatures they liked:[13]

> He pointed out his house, conspicuous on a nearby mountain, and encouraged them to climb the steep and straight road that led to it. He said that they would enjoy there an abundance of good things, but he warned them repeatedly not to go there by any other road. This particular road might seem steep at first, but gradually it would become more level.
>
> Having said this, he went away. The *homunculi* began to climb, but immediately some, in their folly, preferred to look like cattle, asses and quadrupeds. Others, led astray by misguided desires, went on detours through the little hamlets they passed. There, in steep and echoing valleys, impeded by thorns and brambles, faced by impassable places, they turned themselves into assorted monsters, and when they returned to the main road, their friends rejected them because of their ugliness. Consequently, realising that they were all made from the same clay, they put on masks fashioned to look like other people's faces. This artificial method of looking like human beings became so commonly employed that you could scarcely distinguish the fake faces from the real ones, unless you happened to look closely at the eye holes of the masks that covered them. Only then would observers encounter the varied faces of the monsters. These masks, called 'fictions', lasted until they reached the waters of the River Acheron and no further, for when they entered the river they were dissolved in its steaming vapour. So nobody reached the other bank unless he was naked and stripped of his mask. Then Gelastus said, 'Charon, are you making this up as a game, or are you telling the truth?'—'No', said Charon. 'In fact, I plaited this rope from the beards and eyebrows of the masks, and I caulked my boat using their clay.'[14]

The story is markedly strange and sinister. On the one hand it relates to a tradition of moral writing in which people are faced with difficult but worthwhile ascents.[15] On the other it constitutes a highly original variation on the theme of the Fall of Man.[16] The creator offers human beings every opportunity to live a blessed and good life, but many choose not to do so. Some, spurred by foolishness, renounce their humanity and opt instead to live as animals. Others, subject to uncontrollable desires, stray from the right path until they find their progress impeded. There, isolated in the midst of a hostile nature, they transform themselves into monsters. Thus we learn that many men are not really men at all, but monsters wearing elaborate masks. By use of these masks, they may succeed in passing as human beings right up to the moment of death; but not beyond, for in death everyone will be revealed for what he truly is. Gelastus is clearly taken aback by Charon's story and we readily understand his hesitant and surprised response. Charon's reply to him offers little comfort and there is a particular force to the mocking tone in which some humans are reduced to the base physicality of hair and clay.

Of course, the idea that man is given to simulation and dissimulation and that the outward appearance of a person may be chronically at odds with the inner reality, can be found at many places in Alberti's work. A well-known passage in the same *Momus*, in which Momus himself ponders his newfound talent for simulation and dissimulation, is perhaps the clearest statement of this view:

> But now I realise that I must adopt another mask, one more suitable to my circumstances. What will that mask be, Momus? I must show myself to be a friendly fellow, of course, easygoing and affable.... Can you do something so completely against your own nature, Momus? Yes, I can, as long as I want to.
>
> ... What next? Shall I then forget my deep-rooted and almost congenital habit of doing harm? No; but I will control it silently and I shall preserve my old zeal against my enemies, using, however, another way, a new method for entrapping and hurting them. I have come to the conclusion that men who have to live and do business among the multitude must never in their heart of hearts blot out the memory of an injury they have sustained, but they must never make public their anger at this offence. Instead they must be time-servers, practising simulation and dissimulation.[17]

Such men, according to Momus, "will trust no one, but they will pretend to trust everyone. They should fear no man, but should train themselves to applaud and flatter everyone while in their presence."[18] He concludes:

> In short, it will be advantageous above all to call this one thing to mind over and over again: hide all your plans carefully and well, covering them with signs of trustworthiness and innocence. I shall carry this off brilliantly once I get used to moulding and shaping my words, expressions, and my whole appearance so that I seem identical to those who are deemed good and meek, even though I am completely different from them. Oh, what an excellent thing it is to know how to cover and cloak one's true feelings with a painted facade of artificiality and studied pretence![19]

In these passages, Momus recognises the supreme power of dissimulation and the mask. It is immediately to be noted that the impulse towards dissimulation, for Alberti, seems to be distinctly connected to the circumstance of living in human societies—the circumstance, that is, of the city. As Momus says, simulation and dissimulation are the necessary strategies of those who live and do business *intra multitudinem*. Alberti's own subscription to such a view appears to be confirmed by several passages of the *De familia* in which various characters compare the inherently tricky and untrustworthy discourse of the city to the open and honest conversation that is characteristic of the country.[20] In Charon's tale we find the implication that the habit of masking one's true self is not natural to human beings but is rather the result of an originary decision to stray from the right path; to depart, that is, from the order of Nature. This might lead us to question whether Alberti does not sometimes think of cities in the same way, as indeed some earlier thinkers had done. Augustine, for example, seems to have considered that sociability was natural to human beings but that politics was not.[21] Had there been no Fall, the cities of the world, with their political and civic organisations, might never have been necessary. Cities might thus be a manifestation of human imperfection and Augustine makes much of the fact that the first city was built in the wake of the Fall by the fratricide Cain. Alberti never articulates a view of this kind but he does consider the Nature of man's sociability in a passage of the *De iciarchia*. Here, assigning the greater part of the dialogue to himself as a character, Alberti often sounds closer to a 'civic humanist' than he does elsewhere in his writings. He employs a variant of the commonplace maxim that had appeared in the *De re aedificatoria*, asserting that a city is like a large family and a family like a small city. Both exist for the purpose of congregation with a view to providing for those who participate in them, in terms of utility and necessity.[22] After all, every man, from the moment of his birth, finds it necessary to request help from others. But family bonds are perhaps more important than civic ones, Alberti speculates, and indeed Nature has so arranged things that bonds between men arise in the first place in the family.[23] By contrast, cities "were perhaps constituted by chance, and for no other reason than only to be able to live together with sufficiency and comfort". And whereas the foundation of the family is love, and the bonds that hold it together derive from piety, charity and a natural sense of duty towards one's own kin, the city finds its origins in less noble and more selfish concerns. Men congregated into cities with a view to preserving themselves rather than to helping others; thus one might with good reason assert that a person owes more to his family than to his city.[24] In short, the family is natural while the city may not be. Since it is constituted by Nature, the family must exist. The city, on the other hand, may be the product of chance and it is conceivable that it might never have come about.[25]

Alberti's discourse addresses many of the issues raised by Aristotle in the fundamental opening passages of his *Politics*. The philosopher establishes from the first that human beings are by Nature incapable of existing alone and must form couples in order to reproduce.[26] The formation of couples leads to the household and the household to the village, which "comes into being through the process of nature in the fullest sense, as offshoots of a household are set up...."[27] The city (or state) is formed through the combination of a number of villages and thus "every city-state exists by nature as the earlier associations too were natural".[28] Indeed, the city-state is the proper end of the household and the village, and "whatever is the end-product of the coming into existence of any object, that is what we call its nature".[29] This leads to the conclusion that "the city-state belongs to the class of objects which exist by nature, and... man is by nature a political animal".[30] Moreover, since, for Aristotle, the whole must by necessity be prior to the part, it follows that the city-state must be prior to the household and the other relationships which existed before it.[31] In short: "it is clear then that the city-state is both natural and prior to the individual".[32] Alberti takes a great deal from these arguments but the extent of his departures are immediately noticeable. Indeed, Alberti appears to want to call into the question the most central tenets of Aristotle's theory: that the city (or city-state) is natural, that it is the proper end of the family and that it has priority over the household. Moreover, Alberti is keen to stress that the bonds that hold the family together differ greatly in quality to those which bind households into the city.[33] These attitudes would seem to find conformation in many passages in Alberti's writings. He generally appears to be more at ease when talking about the family and the household than when he addresses politics and the city. He finds little trouble in characterising the family as a good thing and approaches the subject in a direct manner, not only in the *De familia* but elsewhere as well. Politics is another matter. Indeed, if the *Momus* is truly to be considered a work of political theory, one cannot help but be struck by the highly complex, figurative and multiform nature of the text. Difficulties in understanding and interpretation abound; the approach to politics is anything but direct.

These observations might be brought to bear on the different accounts given by Alberti and Vitruvius regarding the founding of cities. Vitruvius, as we have seen, emphasised the political nature of man, which he saw as being a necessary condition for the formation of communities, things which preceded even the construction of dwellings. Alberti, on the other hand, appears less convinced about man's political nature. It is not clear that the city should, in Albert's view, be seen as natural and it might even be a sign of man's having stepped apart from the order of Nature. Charon's strange tale suggests an originary decision on the part of some men (rather than mankind as a whole) to abandon their natural state from the outset. Such men adopted the ways that Alberti frequently associates with city life, divorcing appearance from reality, simulating and dissimulating. Politics, the city, urban life as lived in the real world: one feels that a part of Alberti may have considered these things to be aberrations. But Charon's story points to another serious conflict with Vitruvius. Commenting on the passage in his *Rinascite e rivoluzioni* of 1975, Eugenio Garin noted pithily that "nobody has noticed that some decades before Giovanni Pico della Mirandola composed the famous hermetic opening of the oration in praise of man, Alberti had already written the parody."[34] The observation is revealing, for Charon's story is indeed just this. Alberti had written on the dignity of man with genuine force and passion in some of his earlier works. Here, however, he seems at pains to undermine the notion and to do so with a certain violence. Where Pico focuses on man's potential, Alberti concentrates on his failure. Where Pico encourages us to lift our eyes to the heights that God has granted that we may reach, Alberti ends with the disintegration of our pretensions and deceits into a mess of hair and clay.[35] Indeed, it is striking that Alberti on more than one occasion has recourse to the imagery of the mutilation and destruction of the body when considering bad and deceitful men. He often appears to believe that some men are bad in their very inner natures and that their outer forms need not merely to be stripped away, but actually obliterated. Thus, Alberti asks, in the *De iciarchia*:

> Who will be able to admire a slanderous deprecator, a defamer, and not be horrified by his fury? Men ever worse and worse, worthy of being pursued by the entire populace, not, I will say, with bow and arrows, but with ropes and flaming torches, and roasted to such a degree that their bones are left entirely stripped, so that no fiction may yet be latent within that monster.[36]

It cannot be said that Alberti straightforwardly endorses the notion of the dignity of man and in passages such as this he appears to use the graphic imagery of physical mutilation to underline the very *indignity* of some.[37]

This ambivalent approach to what has often been characterised as a central aspect of Renaissance thought would also seem to go to the root of Alberti's disagreement with Vitruvius. For the Roman architect's account of the origins of settlements and architecture clearly relies on a number of well-worn commonplaces regarding man's inherent dignity. First, we should note that in his account, Vitruvius had stressed the role of language, something that a number of ancient philosophers had pointed to as distinguishing men from beasts.[38] More importantly, he had remarked that many men came together into communities "having from nature this boon beyond other animals, that they should walk, not with the head down, but upright, and should look upon the magnificence of the world and of the stars". It is one of the great commonplaces of the theme of the dignity of man, employed from pagan antiquity right through the Christian Middle Ages and into the early modern era. As John V Fleming has written, "rectitude was... one of the crucial qualities which separated man and beast. A natural rectitude of posture was like the immortal soul and reason; men and women had it, dogs and pigs did not. This idea was very ancient—more ancient than Christianity or the particular Christian evolution of Latin *rectitudo*."[39] Alberti would have been familiar with this *topos*, not least from the works of Cicero, and his brusque dismissal of Vitruvius might thus reveal a certain impatience with these ideas. Men formed communities and built buildings because otherwise they would get wet and live in discomfort, not because they were able to gaze upon the stars. It would appear to be an example of Alberti's stubborn determination to reason from what he considers first principles, outside of traditional moral discourse. Yet Alberti himself had employed this commonplace in the *De familia*:

> Less does the saying of the philosopher Aanaxagoras displease me, who, when asked for what reason God created man replied: 'he made us to be contemplators of the heavens, of the stars, the sun and of all of his marvellous, divine works'. And one can readily persuade oneself of this opinion since we see no other animal that is not prone and inclined to bend, with its head to the pasture and the earth; only man do we see upright with his brow and face raised, almost as though he is by his nature so made only to gaze at and know the celestial places and things.[40]

The passage occurs in Book II, where it forms part of Leonardo Alberti's praise of the active life. Leonardo employs the maxims of a number of ancient thinkers to demonstrate that man was made for activity rather than leisure and he clearly expresses approval of what he terms the "*sentenza d'Anassagora*". Importantly, however, the approval is relative; he is less displeased by Aanaxagoras' idea than by Epicurus' assertion that the highest happiness of God rests in doing nothing. These are just the kind of sentiments we would expect to hear from the young, humanist Leonardo.[41]

The theme is revisited in the first book of the *Profugiorum ab erumna* where it is again incorporated into a discussion of the active and contemplative lives. Agnolo Pandolfini argues that man should not be considered as born only, as Anaxagoras had said, to contemplate the heavens, the stars and the whole of nature. First and foremost, man is born to serve God. Importantly, however, service to God is conceived of as favouring the good and upholding justice; that is to say, as a life of activity.[42] It is striking that in this same passage Agnolo cites Seneca's contention that reason and society are God's two highest gifts to man, and even employs the term "*naturale società*".[43] One should strive, Agnolo asserts, to achieve immortality, glory, fame and dignity for oneself, one's family and one's *patria*. Here there might indeed seem to be an implication that the city should be considered naturally constituted and God-given. However, Agnolo's pronouncement is closely followed by the maxim that the true *patria* of man is the entire world, something that will be especially true for the learned.[44] Moreover, one struggles to live freely amongst the multitude and solitude, providing it is not coupled with leisure, is in many ways preferable.[45] That Alberti considered a form of sociability to be natural to man can hardly be disputed. It is far from clear, however, that he thought of cities, as they existed in the real world, to be the most natural manifestation of that sociability. Hence Agnolo's complaints about the difficulties of life "*fra la moltitudine*".

Turning once again to Charon's tale, it is important to remember that the ferryman had insisted that he had not heard the story from a philosopher but from a painter. The painter, he asserted, had learnt more from looking at *lineamenta* than any philosopher had ever done when measuring the heavens. Even here we appear to encounter an attack on one of man's most important claims to intellectual accomplishment. For the man who gazes at the heavens and understands the motions of the stars had long been emblematic of the search for truth and wisdom. To quote Fleming once more, "in the medieval iconology of learning the stars play a decisive role, because the wise man is, *par excellence*, the astronomer, the student of the stars".[46] Indeed, the eighth psalm suggests that the study of the stars might confirm man's special dignity:

> When I consider the heavens, the work of thy fingers the moon and the stars, which thou has ordained; What is man, that thou are mindful of him? And the son of man that thou visitest him? For thou hast made him but little lower than the angels, And crownest him with glory and honour. Thou madest him to have dominion over the works of thy hands; Thou hast put all things under his feet; all sheep and oxen, yea, and the beasts of the field, The foul of the air and the fish of the sea, Whatsoever passeth through the paths of the sea.

The sight of the heavens here initially leads to a consciousness of man's minuteness when compared to the vast complexity of creation. Yet it also serves to underline man's privileged place, "but little lower than the angels", crowned with honour and glory and given dominion over the whole earth. Ultimately, it impels man to praise God.[47] In brushing aside the claims of the philosopher and star-gazer, Alberti declines to engage with this discourse. As we have seen, the story develops in such a way that the privileged position of man, at least man in general, looks far from assured. Instead, Alberti suggests another, seemingly surer means of achieving knowledge. It is the study of *lineamenta*, common to both painting and architecture, that allows the painter to see beyond fictive appearances and to understand the truth about human beings. Rather than being prompted by the stars to praise God, *lineamenta* here act as a spur to decry the foolishness of a large section of humanity. The implications of the idea that knowledge of *lineamenta* might allow for an especially profound kind of knowledge are momentous, but discussion of them must be reserved for another place. It is perhaps enough here to note that in his supposed autobiography, Alberti had claimed of himself that "he could also recognise the faults of a man on sight alone".[48]

The interpretation of Alberti's work is an inherently tricky business. One is faced with a large body of writing on a diverse range of subjects. Different works were written for different purposes, employing a variety of approaches and styles. There is a real danger that by selecting a quotation from here, a quotation from there and removing them from their original context, one might be able to make Alberti say anything. The danger is heightened when we mix together distinct genres, such as the Latin *Momus* or *Intercenales* with the vernacular dialogues such as *De famila* or *De iciarchia*. Indeed, it has sometimes been proposed that works such as the *Momus* should be largely discounted in the attempt to interpret Alberti's thought, since we are unable to decipher them with any certainty. And yet they are there; not only present but seemingly brimming with meaning and inviting interpretation. I do not deny that it would be quite possible to construct an image of Alberti that is at odds with the one that is offered here. As stated above, there are, for instance, times when Alberti is far more forthright regarding the dignity of man. It is not my contention that the various passages cited here are bound together by a kind of invisible thread so that they may be read as though they were intended as the component parts of a complete argument, or as though they form a coherent text of their own. Rather, I have cited these passages because they appear to me to be emblematic of positions that Alberti takes throughout his writings. His thinking about the city is almost always marked by a significant degree of doubt, a persistent ambivalence which takes a variety of different forms. These positions themselves, however, derive from Alberti's most fundamental views about humanity; the problems of the city are in truth the problems of mankind. Alberti is often optimistic about man's potential. The cultivation of *virtù* and the acquisition of *dottrina* are for him the surest way to the *bene e beato vivere*. And yet there are other times when he seems to suggest that even the best of men may not be rewarded for their diligence and moral steadfastness. Moreover, one has the impression that those who are able to cultivate real *virtù* are a small minority. The rest of humanity is in a far less promising position and, as noted above, Alberti seems to imply that some people are simply bad from beginning to end.[49] Entirely lacking in his writings is anything that resembles the traditional theological notion of salvation and there is no indication that the mask-wearers who have wandered from the path can ever truly change the inner monster that they have become. If Alberti is reluctant to exult the city then his reluctance begins with mankind. For all the benefits that it offers, one is left with the impression that the city may be the creation of a humanity which has left the order of Nature.

/ **1.** Vitruvius Pollio, Marcus, *De architectura*, vol 1, trans Frank Granger, London: Heinemann, and Cambridge, MA: Harvard University Press, 1931, 2, I, p. 77: "*Homines vetere more ut ferae in silvis et speluncis et nemoribus nascebantur ciboque agresti vescendo vitam exigebant.*"

/ **2.** Vitruvius, *De architectura*, pp. 78–79: "*... ligna adicientes et id conservantes alios adducebant et nutu monstrantes ostendebant, quas haberent ex eo utilitates. In eo hominum congressu cum profundebantur aliter e spiritu voces, cotidiana consuetudine vocabula, ut optigerant, constituerunt, deinde significando res saepius in usu* *ex eventu fari fortuito coeperunt et ita sermones inter se procreaverunt. Ergo cum propter ignis inventionem conventus initio apud homines et concilium et convictus esset natus, et in unum locum plures convenirent habentes ab natura praemium praeter reliqua animalia, ut non proni sed erecti ambularent mundique et astrorum magnificentiam aspicerent, item manibus et articulis quam vellent rem faciliter tractarent, coeperunt in eo coetu alii de fronde facere tecta, alii speluncas fodere sub montibus, nonnulli hirundinum nidos et aedificationes earum imitantes de luto et virgulis facere loca quae subirent."*

/ **3.** Alberti, LB, *De re aedificatoria*, prologue: "*Fuere qui dicerent aquam aut ignem praebuisse principia, quibus effectum sit, ut hominum coetus celebrarentur. Nobis vero tecti parietisque utilitatem atque necessitatem spectantibus ad homines conciliandos atque una continendos maiorem in modum valuisse nimirum persuadebitur.*" Citations from Alberti's *De re aedificatoria* refer to the English translation in LB Alberti, *On the Art of building in Ten Books*, trans J Rykwert, N Leach, R Tavernor, Cambridge, MA and London: MIT Press, 1988; and the Latin transcription in LB Alberti, *L'architettura*, trans G Orlandi, Milano: Edizioni Il Polifilo, 1966.

/ **4.** Alberti, LB, *De re aedificatoria*, I, 2: "*... hic adeo coepisse meditari, ut tecta ponerent, quo essent a sole et imbribus operti; idque ut facerent, adiecisse deinde parietum latera, quibus tecta imponerentur—sic enim a gelidis tempestatibus et pruinosis ventis se futuros tutiores intelligebant... Itaque quicunque ille fuerit, seu Vesta dea Saturni fila, seu Heurialus Hiperbiusque fratres, seu Gellio aut Traso Cyclopsve Tiphinchius, qui ista principio instituerit, tandem sic puto hos fuisse condendorum aedificiorum primos ortus primosque ordines.*"

/ **5.** Alberti, LB, *De re aedificatoria*, "*Sed omnia ab his, quae recensuimus, principiis manasse negabit nemo.*"

/ **6.** Alberti, LB, *De re aedificatoria*, IV, 1: "*Nam principio quidem, si recte interpretamur, facere opus homines coepere, quo se suaque ab adversis tempestatibus tuerentur. Proxime item prosecuti sunt non modo velle quae ad salutem essent necessaria, verum et siqua etiam ad expeditas quasque commoditates assequendas conferrent, ea nusquam esse praetermissa voluere.*"

/ **7.** The most important work in this regard is M Paoli, *L'idée de nature chez Leon Battista Alberti (1404–1472)*, Paris: Honoré Champion Editeur, 1999.

/ **8.** See C Smith, *Architecture in the Culture of Early Humanism: Ethics, Aesthetics and Eloquence 1400–1470*, New York and Oxford: Oxford University Press, 1992, p. 8, for a similar characterisation of nature in some of Alberti's works; M Paoli, *L'idée de nature chez Leon Battista Alberti (1404–1472)*, on the whole takes a different view.

/ **9.** Alberti, LB, *Opere volgari*, vol 2, C Grayson, ed, Bari, 1960–1966, p. 87. The relationship between Nature and *fortuna* is explored at some length in M Paoli, *L'idée de nature chez Leon Battista Alberti (1404–1472)*, pp. 131–135. Paoli does not see the Albertian concept of *fortuna* as being in conflict with his concept of Nature but instead argues persuasively that there is room for *fortuna* within the order of Nature.

/ **10.** This is not to say that Alberti was influenced by the specifically Christian content of this thought. Indeed, true Christian sentiment finds little place in his writings. Rather, he appears to adopt some of the underlying ideas about man's relationship to the world but largely outside of a Christian context. M Paoli, *L'idée de nature chez Leon Battista Alberti (1404–1472)*, pp. 114–116 argues that Alberti's conception of nature is not significantly influenced by Christian ideas.

/ **11.** Alberti, LB, *Momus*, trans V Brown and S Knight, Cambridge, MA and London: Harvard University Press, 2003, pp. 6–7: "*Nos contra elaboravimus ut qui nos legant rideant, aliaque ex parte sentiant se versari in rerum pervestigatione atque explicatione utili et minime aspernanda.*"

/ **12.** Alberti, LB, *Momus*, pp. 306–308: "*Ex Charonte adeo portitore disce ipsum te nosse. Referam quae non a philosopho—nam vestra omnis ratio nisi in argutiis et verborum captiunculis versatur—sed a pictore quodam memini audivisse. Is quidem lineamentis contemplandis plus vidit solus quam vos omnes philosophi caelo commensurando et disquirendo. Adis animo: audies rem rarissimam. Sic enim aiebat pictor: tanti operis artificem selegisse et depurasse id quo esset hominem conditurus; id vero fuisse aliqui limum melle infusum, alii ceram tractando contepefactam. Quicquid ipsum fuerit, aiunt imposuisse sigillis aeneis binis quibus altero pectus, vultus et quae cum his una visuntur, altero occiput, tergum, nates et postrema istiusmodi impressarentur.*"

/ **13.** Alberti, LB, *Momus*, "*Multas formasse hominum species et ex his selegisse mancas et vitio insignes, praesertim leves et vacuas, ut essent feminae, feminasque a maribus distinxisse dempto ab iis Paulo quantillo quod alteris adigeretur. Fecisse item alio ex luto variisque sigillis multiplices alias animantium species. Quibus operibus confectis, cum vidisset homines aliquos sua non usquequaque forma delectari, edixisse ut* *qui id praestare arbitrarentur quas placuerit in alias reliquorum animantium facies se verterent."*

/ **14.** Alberti, LB, *Momus*, pp. 308–311: "*Dehinc suas quae obiecto in monte paterent aedes monstravit atque hortatus est ut acclivi directaque via quae pateret conscenderent: habituros illic omnem bonarum rerum copiam, sed iterum atque iterum caverent ne alias praeter hanc inirent vias—videri arduam initio hanc, sed continuo aequabilem successuram. His dictis abivisse. Homunculos coepisse conscendere, sed illico alios per stultitiam boves, asinos, quadrupeds videri maluisse, alios cupiditatis errore adductos in transversos viculos delirasse. Illic abruptis constreposisque praecipitiis sentibusque et vepribus irretitos pro loci difficultate se in varia vertisse monstra; et iterato ad primariam viam redisse, illic fuisse ab suis ob deformitatem explosos. Ea de re, comperto consimili quo compacti essent luto, fictas et aliorum vultibus compares sibi superinduisse personas, et crevisse hoc personandorum hominum artificium usu quoad paene a veris secernas fictos vultus ni forte accuratius ipsa per foramina obductae personae introspexeris: illinc enim contemplantibus varias solere occurrere monstri facies. Et appellatus personas hasce fictiones easque ad Acherontis usque undas durare, nihilo plus, nam fluvium ingressis humido vapore evenire ut dissolvantur. Quo fit ut alteram nemo ad ripam non nudatus amissa persona pervenerit. Tum Gelastus: "O Charon, fingisne haec ludi gratia an vera praedicas?" "Quin" inquit Charon "ex personarum barbis et superciliis rudentem hunc intorsi ipsoque ex luto cumbam obstipavi."*

/ **15.** Brown, V and S Knight in LB Alberti, *Momus*, p. 397, fn 20, cite Dante's *Purgatorio*; Petrarch, *Epistole familiari* 4.1; and Seneca, *De providential*, 5 as examples. The notion that the true nature of a person can be seen in the eyes might also be related to Matthew, 6, 22–23: "The light of the body is the eye: if therefore thine eye be single, thy whole body shall be full of light. But if thine eye be evil, thy whole body shall be full of darkness. If therefore the light that is in thee be darkness, how great is that darkness!" This is closely followed at 7, 13 by the command "Enter ye in at the strait gate: for wide is the gate, and broad is the way, that leadeth to destruction, and many there be which go in thereat: Because strait is the gate, and narrow is the way, which leadeth unto life, and few there be that find it."

/ **16.** Writing about the *Momus* and some of the *Intercenales*, M Marassi, *Metamorfosi della storia, Momus e Alberti*, Milan: Mimesis Edizioni, 2004, p. 51, characterises Alberti as viewing humanity as being irredeemably fallen.

/ **17.** Alberti, LB, *Momus*, pp. 100–103: "*Nunc vero aliam nostris temporibus accommodatiorem personam imbuendam sentio. Et quaenam ea erit persona, Mome? Nempe ut comem, lenem affabilemque me exhibeam.... Ne tu haec, Mome, ab tua natura penitus aliena poteris? Potero quidem, dum velim.... Quid tum? Igiturne vero nos insitum et penitus innatum lacessendi morem obliviscemur? Minime; verum id quidem moderabimur taciturnitate, pristinumque erga inimicos studium nova quadam captandi laedendique via et ratione servabimus. Demum sic statuo oportere his quibus intra multitudinem atque in negotio vivendum sit, ut ex intimis praecordiis numquam susceptae iniuriae memoriam obliterent, offensae vero livorem nusquam propalent, sed inserviant temporibus, simulando atque dissimulando."*

/ **18.** Alberti, LB, *Momus*, "*... credent nemini, sed credere omnibus ostentabunt. Nullos vereantur, sed coram quibusque applaudere atque assentari omnibus condocefiant."*

/ **19.** Alberti, LB, *Momus*, pp. 104–105: "*Sed quid plura? Omnino illud unum iterum atque iterum iuvabit meminisse, bene et gnaviter fuscare omnia adumbratis quibusdam signis probitatis et innocentiae. Quam quidem rem pulchre assequemur si verba vultusque nostros et omnem corporis faciem assuefaciemus ita fingere atque conformare, ut illis esse persimiles videamur qui boni ac mites putentur, tametsi ab illis penitus discrepemus. O rem optimam nosse erudito artificio fucatae fallacisque simulationis suos operire atque obnubere sensus!"*

/ **20.** This is particularly evident in the words of Gianozzo in the third book of the dialogue.

/ **21.** On this see RW Dyson's introduction to Saint Augustine, *The city of God against the pagans*, ed and trans RW Dyson, Cambridge: Cambridge University Press, 1998, p. xvii.

/ **22.** Alberti, LB, *Opere volgari*, vol 2, p. 266: "*Quanto m'occorre dalla natura, pare a me che la città com'è constituita da molte famiglia, così ella in sé sia quasi come una ben grande famiglia; e, contro, la famiglia sia quasi una picciola città. E s'io non erro, così l'essere dell'una come dell'altra nacque per congregazione e coniunzione di molti insieme adunati e contenuti per qualche loro necessità e utilità."*

/ **23.** Alberti, LB, *Opere volgari*, "*Le cose in prima necessarie sono quelle senza le quale non si può perseverare bene in vita. E se, come noi tuttora proviamo, dal primo ingresso a questa luce sino all'ultimo fine sempre all'omo sta necessità chiedere aiuto dagli altri omini, certo sempre furono a' mortali utili e necessarie molto le coniunzioni, massime di que' che sono nati e* *allevati insieme e contenuti da un volere esser l'uno pell'altro salvi e in buono stato. Questo simile uso di vivere insieme e ridursi sotto a un tetto si chiama familiarità; e questo numero d'omini così ridutti insieme si dice famiglia. E forse le coniunzioni familiari legate da consanguinità hanno insieme qualche commodità più necessaria che quella qual ci presta la città, massime quando così sia che la natura per sé pose insieme questi onde s'acrebbe in primo la famiglia.*"

/ **24.** Alberti, LB, *Opere volgari*, "*Ma furono poi le città constituite forse a caso, e non per altra ragione che solo per vivere con sufficienza e commodità insieme. E parmi che alla origine della famiglia el primo accesso fu amore, e indi el primario vincolo a contenerli insieme fu pietà e carità e certo officio richiesto dalla natura verso e' suoi. In questi altri della città pare che certo fine, per più conservare sé stessi che per punto beneficar gli altri, li congregasse. Quinci forse e non senza ragione affermerete che tu più debbi alla famiglia tua che al resto della città.*"

/ **25.** For a different view see M Paoli, *L'idée de nature chez Leon Battista Alberti (1404–1472)*, especially pp. 152–154.

/ **26.** Aristotle, *Politics*, 1252a24.

/ **27.** Aristotle, *Politics*, trans TA Sinclair, London: Penguin, 1992, p. 58 (1252b15).

/ **28.** Aristotle, *Politics*, p. 59 (1252b27). Here and in the following quotations I have modified the translation, substituting "city-state" for Sinclair's "state."

/ **29.** Aristotle, *Politics*.

/ **30.** Aristotle, *Politics*, (1253a1); indeed, it is argued at 1253a7 that this quality separates man from other animals such as bees which, although they may be gregarious, are not political.

/ **31.** The type of priority referred to here is what Aristotle terms priority in nature. Although the individual and the household existed before the city, and are thus prior to it in time, the city is prior to the individual and household in nature. In Aristotelian terms, priority in nature refers to the whole being necessary in order for the parts that constitute it to exist. Just as the parts of the body could not exist without the body itself, so the individual, because it is not self-sufficient, could not exist without the city. For a discussion of priority in this sense see Aristotle, *Metaphysics*, I, 8, 989a15, and V, 11, 1019a2.

/ **32.** Aristotle, *Politics*, p. 61 (1253a18).

/ **33.** Leonardo Bruni's commentary on the pseudo Aristotle's *Economicus* likewise explores the differences between the family and the city, or rather the *res publica*. Bruni follows the conventional Aristotelian argument, which also weighs heavily on Alberti's writings, that the purpose of the city is to allow men to live well and comfortably and that it arises out of the natural interdependence of human beings. Interestingly, Bruni, who dedicated his text to Cosimo de' Medici, significantly develops the role of trade and money in the formation and preservation of societies, going rather beyond the actual text that he is commenting on. He argues that "there is thus an exchange of things which holds the city together" and that "money has... been found to be a necessary instrument for holding the city together and supporting social existence". see L Bruni, *The Humanism of Leonardo Bruni: selected texts with introductions and translations by Gordon Griffiths, James Hankins and David Thompson*, Binghampton, NY, Medieval & Renaissance Texts & Studies in conjunction with the Renaissance Society of America, 1987 pp. 308–309. Alberti never places so great an emphasis on trade in explaining the origins of human societies.

/ **34.** Garin, E, "Studi su Leon Battista Alberti" in *Rinascite e rivoluzioni. Movimenti culturali dal XIV al XVIII secolo*, Roma-Bari, 1975, p. 145. Nonetheless, Garin's observations do not appear to be entirely accurate. He describes the creator of Charon's story as impervious, and as being amused by the spectacle of the humans below trying to disguise themselves with mud. Yet there is nothing in the text to suggest the creator's amusement. Garin also describes the painter as standing apart and taking note of the goings on. However, it is not clear from Alberti's text that the painter should be understood as having been present at these events. Rather, it is surely the painter's speciality in the realm of images and understanding of *lineamenta* that allow him knowledge of what went before. On the painter as a specialist in imagery in the wider context of *Momus*, see R Rinaldi, *"Melancholia christiana". Studi sulle fonti di Leon Battista Alberti*, Firenze: Leo S Olschki, 2002, p. 133.

/ **35.** Marassi, M, *Metamorfosi della storia*, p. 51 writes in this regard: "*Se si accostano queste pagine [Intercenales* Fatum et fortuna *and* Fatum et pater infelix*] di Alberti a quelle più celebrate e ormai assunte a canone della figura dell'uomo dell'Umanesimo, scritte da Pico, la distanza è abissale. La filosofia della* dignitas hominis, *che scorge in questa creatura una "realtà sovrannaturale e privilegiata", viene capovolta da Alberti nell'immagine della follia, più atta a descrivere l'ambivalenza dei desideri, l'accecamento delle passioni, proposta in un'antropologia che riposa su un'ironia filosofica complessa, intrisa com'è di elementi ermetici,* *cinici e stoici. Dove Pico celebra dell'uomo la dignità, Alberti ne descrive le nefandezze; dove Dio libera l'uomo dalla caduta e lo affida alla scelta di un modello di esistenza, Alberti ne tratteggia la sorte da cui non può mai svincolarsi, anzi a malapena riesce a celare a se stesso e gli altri i suoi continui scontri con la sventura. L'uomo come assoluta possibilità di Pico ha come contraltare nel* Momus *le bizzarie del disordine e la malvagità delle azioni: l'immagine di uomo che viene proposta è inquiete e inafferabile....*"

36. Alberti, LB, *Opere volgari*, vol 2, p. 234: "*Chi potrà mirare un maledico ottrettatore, calunniatore, e non avere orrore della rabbia sua? Omini ancora e ancora pessimi, degni d'essere persequitati da tutto el populo, non dirò con l'arco e colle saette, ma co' funali e face infiammate, e brustulati tanto che l'ossa rimangono denudate, acciò che niuna fizione possa più in quell mostro essere latente!*" The language here is similar to that used in Charon's story, where men adopt *fictos vultus* but finally end up *nudatus*.

37. In *Somnium*, which contains some of the most vivid imagery to be found in the *Intercenales*, Libripeta enters a wide meadow of human and animal hair, where people are digging up roots that will make them appear learned even though they are not. He is then nearly devoured by a swarm of lice. Here too the physicality of the body and hair specifically, is employed in the mocking of human pretensions.

38. Aristotle, *Politics*, 1253a7; Alberti also proposes that language distinguishes man from beast in the *De iciarchia*, p. 232, although the distinction is more to do with the quality of language rather than the possession of language *per se*. His remarks have something of the flavour of Lucretius' discussion of the issue in *De rerum natura*, 5, 1028. The contrast between civilised man and wild beast is a constant in Alberti's writings. In a passage of the *De iciarchia*, he urges that man was not created to live like an animal, and is distinguished from other mortal beings by his ability to investigate the causes of things, to seek the truth and to understand morality. Ironically, however, it is usually men who live in cities, surrounded by other men, that are described as beasts in Alberti's writings, rather than those who live in the country surrounded by animals.

39. Flemming, JV, "Natura lachrymosa" in *Man and Nature in the Middle Ages*, S Ridyard and R Benson, eds, Sewanee, 1995, p. 29.

40. Alberti, LB, *De familia*, Tenenti and Romano, eds, Torino: Einaudi, 1972, pp. 160–161: "*Manco a me dispiace la sentenza d'Anassagoro filosafo, el quale domandato per che cagione fusse da Dio procreato l'uomo, risposse: "Ci ha produtto per essere contemplatore del cielo, delle stele, e del sole, e di tutte quelle sue meravigliose opere divine." E puossi non poco persuadere questa opinione, poiché noi vediamo altro niuno animante non prono e inclinato pendere col capo al pasco e alla terra; solo l'uomo veggiamo ritto colla fronte e col viso elevato, quasi come da essa natura sia cosí fabricato solo a rimanere e riconoscere e' luoghi e cose celeste.*"

41. Slightly further on in the *De familia*, Alberti undertakes a short diversion in order to discuss the origins of human societies. Here too he dismisses the notion that water or fire were responsible for bringing men together and instead advances the Aristotelian theory of mutual interdependence: "*Non fece la natura gli uomini tutti d'una compressione, d'uno ingegno e d'uno volere, né tuti a un modo atti e valenti. Anzi volse che in quello in quale io manco, ivi tu supplisca, e in altra cosa manchi la quale sia apresso di quell'altro. Perché questo? Perch'io abbia di te bisogno, tu di colui, colui d'uno altro, e qualche uno di me, e cosí questo aver bisogno l'uno uomo dell'altro sia cagione e vinculo a conservarci insieme con publica amicizia e congiunzione. E forse questa necessità fu esordio e principio di fermare le republice, di costituirvi le leggi molto piú che come diceva... fuoco o d'acque essere stato cogione di tanta fra gli uomini e sí con legge, ragione e costume colligate unione de' mortali.*" Unlike Alberti's forceful assertion in the *De re aedificatoria* that it was the need for shelter that brought men together, these words have a somewhat formulaic feel. As M Paoli, *L'idée de nature chez Leon Battista Alberti (1404–1472)*, p. 145, puts it: "*... il s'agit là d'habitudes rhétoriques*".

42. Alberti, LB, *Opere volgari*, vol 2, p. 122: "*Non premediterò io assiduo me essere nato non solo, come rispose Anassagora, a contemplare el cielo, le stelle e la universa natura, ma e ancora in prima, come affermava Lattanzio, per riconoscere e servire a Dio, quando servire a Dio non sia altro che darsi a favoreggiare e' buoni e a mantenere giustizia?*"

43. Alberti, LB, *Opere volgari*, "*Queste due cose qual dicea Seneca filosofo esserci date da Dio sopra tutte l'altre validissime, la ragione e la società, lascerolle io estinguere per desidia e inerzia e nulla valere in me?*" Later: "*Quinci saremo in ogni officio d'umanità e culto di virtù ben composti, e ben serviremo alla naturale società e vera religione, e preporrenci in ogni nostra vita esser constanti e liberi.*"

44. Alberti, LB, *Opere volgari*, p. 124: "*Ma e' dicono ancora che la patria dell'uomo si è tutto* *el mondo, e che 'l savio, in qualunque luogo sarà constituto, farà quell luogo suo...."*

/ **45.** Alberti, LB, *Opere volgari*, "*Fra la moltitudine puoi né stare né andare che tu non sia urteggiato.... La solitudine sempre fu amica della quiete; e questo vero quando la sia non oziosa. L'ozio—chi dubita?—nutrisce ogni vizio; e nulla più peturba che' l vizio.*"

/ **46.** Flemming, JV, "Natura ridens" in *Man and Nature in the Middle Ages*, p. 7.

/ **47.** See JV Flemming, "Natura ridens" in *Man and Nature in the Middle Ages*, pp. 4–5ff. For an interesting commentary on the eighth Psalm in the context of the relationship between man and nature.

/ **48.** Alberti, LB, *Vita*, in R Neu Watkins, "Lcon Battista Alberti in the mirror: an interpretation of the *Vita* with a new translation" in *Italian Quarterly*, 30, 1989, p. 15; also R Fubini and A Menci Gallorini, "L'autobiografia di Leon Battista Alberti studio e edizione" in *Rinascimento*, 68, 1972, pp. 36, 76: "*... ex solo intuitu plurima cuiusque praesentis vitia ediscebat*".

/ **49.** In the *Profugiorum*, Agnolo warns against believing that all men are good. Alberti, *Opere volgari*, vol 2, p. 127: "*E con tutti conviensi esser tardi al credere e persuaderti ch'ogni uomo sia buono.*"

THE DARK SIDE OF ARCHITECTURE

Kari Jormakka

God made the world out of nothing. But the nothingness shows through.
Paul Valéry, *Ex nihilo*[1]

Vitruvius traces the birth of architecture to the moment when men, still living in woods and caves like wild beasts, discovered flames burning in the forest. Realising how comfortable it was to stand before the warm fire, they brought up more people to it, and in this first assembly, invented language and started to construct shelters.[2] This narrative implies that architecture is on par with language a *definiens* of humanity. Later thinkers have sometimes concurred with this generous judgment on architecture. Sigmund Freud, for one, lists the three first acts of civilisation as the making of fire, the manufacture of tools, and the construction of dwellings after the model of the mother's womb.[3]

The Vitruvian account set an even more important precedent in suggesting that architecture was invented to provide weather protection. This idea has also survived across the centuries. In 1753, to give an example, Abbé Laugier asked us to consider "man in his earliest origins, without any other help, without other guide than the natural instinct of his needs". To provide himself with shelter from the scorching sunshine and fearful rains, primitive man constructed a simple roof that set the paradigm for the entire subsequent development of architecture.[4] Following this lead, Otto Wagner in *Modern Architecture* of 1896 confidently declared that "the need and necessity for protection against inclement weather and against men and animals was certainly the first cause and original purpose of building".[5] In *Towards a New Architecture* of 1924, Le Corbusier claimed that architecture is a direct function of human instinct and that it serves the human need for shelter.[6] Despite its popularity, this idea is not as self-evident as it may seem at first glance. As early as 1755, Jean-Jacques Rousseau observed in his second discourse that climate protection could not have necessitated the construction of the first dwellings, for architecture was invented in the same regions where humans were already living in temporary or natural shelters.[7]

SHAME AND FEAR

Not surprisingly, then, other explanations for the origin of architecture have also been proposed. In 1741, John Wood the Elder, the architect of Bath, sought to revise the classical theory of architecture in his treatise *The Origin of Architecture, or the Plagiarism of the Heathen Lies Detected.*[8] Wood explains that:

> VITRUVIUS, at the very Time that *Augustus* became *High Priest*, and EXAMINED into the PROPHETICK BOOKS, composed his Works on *Architecture*, for *Caesar's* Instruction in it; and as the Emperor burnt above 2,000 Volumes of those Books, preserving only some of the *Sibylline*, can there remain the least Doubt, but that *Vitruvius* attributed to the *Grecians* whatever was found recorded, concerning *Architecture*, in the *Jewish* history? Here was a sufficient Cloak for his divesting the Jews, and giving to the *Heathens* the Invention of every Thing curious in *Architecture*: And this PLAGIARISM will more strongly appear, when we come to explain the proper *Orders* of Columns, with the *Forms* and *Proportions* of the Heathen *Temples*.[9]

Wood claimed that God revealed to Moses "how we should supply our Necessities in Building, with the Materials of the Earth, and even reconcile Art with Nature... to which purpose, as the pillars imitated trees, so they were made with a Base at the Bottom, to answer the Root End and with a Capital at the Top to represent the Head of the Tree...."[10] Although the orders were of divine origin, the Greeks adopted them and fabricated a false account of them: "being a People naturally inclined to Fiction, they so dressed up their Story of the Origin of the Orders that the Romans very readily had given the Invention of these beautiful Parts to them, as appears by the Writings of Vitruvius".

Wood's attempt to demonstrate that the Vitruvian books were plagiarised may owe something to Clement of Alexandria who in the sixth book of the *Stromata* accuses Greek poets and philosophers of stealing their wisdom from each other and from the Christians.[11] Not only do both authors condemn the plagiarisms but they also point out that the true message usually gets distorted in the process. Thus, Wood argues that the Vitruvian triad of *utilitas*, *firmitas* and *venustas* is a misrepresentation of the real causes of architecture. Through a close reading of the Genesis, he attempts a reconstruction of the original theory of architecture and names the two most important principles of architecture:

> The First received its Origin at the Time of the *Fall*, when Man, ashamed of his Disobedience, *screened himself under Trees*; the Second took its Birth in the Third Generation, when *Cain*, in fear of Reprisals for the Murder of his Brother *Abel, built Huts to keep his Family in one collected Body*, thereby to enable him to prevent the other Part of the Issue of *Adam* from taking Vengeance upon him which the Nature of his Crime deserved. *Convenience of Shelter* was therefore *the First Principle of Architecture*, and *Strength the Second*: Dreadful Effects of Disobedience to GOD![12]

In Wood's interpretation, the first principle of architecture, shame, corresponds to the Vitruvian *utilitas*, and the second, fear, to *firmitas*. He goes on to articulate three more principles on the basis of the Biblical account: "BY the *Tower of Babel*, which was erected to shew the *Piety of Man, Architecture* receiv'd a *third Principle*." Although this principle, unlike the first two, was revealed to Mankind by God, it still led to a disaster, as the attempts of the Builders of the Tower "ended in nothing but CONFUSION".[13] At this time, "those Cities, which, upon the Confusion of Languages, were founded for *Convenience*, were afterwards judg'd as necessary for *Defence*; and therefore the principal Care of the People was to inclose every City with a Bank of Earth, or with a Wall..." but "the Manner of Building remain'd in its primitive Simplicity, without Order, Proportion, or any other Character that could render it beautiful".[14]

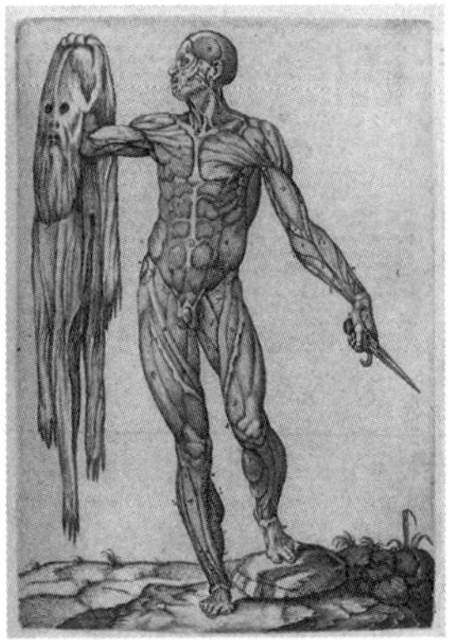

left/ John Wood the Elder, *The Order of the Temple of Solomon*.
right/ Juan de Valverde de Amusco, *Anatomia del corpo humano*, 1560.

Soon therafter, according to Wood's exegesis, "ARCHITECTURE however receiv'd two other Principles by these early Works; and such as regarded the *Gratitude*, and the *Fidelity* of Man: The former took its Rise when *Jacob* had his Vision [of collecting stones into heaps and erecting a pillar on the grave of Rachel],[15] and the latter when he made his Covenant, with *Laban*."[16] Finally, Wood concludes: "all the Causes of Building are Five, to wit, *Shame*, *Fear*, *Piety*, *Gratitude*, and *Fidelity*; and these produced three Precepts of Building, namely, *Convenience*, *Strength*, and *Beauty*. The two first whereof Mankind soon attain'd, but the last was REVEALED to them...."[17]

CAIN'S HOUSE

Although to us, Wood's reasoning may appear idiosyncractic, the notion that architecture is a "Dreadful Effect" of sin has a long history. Myths about the origin of architecture reinforce the pattern linking architecture—or the city—to either an original act of violence or to the concealment of a sin. The Greeks sometimes attributed the invention of architecture to Daidalos who built a labyrinth to hide the Minotaur, the result of an impure union between Queen Pasiphaë and a white bull. The violence of the monster was not canceled even when contained within the walls of the first building but instead indefinitely perpetuated and organised as sacrifice. The architectural institutionalisation of violence does not only apply to such monuments as the labyrinth but even much later to the canonic ornamentation of classical architecture. George Hersey has pointed out that familiar classical ornaments constitute an elaborate architectural representation of human or animal sacrifices: *guttae* for example stand for drops of blood or fat.[18] For Clement of Alexandria, the temples of the pagan gods were "in reality tombs" and the pagan mysteries were "in short, murders and funerals".[19]

Clement is not alone among the Early Christians to view ancient monuments with suspicion. The reasons for the Christian anathematisation of architecture go back to the Old Testament and later Judeo-Christian writers. Summing up this tradition, the fifteenth century *Cooke Manuscript* explains that "Jabal was the first man that ever found Geometry and Masonry, and he made houses.... And he was Cain's Master Mason and governor of all his works, when he made the City of Enoch—that was the first City that ever was made, and that made Cain, Adam's son."[20] Jabal's father was Lamech, a descendant of Cain in the seventh generation and the first one to violate the divine institution of monogamy. One day Lamech said to his two wives, "Adah and Zillah, Hear my voice; ye wives of Lamech, hearken unto my speech: for I have slain a man to my wounding, and a young man to my hurt."[21] The Talmud and Midrash, as well as the Second Book of Adam and Eve, explain that Lamech accidentally killed his forefather Cain with an arrow, and soon thereafter his son Tubal-Cain, the inventor of the sword, by smashing his head with a rock.

Thus, in the Biblical tradition the origins of geometry and architecture are compromised, to say the least. Before the Fall, there was no need for architecture in the Garden of Eden, nor are there any buildings in the Heavenly Jerusalem, according to the Book of Revelation: "And I saw no temple therein: for the Lord God Almighty and the Lamb are the temple of it."[22] After the Fall, things changed. The Book of Genesis tells that once *elohim*, the band of gods, refused his agricultural offering, Cain killed his nomadic brother Abel and was expelled. In response, he founded a city for his family and named it Enoch, after his son.[23] Flavius Josephus claims that Cain

> did not accept of his punishment in order to amendment, but to increase his wickedness; for he only aimed to procure every thing that was for his own bodily pleasure, though it obliged him to be injurious to his neighbours. He augmented his household substance with much wealth, by rapine and violence; he excited his acquaintance to procure pleasures and spoils by robbery, and became a great leader of men into wicked courses. He also introduced a change in that way of simplicity wherein men lived before; and was the author of measures and weights. And whereas they lived innocently and generously while they knew nothing of such arts, he changed the world into cunning craftiness. He first of all set boundaries about lands: he built a city, and fortified it with walls, and he compelled his family to come together to it; and called that city Enoch, after the name of his eldest son Enoch.[24]

Notably, St Augustine comments on Enoch:

> The founder of the earthly city was a fratricide. Overcome with envy, he slew his own brother, a citizen of the eternal city, and a sojourner on earth. So that we cannot be surprised that this first specimen, or as the Greeks say, archetype of crime, should, long afterwards, find a corresponding crime at the foundation of that city which was destined to reign over so many nations, and be the head of this earthly city of which we speak. For of that city also, as one of their poets has mentioned, 'the first walls were stained with a brother's blood' or, as Roman history records, Remus was slain by his brother Romulus.[25]

Of course, mythologies tell not only of fratricide founders of cities, such as Cain or Romulus. There are also parricide founders, such as Theseus, as well as child murderers.[26] Walter Burkert explains that "a house, a bridge or a dam will stay strong only if something lies slaughtered beneath it... any new birth... requires ritual killing".[27]

The harvest of the city founders' guilt was more violence. Augustine argues that the *civitas terrena* "is often divided against itself by litigations, wars, quarrels, and such victories as are either life-destroying or short-lived".[28] The aggression is also directed outwards. From Plutarch we learn that four months after Romulus had built Rome he abducted 30 daughters of the Sabines, not because there were not enough women in Rome but because he realised that the greatness of the city depended on the benefit of war.[29]

In the Augustinian vision, the denizens of the earthly city ultimately cause the end of the world. The saint believed that the evil forces of the Apocalypse, Gog and Magog, are not to be understood as some barbarous nations, such as the Getæ and Massagetæ; rather "the meaning of these names we find to be, Gog, 'a roof', Magog, 'from a roof'—a house, as it were, and he who comes out of a house". He implies that Gog and Magog are the sedentary house-dwellers who attack the nomadic "camp of the saints".[30] Perhaps the inextricable connection between cities and violence is the reason why nomads were equally appalled by cities as by graves, as Ammianus relates about the Huns.[31]

GOLDEN YEARS

In contrast to the violence of the cities, many mythologies postulate an original paradise or a golden age which often bears the hallmarks of a nomadic way of life. Summarising the view of Dicaearchus, a student of Aristotle, Porphyry Malchos characterises the Golden Age thus:

> men did not procure any thing by labour, because they were unacquainted with the agricultural thing by labour, because they were unacquainted with the agricultural art, and, in short, had no knowledge of any other art. This very thing, likewise, was the cause of their leading a life of leisure, free from labours and care; and if it is proper to assent to the decision of the most skillful and elegant of physicians, it was also the cause of their being liberated from disease.... Moreover, there were neither any wars among them, nor seditions with each other. For no reward of contention worth mentioning was proposed as an incentive, for the sake of which some one might be induced to engage in such dissensions. So that the principal thing is that life was leisure and rest from necessary occupations, together with health, peace, and friendship.[32]

But then the original paradise was lost forever—until archaeologist Juris Zarins announced in 1980 that through an analysis of textual evidence, ancient language patterns, geological and hydrological research as well as satellite photos he had finally discovered the Biblical Garden, or that what was left of it, at the tip of the Persian Gulf. Zarins was not content with merely pointing out the location but also proposed an interpretation of the Fall which he said represented the farmers taking over the land from the foragers.[33] The idea that myths about the paradise or the golden age actually describe a nomadic lifestyle has since been perpetuated in the writings of a number of modern anthropologists.

In a celebrated 1988 book, *The Domestication of the Human Species*, the anthropologist Peter Wilson talks about the "revolutionary significance of architecture" for human evolution.[34] He focuses essentially on permanent settlements appearing about 15,000 years ago during the Mesolithic period and links the construction of permanent shelters with the agricultural revolution. Wilson points out that even though contemporary hunter-gatherers have been forced to climates and areas that are far less ideal living environments than the ones they occupied before the sedentary revolution, they can be said to live a life of leisure, health and peace. For example, !Kung Bushmen women (who are usually responsible for most of the food) are reported as needing anyhere from five to 20 hours a week to gather enough for the whole family. In addition to that, they may use a few hours to construct simple shelters. Lorna Marshall estimates that it takes the women of the !Kung San (or Zhu/wasi as they call themselves) no more than 45 minutes to build their shelters but more than half of the time the women decide not to build any. In this case, they sometimes put up two sticks to symbolise the entrance of the shelter so that the family may orient itself as to which is the men's and which the women's side of the fire.[35]

The diet is healthy; paleopathologists agree that the skeletons of ancient hunter-gatherers tend to be larger and more robust and show fewer signs of degenerative disease than do those of agriculturalists. Daily life goes on usually in full view of the camp; the constant interactive monitoring of behaviour produces a special sensitivity to other people and makes serious conflict very rare[36]—although Laurens Van der Post cites a Bushman tradition according to which there once was a war so terrible that eventually one man was killed, and the parties involved were so appalled that they drew a line in the desert never to be crossed.[37]

Noteworthy are also the nomadic conceptions of self, kinship and property. The social composition of the band is fluid: individuals and hearth-holds come and go. The mobility of nomadism allows for a constantly shifting locus of authority, a constant realignment of friendships and work units, and for the dissipation of latent disputes. The concept of territory is vague; instead of boundaries there are foci, such as water holes, to which members of the band belong. Similar fluidity characterises social relations. Ties between spouses or between a father and a child can be very loose. Instead of biological kinship, the responsibilities of the present moment are emphasised. Social commitments are personal rather than institutionalised and fixed. There are agreed procedures for making decisions but no authority is designated by assigning precedence to age, sex, birth, expertise, or wealth.[38]

In its fluidity, the nomadic lifestyle promotes non-hierarchical thinking—or what Gilles Deleuze, an enthusiast for philosophical nomadology, called non-arboreal or rhizomatic thought: it is characterised by an ill-defined sense of boundaries and "memorate knowledge", inexact and unsystematic information based on focus and lacking in coherent and socially shared categories.[39] The games of the Inuit Eskimo, for example, employ contradictory feelings that help to destroy any compartmentalisation.[40] As a result of nomadic social organisation, hunter-gatherers lack a developed sense of individuality; the origin of personhood or individuality and the concomitant arboreal thought can be situated at a time after the fall into agriculture and domestic life.

The characteristics of nomadic thought have been divined in the religious texts. St Augustine, for example, argued that in Paradise Adam was not a single individual but a multiplicity, all men and women in one body: "we did not yet have individually created and apportioned forms in which to live as individuals". The Fall divided this multiplicity into two opposite sexes (Dorothy L Sayers once asked why the sexes are said to be opposites, continuing: "what is the 'neighbouring sex'?"[41]) and brought about the general tendency to think in dualisms, including the knowledge of good and evil. The Gnostic Gospel of Philip interprets the Fall as the moment in which death emerges as Eve is separated from Adam, and condemns such deceptive discriminations that divide things that in truth are inseparable, such as right and left, light and darkness, or life and death.[42]

AGRICULTURAL REVOLUTION

Wilson explains that after the Ice Age, as a result of climate changes, big game became scarce and the nomadic lifestyle was less convenient than before. Women who gathered seeds of wild barley, wheat, and other grasses gradually developed farming. For an individual, agriculture meant a certain loss in the quality of life: one has to work many more hours for a much less healthy diet. Still, while gathering produces more food per hour worked, agriculture produces far more food per acre and can thus sustain more people. Moreover, a sedentary lifestyle and diet make women more fertile and also provides economic incentives to want more children as labourers. As a result, the agricultural revolution was practically irreversible.

Simultaneously, it had social consequences. Instead of a system of immediate return typified by hunter/gatherer societies, farming implied postponed gratification. It took the planning and cooperation of a stable community and required considerable material investment. The first permanent villages were built to provide a place for storing the grain, grinding it into flour, and converting it into cakes or porridge. The storage pits, roasting ovens, heavy grinders and houses could not easily be given up.[43]

In this sense, the invention of agriculture was contingent upon the development of architectural structures that separated private property from the public domain, the natural and ownerless environment. It is not until the Upper Paleolithic Age that archaeologists begin to detect traces of economic inequality. A dramatic early case is Sungir, northeast of Moscow, a burial ground 20,000 to 25,000 years old which contains the remains of a man, a woman and two boys, decorated with thousands of pierced mammoth-ivory beads, arctic-fox canine teeth, assorted rings and bracelets of mammoth ivory, and 16 spears, darts, and daggers.[44]

Private property establishes permanent differences among the members of the band, upsetting nomad relationships. Plato notes as much, writing that the "treasure house which each possesses filled with gold destroys that polity" and adding that "such men... will be avid of wealth, like those in an oligarchy, and will cherish a fierce secret lust for gold and silver, owning storehouses and private treasuries where they may hide them away, and also the enclosures of their homes, literal private love-nests in which they can lavish their wealth on their women".[45] In the *Republic*, he demands that the guardians of the polis must own nothing but their own bodies; in the *Laws* he argued that a state of leisure cannot be "fully realised... so long as women and children and houses remain private, and all these things are established as the private property of individuals".[46] Private property imprisons the individual and turns him into a thing as well; Plato's example is the tyrant who collects gold and silver in his house but is the "only one of all the citizens who may not travel abroad or view any of the sacred festivals that other freemen yearn to see, but he must live for the most part cowering in the recesses of his house like a woman".[47] Plato's view was shared by many Judeo-Christian writers. Philo of Alexandria and St Augustine, to name just two, suggest that the earthly city of sin and violence results from ownership and derive the name of Cain from the Hebrew word for "possession".[48]

Jean-Jacques Rousseau traces every civil institution to the original separation of private property. He wrote:

> The first man who, having enclosed a piece of ground, bethought himself of saying 'This is mine', and found people simple enough to believe him, was the real founder of civil society. From how many crimes, wars, and murders, from how many horrors and misfortunes might not any one have saved mankind, by pulling up the stakes, or filling up the ditch, and crying to his fellows: 'Beware of listening to this impostor; you are undone if you once forget that the earth belongs to us all, and the earth itself to nobody.'

top/ Peter Comestor, "Lamech kills Cain by accident" in *Bible Historiale*, 1372.
centre/ Peter Comestor, "The ark of Noah drifting on the water" in *Bible Historiale*, 1372.
bottom/ Peter Comestor, "Expulsion from Paradise" in *Bible Historiale*, 1372.

Presumably there were objections to such claims on property and land but the economic advantages of private ownership outweighed the horror of war and crime.

The invention of agriculture brought with it hierarchic social organisation; writing in the form of inventories of grain stocks, interspersed with accounts of battle; private property and architectural structures to separate and protect it; as well as organised warfare.[49] While "there is no injustice when there is no property", as John Locke remarks, an agricultural society is always at risk, not only from a poor harvest, but also from neighboring communities that covet the crops.[50] Hence, organised warfare is another consequence of agriculture. The aggression typical of agricultural societies is also reflected in the fact that while hunter-gatherers sometimes indulge in endogamous cannibalism, agricultural peoples rather choose the exogamous form. The difference is that eating one's ancestors is usually understood as an expression of ancestral worship but devouring others is practised as a way of totally annihilating the enemy. Rousseau concludes that iron and wheat civilised men, and ruined Mankind.[51]

ETYMOLOGIES OR ORIGINS

Architecture makes it possible to store property. "Why does a house exist?" asks Aristotle. He answers: "For the preservation of one's goods."[52] In Indo-European etymologies, the house often grouped together with hollow vessels used to store things. The Greek word *keuthmos*, "dwelling" is related to the Sanskrit *kotah*, "shed, hut"; *kutah*, "house", *kutaruh* "tent" and *kutih*, a "hut" (whence also words such as "cote" and "cottage" in English). These in turn are related to the Sanskrit word *kupah* or a "hole', "cave', "well"; *kutah* or a "pot" or a "pitcher"; *kundam* or a "pitcher" or "pot", or "hollow" and *kuharah* or *kuharam* or "a cavern, hole", a place for storing wheat or property.[53] Storage space makes it possible to have private property, hidden away from the eyes of others. The verb "to hide" goes back to the Greek *keuthein*, "to conceal" (akin to *keuthmos*), deriving from the Sanskrit words *kutah*, "house", homonymous with *kutah*, "false, untrue, deceitful", related to *kutam*, "illusion, trick", *kuhakah*, "a cheat".[54] It should also be remembered that the English noun "hide" either means "skin", as in English "cuticle", Greek *kutos* and Latin *cutis*, or refers to the measure of land reckoned as that sufficient to support a free family with dependants, in which case it is related to the Latin *civis*, "citizen".

In the absence of mutual visual control that characterises a nomadic lifestyle, groups of sedentary people break into smaller and more permanent entities. Instead of fluid associations between group members, a stable, fixed separation emerges between family and outsider, between "us" and "them", between the familiar, trustworthy and compassionate versus the alien, perfidious and corrupt, between the *heimlich* or homy and *unheimlich* or uncanny, terrible. The separation between "us" and "them" breeds "contempt", a term derived from the Greek *temnein*, "to separate". In its most ancient sense, to be outdoors means to be a foreigner: the word "foreign" derives from the Sanskrit dvar, meaning "door"; the same root also gives us "forest" and "forum", the outdoor space of nature and the public space between the hills and hence outside of the villages. *Dvar* or "door" goes back to **dhwer*, to "mislead", to "hide", to "deceive": a door is, of course, a frustrating illusion, being at the same time a wall or an enclosure and its opposite, an opening.[55] The door defines the outside as foreign but the separation it provides also enhances awareness of the self, the in-group and the home or dwelling. Indeed, from the Sanskrit **dhwer* one also gets the Old High German *twellan*, to "be in error" or to "retard", to "delay"; and ultimately the English word "dwelling".

In the earliest houses, the continuity of the family extends over generations. Since the 1960s, archaeologists have unearthed more than 400 skeletons under the houses in Çatalhöyük—one dwelling alone had 64 skeletons.[56] Pointing out that burying the dead under houses was common at early agricultural villages in the Near East, Ian Hodder suggests that the earliest function of the domus was to negotiate death and keep the inhabitants aware of death at all times—the frescoes and bull skulls of Çatalhöyük are further reminders of the same.[57] In a similar fashion, Peter J Wilson argues that "the pivotal juncture of domestication, architecture, and kinship comes in the tomb which is architecturally... and ideologically the... centre point of many domesticated societies". Burial feasts and ceremonies allow a display and expansion of social power.[58] Also Hodder speculates that the storage and preparation of food in the house would also have made it possible to arrange feasts to strengthen community bonds. Thus, in contrast to the classical view which sees architecture as the product of the agricultural revolution, Hodder and Wilson claim that domestication in the symbolic and social sense occurred before domestication in the economic sense and actually made the invention of agriculture possible.[59]

DOMESTIC VIOLENCE

In addition to fostering notions of secrecy, privacy and the individual, the visual obstruction by architectural structures also generates power. The more hidden one is the less vulnerable and the more powerful one becomes. The pseudo-Aristotelian treatise, *On the World*, describes how the kings of Persia remained invisible behind the mighty walls of their opulent palace, reigning through their servants, guardians, and spies who let them see and hear all things; the author infers that the most powerful of kings, God, must rule the universe even more indirectly and invisibly.[60] Aristotle himself names two other devices that tyrants use to defend themselves against their own subjects: keep the people busy and poor by making war and building large architectural projects: "the Pyramids of Egypt afford an example of this policy; also the offerings of the family of Cypselus, and the building of the temple of Olympian Zeus by the Peisistratidae, and the great Polycratean monuments at Samos; all these works were alike intended to occupy the people and keep them poor".[61] This explanation of the original function of the pyramids anticipates the thesis proposed in the 1970s by Kurt Mendelssohn.[62]

Of course, the visual obstruction that architecture provides also brings about the fear of conspiracy, of the evil eye and of occult powers—whence arises the need for surveillance both outside and inside the house. The use of the house as a control mechanism is clearly written in language. The Latin *domus* and Greek *domos* derive from the Sanskrit *damah*, "house, home" and *damah*, "taming, control, discipline" which also yields *damunah*, "householder, master", and *damayati*, "subdues, overpowers, controls one's self" which in Latin becomes *domo*, *domare*, "tame". The house is the place where animals are overpowered, tamed or disciplined; next, domestication is extended to human beings which produces the concomitant concept of *famula*, *famulus*, a client, servant or slave; an apocryphal etymology links the Latin *famula* to the Oscan *famel*, servant, and *faama*, house, and ultimately to another Sanskrit word for house, *dhaman*. As the process of domestication progresses, *familia* first adopts the meaning of "household", meaning master, mistress, children, servants and slaves. Ultimately, *familia* takes on its modern sense, referring to the nuclear family: discipline is then completely interiorised.

Athanasius Kircher, *Musurgia Universalis*, 1650.

In particular, the house as a place of confinement contributes to the domestication of women who, in the Biblical Tenth Commandment, are grouped together with houses, slaves, and domesticated asses. The Greek verb *damain*, akin to *domos*, connotes this most forcibly since it translates both as "to overpower", "to subdue", "to break", "to tame", and "to give in marriage": the legal term for a wife, *damar*, survives in the English as "dame" which signifies a tamed woman.[63]

SECRETS OF WOMEN

While the house is one of the means to domesticate and control women, it also bears feminine connotations. An examination of another etymological family suggests why. The words "house" and "hut" have the same root as the words "hose" and "shoe", namely the Indo-European **(s)keu-*, **(s)keuə-*, **(s)ku*, meaning "to cover, to enclose", which also yields the words "skin" and "sky".[64] In effect, then, we can postulate levels of enclosure from skin to clothes to dwellings and to the sky. The essence of such enclosure is concealing, obscuring, making something visually inaccessible.

The skin makes the body beautiful by hiding that which is inside: if men could see through stone walls, Boethius argues, they would find the superficially beautiful body of Alcibiades to be most vile upon seeing his entrails.[65] In this sense, the eyelid (*cilium*) conceals (*celare*) the eye, as Isidore of Seville teaches.[66] Isidore argues that the word *pulcher*, "beauty", comes from *pellis*, "skin", but he also cautions that from the same root, *pellis*, we get the word *pellax*, "seductive" or "deceitful".[67] The skin (or animal hide) can also function as a disguise, as in the universal myths about the *versipellis* that can change its skin. To add another immoral connotation to the word "skin", Isidore adds that another Latin word for skin, *scortum*, is also used of prostitutes or escorts.[68]

What is true of the skin can also be applied to vestal and architectural covers. Isidore explains that the chasuble or "the *casula*... is a diminutive of *casa*, because it covers the whole person like a little house, whence also the cowl is *cuculla*, as if a small room, *cella*".[69] The *cella* is for Isidore a device for hiding things: "*Cella dicta quod nos occultat et celat.*"[70] Like the *cella*, clothing conceals the person and allows for disguises. Famously, Joan of Arc was condemned as a fraud because she insisted on wearing man's clothing.[71] Even the sky may function as a concealment, at least if we believe the *Catholicon* by Johannes Balbus who claims that "the word for heaven, *celum*, comes from the word *celo* 'hide', because it hides secrets from us—*celum a celo, quia celat nos secreta*".[72]

To complete this layering, however, another level must be added to the innermost core: the Latin *cunnus*, or "vulva", also derives from the same Sanskrit word *skutas*, "covered" and the root **(s)keu*; finally, so does the word *obscurus*. The female womb forms the most hidden space in the layering of enclosures. St Augustine refers to the virginal womb as a *hortus clausus* or a walled garden "the gate to which shall remain locked".[73] The control of passage into this garden assumes a crucial significance in the sedentary society with its stabilisation of the family structure.

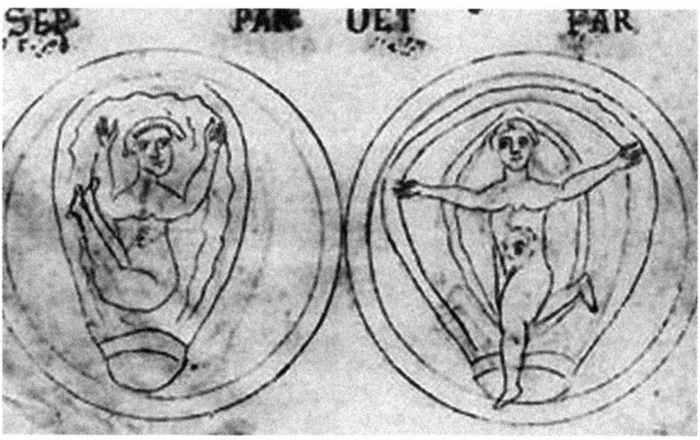

Fœtus in womb, twelfth century illustration after Soranus (first century AD).

The image of the womb as an architectural structure is a recurring metaphor. Hildegard of Bingen, for example, likens the reproductive system of young girls to an unfinished house "where only the foundations have been laid, and the walls are not yet completed" while between the ages of 15 and 20 the womb is "like a house which is already finished on the outside and roofed in, and which is now being furnished". Eventually, "after the seed of the man, which can be visualised as a man, has safely reached its destination, then around it there develops out of the woman's menstrual blood a membrane which surrounds it like a little vessel... so that the form lies in the midst of it, like a man in the innermost chamber of his house".[74]

Many other texts regard the womb as an architectural storage space. For example, the *Anatomia porci*, an apocryphal Galenic text produced at the medical school in Salerno during the twelfth century, begins the discussion of the matrix as an organ contrived so that whatever superfluities a woman generates during the month, her menstrual flow, could be sent there "like the bilge water of the entire body".[75] Similarly, Galen compares the stomach with the womb as large, hollow spaces in which things can be retained for a long time; the uterus is for him the best example of the retentive function.[76]

Another trope that Galen popularised is the one-sex theory. For Galen, the genitals of both sexes have exactly the same parts, the only difference being that a woman's genitals are hidden inside while a man's are visible on the outside. Women are thus related to both domesticity and secrecy.[77] At the same time, women's bodies are thought to be more open than men's, hence more vulnerable to the dangerous outside.[78] The additional doorways in the female body undermine the security of the fetus in the *hortus clausus*. Hildegard claims that women's bodies are punctuated by "openings, windows, and wind-passages".[79] Heloise quoted Macrobius' claim that women's bodies are pierced with more holes, channels and outlets than men's.[80] Also Albertus Magnus takes it for granted that "the body of a woman is more porous and the body of the man is denser".[81] In the Classical and Medieval tradition, architecture contributes to the subjection of the woman, at once imitating and outlawing the female body.

Given the metaphor of the womb as inner space or a room in a house, it is to be expected that women stand for dark shadows while men stand for light in many traditional models of thinking, e.g. Pythagoreanism. The dark womb-like hut needs fenestration; the word *fenestra*, "a window", is related to the Latin *penes*, "within", and its derivatives, *penetrare*, "to go inside", Penates, and, of course, penis. Just as a rapist uses forced penetration as a way of asserting his authority, power, or control over the woman, the original function of fenestration is to extend the inhabitant's control to the area surrounding the home. Windows were not originally punched into the wall only to let light in the home—this could have been achieved by fire or candles or a simple skylight which could also double as a chimney—but to magnify the domestic or private sphere by including the yard in the visual dominion of the master. The Finnish word for "window", *ikkuna*, goes back to its Russian equivalent, *okno*, a derivation of *oko*, eye. Likewise, "window" derives from *vindauga*, "eye of the wind", a word which articulates both functions of fenestration.

In many early cultures, the eye was believed to be an active organ which sent its rays to the outside world; we can find this doctrine as late as the *Optics* of Euclid. This also explains the concept of the evil eye. According to Calasiris in Heliodorus' novel *Aethiopica*, when one looks upon a beautiful object with envy he fills the surrounding air with this malignant quality and transmits his own pernicious breath to whatever is near.[82] Furthermore, the ancients often associated the eye with the erect male organ. In Greek art, the phallus with an eye often stares at naked women.[83] This motif may assert masculine dominance, for the phallus is as aggressive and expansive (but also as vulnerable) as an *oculus malignus*. The Romans, for example, occasionally collapsed the difference between the eye, the *fascinum* (or the object of vision which captivates the eye) and the male organ.[84]

Insofar the house is seen as a womb it is also relevant to point out that in a stable, sedentary society, the womb holds the secret of paternity; it is the *arché* of the family. Thus, the status and the authority of the father depend on controlling the potential infidelity and mobility of his opposite, the mother. Women in Classical Greece and afterwards have always been subjected to a stricter code of clothing, designed to keep the skin and the sexual organs hidden. Likewise, architectural coverings have also been used to protect or confine women more than men and keep them away from the eyes of strangers. In ancient Greek houses, women were segregated to separate quarters; Aeschines reports how an Athenian father walled his daughter up alive in a deserted house after finding out she was no longer a virgin.[85]

Tobias Cohn, *Ma'aseh Toviyyah*, 1707.

The ancient Roman marriage ceremony, modelled closely on the Greek, consisted of three acts: the sacrifice of the daughter or her extrication from her family by her father (*traditio*); the conduction of the bride to the groom's house (*deductio in domum mariti*); the couple's sacrifice to the Penates, the husband's domestic gods and the ancestors, as well as a ritual meal (*confarreatio*). The second, transitional stage actually simulated abduction. The husband feigned forceful seizure of his screaming bride; the women accompanying the bride pretended to defend her in vain. Finally, the husband carried the wife into his house, taking great care that her feet did not contaminate the doorsill for she was still impure, unconnected to any hearth and therefore supremely dangerous.[86] Even though most Roman rituals connected to the "sacred marriage" gradually vanished as the ancient beliefs died out, the abduction ritual of carrying the bride over the threshold has, significantly enough, survived to our day.[87]

CONCLUSION

The semi-occult tradition outlined here has survived and even stepped out of the closet, thanks to the writings of Rem Koolhaas, Bernard Tschumi and other avant-gardists who link architecture to sin, violence, and power. In his 1970 diploma for the AA, Koolhaas proposed rewriting the history of architecture based on the premise that the paradigmatic building would not be Laugier's primitive hut but rather the Berlin wall, a kind of 'pure' architecture with a minimum of beauty and a maximum of control.[88] In a similar vein, Tschumi has argued that architecture's violence is fundamental and unavoidable and concluded that "to really appreciate architecture, you may even need to commit a murder".[89]

Both Tschumi and Koolhaas were inspired by Georges Bataille who in 1929 claimed that the origin of architecture is not the temple or the house but the prison. He believed that buildings are the true masters of men and suggested that "in morphological progress men apparently represent only an intermediate stage between monkeys and great edifices. Forms have become more and more static, more and more dominant. ... And if one attacks architecture, whose monumental productions are at present the real masters of the world, grouping servile multitudes in their shadows... one is, as it were, attacking man."[90]

For Georges Bataille, as for Davíd Carrasco, René Girard, and many other authors, every form of architecture, every city and every culture is founded on violence that is necessary to restore the sacredness of the world and save it from mere utilitarian thingness.[91] We can wonder with Freud whether this is a reasonable price to pay for civilisation but at least we can agree with Seneca, who in a letter to Lucilius, speaks of "the towering tenements, so dangerous to the people who live in them. Believe me, that was a happy age, before the days of architects, before the days of builders."[92]

/ **1.** Valéry, P, "Mauvaises pensées et autres", *Oeuvres* II, Édition établie et annotée par J Hytier, Paris: Gallimard, 1960, p. 907: "Dieu a tout fait de rien. Mais le rien perce."

/ **2.** Marcus Vitruvius Pollio, *The Ten Books on Architecture*, trans M Hicky Morgan, New York: Dover, 1960, II, I, pp. 1–2.

/ **3.** Freud, S, *Civilization and Its Discontents*, trans J Riviere, New York: Dover, 1994, pp. 22–23.

/ **4.** Laugier, MA, *An Essay on Architecture*, trans W and A Herrmann, Los Angeles: Hennessey & Ingalls Inc., 1977, pp. 11–12.

/ **5.** Wagner, O, *Modern Architecture*, trans HF Mallgrave, Santa Monica, CA: Getty Center/ University of Chicago Press, 1993, p. 91.

/ **6.** Le Corbusier, *Towards a New Architecture*, 68; cf. R Banham, *The Architecture of the Well-Tempered Environment*, Chicago: University of Chicago Press, 1984, p. 154.

/ **7.** Rousseau, JJ, "Discourse on the Origin of Inequality", II, 12, in JJ Rousseau, *The First and Second Discourses and Essay on the Origin of Languages*, V Gourevitch, ed, New York: Harper & Row, 1986, p. 147.

/ **8.** Wood the Elder, J, *The Origin of Building or the Plagiarism of the Heathens Detected in Five Books*, Bath: S and F Farley, 1741.

/ **9.** Wood, *The Origin of Building or the Plagiarism of the Heathens Detected in Five Books*, Bk IV, p. 177.

/ **10.** Wood, *The Origin of Building or the Plagiarism of the Heathens Detected in Five Books*, Bk IV, p. 70.

/ **11.** Clement of Alexandria, *Stromata*, Bk VI: "From Pythagoras, Plato derived the immortality of the soul; and he from the Egyptians. And many of the Platonists composed books in which they show that the Stoics, as we said in the beginning, and Aristotle, took the most and principal of their dogmas from Plato. Epicurus also pilfered his leading dogmas from Democritus. Let these things then be so. For life would fail me, were I to undertake to go over the subject in detail, to expose the selfish plagiarism of the Greeks, and how they claim the discovery of the best of their doctrines, which they have received from us."

/ **12.** Wood, *The Origin of Building or the Plagiarism of the Heathens Detected in Five Books*, Bk I, p. 13.

/ **13.** Wood, *The Origin of Building or the Plagiarism of the Heathens Detected in Five Books*, Bk I, p. 27.

/ **14.** Wood, *The Origin of Building or the Plagiarism of the Heathens Detected in Five Books*, Bk I, p. 33.

/ **15.** Wood, *The Origin of Building or the Plagiarism of the Heathens Detected in Five Books*, Bk I, p. 38: "Jacob took a Stone and set it up for a *Pillar*; He then order'd his Brethren to gather Stones, and make an Heap, as a Table, whereon they might eat. ... *Jacob* then offer'd Sacrifices, and after that they all sat down together to eat. ... THESE Things were soon imitated by the Heathens, who every where rais'd *Heaps of Stones*, and set up *Pillars* to the Idols." ... "BEFORE *Jacob* had accomplish'd his Journey, he lost his beloved Wife *Rachel*; on whose Grave he set up a *Pillar*, which is the first *Sepulchral Monument* we have any Account of: This was imitated by the Heathens, when they came to deify their Dead...."

/ **16.** Wood, *The Origin of Building or the Plagiarism of the Heathens Detected in Five Books*, Bk I, p. 39. Wood explains in more detail: "Then GOD REVEALED Himself to him [Noah], gave him a Land for the future Abode of himself and Family, and promised, THAT IN HIS SEED ALL THE FAMILIES OF THE EARTH SHOULD BE BLESSED: And in Token thereof *Abram* built an *Altar*. This Promise GOD renewed to *Isaac*, the youngest Son of *Abraham*, who, following the Example of his Father, erected a *Pillar*, poured a Libation of Oil thereon, and these named the Place where that *Pillar* was erected, The HOUSE of GOD: And thus Places separated for the Adoration of GOD took their Rise, and were the Marks of the *Gratitude* of the Founder. THESE were succeeded by other Monuments, and such as affected the *Fidelity* of Man; *Abraham* planted a *Tree*, when he made his Covenant with *Abimelech*; and *Isaac* raised a *Pillar*, and a *Heap of Stones*, when he entered into a League with his Father-in-Law *Laban*; and so *Moses*, when he made the Covenant between GOD and the *Israelites*, set up 12 *Pillars* as Monuments thereof.", Wood, *The Origin of Building or the Plagiarism of the Heathens Detected in Five Books*, Bk I, p. 232.

/ **17.** Wood, *The Origin of Building or the Plagiarism of the Heathens Detected in Five Books*, Bk I, p. 39.

/ **18.** Hersey, GL, *The Lost Meaning of Classical Architecture*, Cambridge, MA: MIT Press, 1988, pp. 31, 40, 42. Hersey describes the "disguised murders and burials" in classical architecture by tracing its ornaments back to the ritual display of the remains of slaughtered enemy. He links the origin of the Doric order, for example, to spears and to the female genitals; such details as the guttae are actually drops of blood.

/ **19.** Clement of Alexandria, *The Exhortation to the Greeks. A Rich Man's Salvation. To the Newly Baptized*, trans GW Butterworth, Cambridge, MA: Harvard University Press/London: Heinemann, 1982, ii, 16, p. 39; iii, 40, p. 99. "If you wish to inspect the orgies of the Corybantes, then know that, having killed their third brother, they covered the head of the dead body with a purple cloth, crowned it, and carrying it on the point of a spear, buried it under the roots of Olympus. These mysteries are, in short, murders and funerals. "Superstition, then, as was to be expected, having taken its rise thus, became the fountain of insensate wickedness; and not being subsequently checked, but having gone on augmenting and rushing along in full flood, it became the originator of many demons, and was displayed in sacrificing hecatombs, appointing solemn assemblies, setting up images, and building temples, which were in reality tombs: for I will not pass these over in silence, but make a thorough exposure of them, though called by the august name of temples; that is, the tombs which got the name of temples. But do ye now at length quite give up your superstition, feeling ashamed to regard sepulchres with religious veneration. In the temple of Athene in Larissa, on the Acropolis, is the grave of Acrisius; and at Athens, on the Acropolis, is that of Cecrops, as Antiochus says in the ninth book of his *Histories*. What of Erichthonius? Was he not buried in the temple of Polias? And Immarus, the son of Eumolpus and Daira, were they not buried in the precincts of the Elusinium, which is under the Acropolis; and the daughters of Celeus, were they not interred in Eleusis? Why should I enumerate to you the wives of the Hyperboreans? They were called Hyperoche and Laodice; they were buried in the Artemisium in Delos, which is in the temple of the Delian Apollo. Leandrius says that Clearchus was buried in Miletus, in the Didymaeum. Following the Myndian Zeno, it were unsuitable in this connection to pass over the sepulchre of Leucophryne, who was buried in the temple of Artemis in Magnesia; or the altar of Apollo in Telmessus, which is reported to be the tomb of Telmisseus the seer. Further, Ptolemy the son of Agesarchus, in his first book about Philopator, says that Cinyras and the descendants of Cinyras were interred in the temple of Aphrodite in Paphos. But all time would not be sufficient for me, were I to go over the tombs which are held sacred by you, And if no shame for these audacious impieties steals over you, it comes to this, that you are completely dead, putting, as really you do, your trust in the dead."

/ **20.** "The elder son Jabal was the first man that ever found Geometry and Masonry, and he made houses, and is named in the Bible "Pater habitantium in tentonis atque pastorum "—that is to say, the father of men dwelling in tents, that is dwelling houses. And he was Cain's Master Mason and governor of all his works, when he made the City of Enoch—that was the first City that ever was made, and that made Cain, Adam's son. And gave it to his own son, and called it the City of Enoch, and now it is called Ephraim. And there was the Science of Geometry and Masonry first employed and contrived for a Science and for a Craft. And so we may say that it was the first cause and foundation of all Crafts and Sciences."

/ **21.** The Bible continues: "If Cain shall be avenged sevenfold, truly Lamech seventy and sevenfold."

/ **22.** Revelation, 21:22.

/ **23.** Genesis, 4:17; cf. St Augustine, *Civitas Dei*, XV, 1.

/ **24.** Philo of Alexandria explains the evil by claiming that Cain's deepest problem is his flawed conception of God, which is reflected in his very name. For Cain believes himself to possess all things. In contrast, Abel's "name means one who refers (all things) to God". (Sacr. 2). The brothers' chosen professions reflect and reinforce their fundamental differences. Philo emphasises that Cain's chosen profession involves him with earthly and inanimate objects. So he does not choose to prepare for a future life and to pay attention to living things. Similarly, Philo points out that Cain is called a tiller of the soil because he refers all things to himself and to his own mind (Sacr. 51). In fact, it is Cain's lack of understanding that the land is really foreign and belongs only to God that misleads him in the direction of a self-loving character trait and ultimately causes the destruction of his soul. In contrast, Abel chooses to tend living beings.

/ **25.** St Augustine, *Civitas Dei*, XV, 5. The reference that Augustine has in mind is Lucan, Phar., i, p. 95.

/ **26.** Joseph Rykwert notes that "town foundations always seem to carry the burden of guilt". J Rykwert, *The Idea of Town*, London: Faber and Faber, 1976, p. 174.

/ **27.** Burkert, W, *Homo Necans: the Anthropology of Ancient Greek Sacrificial Ritual and Myth*, trans P Bing, Berkely/Los Angeles: University of California Press, 1983, p. 39. He suggests that the more gruesome the ritual, the stronger the bond within the community. W Burkert, *Homo Necans: the Anthropology of Ancient Greek Sacrificial Ritual and Myth*, p. 36. Deuteronomy, 19:21, explains that "life shall go for life, eye for eye, tooth for tooth, hand for hand, foot for foot".

/ **28.** St Augustine, *Civitas Dei*, Book XV, 4, p. 481.

/ **29.** Plutarch, "Romulus" in *The Lives of the Noble Grecians and Romans*, trans J Dryden, revised by AH Clough, New York: Modern Library, sd, p. 33.

/ **30.** St Augustine, *Civitas Dei*, XX, 11, p. 729; *Apocalypse*, 20, pp. 8–9.

/ **31.** In foreign lands, the Huns also refused to go under a roof because they felt it was dangerous. Ammianus Marcellinus, *The Later Roman Empire (AD 354–378)*. Selected and trans by W Hamilton, Harmondsworth: Penguin, 1986, xxxi, 2, p. 411.

/ **32.** Porphyry, *On Abstinence from Animal Food*, bk. iv, p. 2.

/ **33.** Zarins concluded that Euphrates and Tigris were once met by two other rivers, one of which is now dammed and the other a dry bed. Additional support for the identification of the site with Paradise was provided by the findings that seven to eight thousand years ago the area was fertile, covered with dense forests and also rich with gold and bdellium, an aromatic gum resin, just as the Bible reports. The Bible says: "A river went out of Eden to water the garden; and from thence it was parted, and became into four heads. The name of the first is Pison: that is it which compasseth the whole land of Havilah, where there is gold; and the gold of that land is good: there is bdellium and the onyx stone. And the name of the second river is Gihon: the same is it that compasseth the whole land of Ethiopia. And the name of the third river is Hiddekel: that is it which goeth toward the east of Assyria. And the fourth river is Euphrates." Genesis, 2:10–14. Havilah is in the southwest of Mesopotamia, and gold was indeed mined there. The Pison could be the present-day Wadi Batin which is now a dry riverbed. "Ethiopia" probably refers to an area of southwest Mesopotamia, in which case the Gihon could be the present-day Karun, which, before it was dammed carried most of the sediment out of the highlands of Iran to form the delta of the modern Persian Gulf. Hiddekel is the Tigris. These four rivers converged at a spot that now lies several kilometers offshore in the Persian Gulf but eight thousand years ago was still dry land. C Tudge, *The Time Before History. 5 Million Years of Human Instinct*, New York: Scribner, 1996, p. 276; R Heinberg, *Memories and Visions of Paradise*, Los Angeles: Jeremy P Tatcher, 1989, p. 165.

/ **34.** Wilson, PJ, *The Domestication of the Human Species*, New Haven and London: Yale University Press, 1988.

/ **35.** Marshall, L, "!Kung Bushmen Bands," *Africa*, vol 30, no 4, 1960, p. 342. As quoted by D Preziosi, "Architectonic & Linguistic Signs" in W Steiner, ed, *Image and Code*, Ann Arbor: University of Michigan, 1981, p. 169.

/ **36.** Wilson, PJ, *The Domestication of the Human Species*, pp. 26–27. For a more critical view of violence among the !Kung San, see also: RB Lee, *The Dobe !Kung*, New York: Holt, Rinehart and Winston, 1984, pp. 90–102.

/ **37.** Heinberg, R, *Memories and Visions of Paradise*, p. 169.

/ **38.** Wilson, PJ, *The Domestication of the Human Species*, pp. 27, 33, 49.

/ **39.** See G Deleuze and F Guattari, *A Thousand Plateaus, Capitalism and Schizophrenia*, trans B Massumi, Minneapolis: University of Minnesota Press, 1997, *passim*.

/ **40.** Wilson, PJ, *The Domestication of the Human Species*, p. 31.

/ **41.** Sayers, DL, "The Human-Not-Quite-Human" as quoted in T Laqueur, *Making Sex. Body and Gender from the Greeks to Freud*, Cambridge, MA: Harvard University Press, 1990, p. 1.

/ **42.** St Augustine, *Civitas Dei*, 13, 14; Elaine Pagels, *Adam, Eve, and the Serpent*, New York: Random House, 1988, pp. 71, 120. 100. God [created] a garden-paradise. [...] This garden [is the place] where it will be said to me: [Thou may eat] this or not eat [this, according to thy] desire. This is the place (where) I shall consume every different (thing)—there, where is the tree of knowledge which slew Adam. [...] It has (the) capability in itself to bestow the knowledge of good and evil. It neither cured him of the evil nor preserved him in the good, but rather it caused those who had ingested it to die. [...]; 76. In the days when Eve was within Adam, there was no death. When she was separated from him, death came to be; 86. If the female had not separated from the male, she would not afterward have died with the male. Their separation was the inception of death; 9. The light with the darkness, life with death, the right with the left are brothers one to another. It is not possible for them to be separated from one another. Because of this, neither are the good good, nor are the evils evil, nor is the life a life, nor is death a death. The Gospel of Philip. http://www.metalog.org/files/philip.html.

/ **43.** Harris, M, *Cannibals and Kings. The Origin of Cultures*, New York: Random House, 1977, pp. 25, 27. It should perhaps be emphasised that not all-pre-agricultural people lived nomadic lives. The villagers of Lepenski Vir on the Danube lived well on the abundant sturgeon and carp and built trapezoidal houses with paved floors and stone-lined hearths. See RE Leakey and R Lewin, *People of the Lake. Mankind & Its Beginnings*, New York: Avon Books, 1978, p. 234. Another example are the Port au Choix Indians on the western coast of Newfoundland, a sedentary community living on seal hunting and the mass killing of karibou, and exhibiting a more tightly organised and authoritarian social system than the islanders.

/ **44.** Pfeiffer, JE, *The Creative Explosion. An Inquiry into the Origins of Art and Religion*, New York: Harper and Row, 1982, pp. 65, 67.

/ **45.** Plato, *Republic*, 550d, 548a.

/ **46.** Plato, *Republic*, 464d; *Laws* 807b. Plato criticises both private houses and the principle of building a wall around a city for defensive purposes, but he also acknowledges that "if men really must have a wall, then the building of the private houses must be arranged from the start in such a way that the whole city may form a single wall; all the houses must have good walls, built regularly and in a similar style, facing the roads, so that the whole city will have the form of a single house, which will render its appearance not unpleasing, besides being far and away the best plan for ensuring safety and ease for defence." (Plato, *Laws*, 779a). Aristotle based the identity of the city on its defenses, demanding that the protective wall around the city must become its main ornament that advertises its glory to the world. Interestingly, he also proposed cross-programming the towers to provide refuge for the poor: "as the walls are to be divided by bulwarks and towers built at suitable intervals, and the body of citizens must be distributed at common tables, the idea will naturally occur that some of the common tables should be housed in the guard-houses." (Aristotle, *Politica*, 1331a. pp. 10–24). In Aristotle's scheme, then, social roles are subverted: the outsiders are to protect the city that has exploited and excluded them. This ambiguity of the wall is well attested by the Roman tradition of triumphal arches. As virtual city gates, the triumphal arches are watched over by Janus, a two-faced god who does not appear in any other mythology. While in most civilisations gates and city walls were erected to provide protection against dangerous outsiders, Janus watches Romans as closely as barbarians. In the *Politica*, Aristotle points out that when planning a city for a tyrant, it is the most important single factor to protect the ruler from his subjects.

/ **47.** Plato, *Republic*, 579b.

/ **48.** St Augustine, *Civitas Dei, The City of God*, trans M Dods, intro T Merton, New York: Modern Library, 1950, Bk XV, 17, pp. 503–504.

/ **49.** Porphyry, *On Abstinence from Animal Food*, Bk IV, p. 2. "A pastoral life succeeded to this, in which men procured for themselves superfluous possessions, and meddled with animals. ... At the same time, together with this life, war was introduced. And these things, says Dicaearchus, are not asserted by us, but by those who have historically discussed a multitude of particulars. For, as possessions were now of such a magnitude as to merit attention, some ambitiously endeavored to obtain them, by collecting them, and calling on others to do the same, but others directed their attention to the preservation of them when collected. Time, therefore, thus gradually proceeding, and men always directing their attention to what appeared to be useful, they at length became conversant with the third, and agricultural form of life." Summing up, Porphyry claims that in the Golden Age, "there was no war, because injustice was exterminated. But afterwards, together with injustice towards animals, war was introduced among men, and the endeavor to surpass each other in amplitude of possessions."

/ **50.** Locke, J, *Essay Concerning Human Understanding*, New York: Prometheus Books, 1995, Bk IV, Ch. III, § 18, p. 448.

/ **51.** Locke, J, *Essay Concerning Human Understanding*, II, 1. p. 170; II, 20, p. 177.

/ **52.** Aristotle, *Posterior Analitics*, II, p. 11.

/ **53.** From this family, a number of words in other Indo-European languages are derived, including the Tamil word *kuti* meaning "hut", "house", "village", "family"; and *koti*, meaning "city", as well as the Latin *custodia*, "a guarding, a hut", and the Serbian *kuca*, "a house".

/ **54.** The verb "to hide" comes from OE *hydan*, W.Gmc. **khuthjanan*, PIE **keudh-*, and base **(s)keu-*. Cf. Greek *keuthein* (to hide), whereas the noun "hide", cf. German *Haut* from P.Gmc. **khudiz*, PIE base **(s)keu-*. It is worth noting that the Egyptian hieroglyph that means "to hide", *hap*, depicts an architectural configuration, a corner (or three nestled L's, and resembles the hieroglyph meaning "corner" and the one meaning "official", *genb*, see Sir EA Wallis Budge, *Egyptian Language. Lessons in Egyptian Hieroglyphics*, New York: Dorset Press, 1993.

/ **55.** "Frustration" derives from Latin *fraus, frustra*, "false", "futile" which also comes from the Sanskrit *dhwer*.

/ **56.** Hodder's team found the earliest example of a plastered skull. Moreover, it was buried with another human skeleton. To Hodder, the co-burial was a hint at an emotional bond between two people.

/ **57.** He suggests that the transition to settled life required "the domestication of the wild by bringing it into the house, at least the symbolism of the wild, and controlling it". Paintings were especially common on earlier layers of plaster that coincided in time with the burials of children. Hodder believes that this close association between paintings and burials is no coincidence. The city is about domesticating the people and the life and death argument plays here a role, just as the link to the ancestors. Symbols and family might have been the "glue" that held the early society at Çatalhöyük together.

/ **58.** Wilson, PJ, *The Domestication of the Human Species*, p. 114.

/ **59.** Hodder, I, *The Domestication of Europe*, Oxford: Blackwell, 1990, p. 31; see also M Balter, *The Goddess and the Bull*, New York: Free Press, 2005.

/ **60.** Pseudo-Aristotle (Apuleius), *De mundo*, 398a2–398b10. "We are told that the outward show observed by Cambyses and Xerxes and Darius was magnificently ordered with the utmost state and splendor. The king himself, so the story goes, established himself at Susa or Ecbatana, invisible to all, dwelling in a wondrous palace within a roof gleaming with gold and amber and ivory. And it had many gateways one after another, and porches many furlongs apart from one another, secured by bronze doors and mighty walls. Outside these the chief and most distinguished men had their appointed place, some being the king's personal servants, his bodyguard and attendants, others the guardians of each of the enclosing walls, the so-called janitors and listeners, that the king himself, who was called their master and deity, might thus see and hear all things. ... and there were couriers and watchmen and messengers and superintendents of signal-fires. ... Now we must suppose that the majesty of the Great King falls as far short of that of the God who possesses the universe, as that of the feeblest and weakest creature is inferior to that of the king of Persia. Wherefore, if it was beneath the dignity of Xerxes to appear himself to administer all things and to carry out his own wishes and superintend the government of his kingdom, such functions would be still less becoming for a god." In *Politica*, Aristotle discusses the principles how a tyrant can maintain his power by similar means. He writes: "A tyrant should also endeavor to know what each of his subjects says or does, and should employ spies, like the 'female detectives' at Syracuse, and the eavesdroppers whom Hiero was in the habit of sending to any place of resort or meeting; for the fear of informers prevents people from speaking their minds, and if they do, they are more easily found out. Another art of the tyrant is to sow quarrels among the citizens; friends should be embroiled with friends, the people with the notables, and the rich with one another." Cf. Walter Burkert, *Creation of the Sacred*, Cambridge, MA: Harvard, 1998, p. 98.

/ **61.** Aristotle, *Politica*, 1313b, pp. 18–25.

/ **62.** Mendelssohn, K, *The Riddle of the Pyramids*, New York: Praeger Publishers, 1974, pp. 141–200. Mendelssohn starts with the information from Herodotus that the pyramids in Giza were tombs for the pharaohs but points out that it seems excessive to spend 25 million tons of limestone only to bury three pharaohs. The problem becomes more puzzling when we realise that the pyramid age was relatively brief, at least by ancient Egyptian standards: the five largest pyramids were built in one century. Before and after this period, such expenditure was apparently not found acceptable, since pharaohs were buried less ostentatiously for centuries. Moreover, in the fourth dynasty, for example, there were more large pyramids than pharaohs to be buried in them. The conspicuous uselessness of Egyptian monuments is nowhere more striking as in the first one, Zoser's complex in Saqqara. Immovable doors were hung on hinges carved out of stone; most of the entries on the facade were false; the interiors of several dummy temples were packed with rubble. Some archaeologists postulate a hypothetical Old Kingdom belief that a work of art, a building or a chant had power and utility in the afterlife in direct proportion to its uselessness in this world: each false door worked in the afterlife precisely because it did not work now. (See D Roberts, "The Age of the Pyramids", *National Geographic*, January 1995, p. 14.) There are other theories as well. The thirteenth century work *Hitat* by the Cairo historian al-Maqrizi records Arab legends according to which the pyramids were antediluvian repositories of knowledge, designed by Hermes Trisgemistos after he read in the stars the coming of the Great Flood; other texts claim that King Saurid built the pyramid in such a way that it embodies all knowledge of geometry, astronomy and medicine. (See Al Maqrizi, *"Das Pyramidenkapitel in al-Makrizi's 'Hitat'" Herausgegeben und übersetzt von Erich Graefe*, Leipzig: JC Hinrich'sche Buchhandlung, 1911, pp. 69–76.) Ever since al-Maqrizi's *Pyramid Chapter* became available in French translation in the early nineteenth century, 'pyramidology' has flourished, culminating on the one hand in Charles Piazzi Smyth's system of reading prophecies about the end of the world from the measurements of the inner corridors and chambers and, on the other, in Erich von Däniken's conviction that the pyramids are the work of aliens from outer space. Mendelssohn begins his alternative explanation by pointing out that before the pyramid age, the majority of the population in Egypt lived in more or less independent villages. During the annual flooding of the Nile, farmers could not work and used the time to raid other villages for cattle and women. The architect of the first pyramid, Imhotep, employed the villagers during this restless time of tribal warfare. For three or four months every year, some 70,000 men took orders from the central administration and were fed and clothed by the administration. In Egypt, the government stabilised the country by usurping the role of the villages and the tribes; thus the first seeds of a nation state organisation were sown. When government was centralised to a degree not encountered before in history, pyramid building stopped. The symbolic or referential meaning of the pyramid, whatever that may have been for the Egyptians, was used as a foil to avert gazes from its performative or ritualistic meaning, the consolidation of nascent state power.

/ **63.** Keuls, E, *The Reign of the Phallus: Sexual Politics in Ancient Athens*, New York: Harper & Row, 1985, p. 209. Eva Keuls proposes that in Athens there was a special women's police, *gynaikonomoi*, whose task was to restrict the movements of women in the cities.

/ **64.** The same is true of the German words *Haus, Hütte, Hort, Hose, Schuh* and *Haut*. In Latin, the words *scutum*, shield, and *scutra*, water vessel.

/ **65.** Boethius, *The Consolation of Philosophy*, trans R Green, New York: Macmillan, 1962, III, p. 8. Boethius refers to the Aristotelian *Protrepticus* suggests that "beauty seems to be the sort of thing it is only because we see nothing accurately. For if one were able to see as keenly as they say Lynceus did, who saw through walls and trees, how could one ever stand to look at people if one saw of what sort of bad things they are composed?"

/ **66.** The Latin word for eyelid, *cilium* comes from the IE base **kel-*. Isidore notes as much, writing: "*Cilia sunt tegmina quibus operiuntur oculi, et dicta cilia quod celent oculos tegantque tuta custodia.*" Isidore, *Etymologies*, XI, I, p. 42, cf. also XI, p. 86, where Isidore points out that the skin hides the bones everywhere else but in the mouth: "*Ossa sunt corporis solidamenta. In his enim positio omnis roburque subsistit. Ossa autem ab usto dicta, propter quod cremarentur ab antiquis; sive, ut alii putant, ab ore, eo quod ibi pateant. Nam ubique cute visceribusque obtecta celantur.*"

/ **67.** Isidore, *Etymologies*, X, pp. 204, 224.

/ **67.** Isidore, *Etymologies*, X, p. 279. In "Genesis", the agent of evil is the serpent whose dishonesty is reflected in its ability to shed its skin. Perhaps this is the reason why "it is said that a serpent does not dare to touch a nude person," as Isidore remarks, (Isidore, *Etymologies*, XI, 4, p. 48.)

/ **68.** Isidore, *Etymologies*, XIX, 24, p. 17. "*Casula est vestis cucullata, dicta per diminutionem a casa, quod totum hominem tegat quasi minor casa. Inde et cuculla, quasi minor cella.*"

/ **69.** Isidore, *Etymologies*, XV, III, p. 9. With this etymology Isidore is actually right: Latin *cella* is related to *celare* "to hide, conceal", from PIE base **kel-* "conceal". From the same root we get Sanskrit *cala* "hut, house, hall"; Greek *kalia* "hut, nest", *kalyptein* "to cover", *koleon* "sheath", Latin *coleus* "sheath", *clam* "secret", OE *hol* "orifice, cave", as well as modern English "hole", "hollow", "holster", "hall" and "hell", as well as "cell" and "cellar".

/ **71.** Pope Pius II (Aeneas Sylvius Piccolomini) declared in 1459 that he had found nothing reprehensible in Joan of Arc save her wearing men's clothing. The prohibition goes back to the Bible: "The woman shall not wear that which pertaineth unto a man, neither shall a man put on a woman's garment: for all that do so are abomination unto the LORD thy God." (Deuteronomy 22:5) Thomas Aquinas explains that "it is sinful for a woman to use male clothing or *vice-versa*" unless by necessity (*S.T.* IIa-IIae, p. 169, a2, ad3), and the save position is adopted by Hildegard of Bingen: "A man should never put on feminine dress or a woman use male attire.... Unless a man's life or a woman's chastity is in danger; in such an hour a man may change his dress for a woman's or a woman for a man's...." *Scivias*, Part II, Vision, pp. 6, 77.

/ **72.** Balbus is wrong, although the same spurious etymology was proposed earlier in Uguccione da Pisa's *Derivationes*. Remarking that "a stammerer is named balbus... for he does not express words... he breaks words," (X.29) Isidore derives *caelum* more plausibly from "shining" or "bright" (IE base **(s)kai-*. (XIII, 4.1).

/ **73.** In *Adversus Jovinianum*, St Jerome declared that the *hortus conclusus* is "an image suggesting Mary, Mother and Virgin". Later, Albertus Magnus described Mary as an enclosed garden into which Christ descended like dew. *Opera Omnia*, 36:707, as quoted in J Delumeau, *History of Paradise. The Garden of Eden in Myth and Tradition*, trans M O'Connoll, New York: Continuum, 1995, p. 124. The thirteenth century writer Bartholomew of England described the womb as a dwelling places with two cells or rooms and also likens the "little chamber" of the uterus to the Temple of Jerusalem, writing: "Thus it is 46 days after the conception of the child that it comes of life and is perfectly formed... just so did Saint Augustine reckon the building of the Temple of Jerusalem, which was made in 46 years, the [which] temple he compares with the body of Jesus Christ.... He shows that, just as the temple was built in 46 years, so the human body is made and formed in 46 normal days." As quoted in J Delumeau, *History of Paradise. The Garden of Eden in Myth and Tradition*, p. 136.

/ **74.** As quoted in MC Pouchelle, *The Body and Surgery in the Middle Ages*, trans R Morris, New Brunswick, NJ: Rutgers University Press, 1990, p. 135.

/ **75.** *tamquam ad sentinam totius corporis.* T Laqueur, *Making Sex. Body and Gender from the Greeks to Freud*, p. 251 fn.2.

/ **76.** "Now those parts of the animal which are especially hollow and large are the stomach and the organ which is called the womb or uterus. ... Now it is impossible to speak of both organs at once, so we shall deal with each in turn, beginning with the one which is capable of demonstrating the retentive faculty most plainly. For the stomach retains the food until it has quite digested it, and the uterus retains the embryo until it brings it to completion, but the time taken for the completion of the embryo is many times more than that for the digestion of food." (Galen, *On the Usefulness of Parts.*)

/ **77.** In his glossary, Du Cange cross-references *secretum naturae* or the "secret place of nature" to *secessus*, Old French *lieux secrez* or latrines, while "secret places of women" means the female reproductive organs, MC Pouchelle, *The Body and Surgery in the Middle Ages*, pp. 134, 242, fn.50.

/ **78.** Isidore, *Etymologies*. Often, the openings of the body are understood as doorways. Isidore explains that "the mouth is called os because, as if through a door, ostium, we send in food, and fling forth sputum; or because foods enter, and speech exits through it". He goes on to make the point that "the vulva is named as if valva, door of the belly, either because it receives semen or because the fetus comes forth from it."

/ **79.** Pouchelle, MC, *The Body and Surgery in the Middle Ages*, p. 148. Hildegard found a special affinity between the airy temperament and the nature of woman. God created Adam from the earth, earthy, for he was to till the earth and subdue it; "but Eve, taken from his marrow, was soft and possessed an airy mind and a keen, delicate life, for the weight of the earth did not oppress her". Hildegard of Bingen, *Heilwissen. Von den Ursachen und der Behandlung von Krankheiten nach der Hl. Hildegard von Bingen. Übersetzung des Causae et curae von Martin Pawlik*, Augsburg: Pattloch Verlag, 1990, p. 73. The female body needs to be airy—permeable and spacious—to accommodate children in the womb. (Hildegard of Bingen, *Heilwissen*, p. 88). Eve, the first mother, "was made like the purest air, for as ether enfolds the inviolate stars, so she—inviolate, incorrupt, without pain—held the human race within her." (Hildegard of Bingen, *Heilwissen*, p. 137). In consequence, women are especially vulnerable to ailments provoked by the weather, making their health more fragile than that of men. Since the Fall, however, woman's airy nature has caused problems. Hildegard writes that women are open like the cither, and *fenestrales et ventosae*: their bodies are like windows which freely admit the stormy elements raging without (Hildegard of Bingen, *Heilwissen*, p. 138.)

/ **80.** Radice, B, ed, *The Letters of Abelard and Heloise*, trans and intro by B Radice, New York: Penguin, 1974, p. 166.

/ **81.** Caciola, 154, *Albertus Magnus, De animalibus libri XXVI 9.1*, H. Stadler, ed, 2 vols, Münster, 1916, I, p. 676.

/ **82.** Heliodorus of Emesa, *An Ethiopian Romance*, trans M Hadas, Philadelphia: University of Pennsylvania Press, 1999, Bk. III, p. 75.

/ **83.** Françoise Frontisi-Ducroix speculates that the phallus may have an eye because it is a living being and in Greece life was defined in terms of sight; or because man (unlike woman) sees his organ and vision is reciprocal; or because the eye of the phallus represents the masculine right to look at woman. She points out that the phallus with an eye never appears in the company of man in Greek art. F Frontisi-Ducroix, "Eros, Desire, and the Gaze" in *Sexuality in Ancient Art*, N Boymel Kampen, ed, Cambridge: Cambridge University Press, 1996, pp. 93–95, 99.

/ **84.** Broxton, R, *Onians, The Origins of European Thought about the Body, the Mind, the Soul, the World, Time, and Fate*, Cambridge: Cambridge University Press, 1994, pp. 78–87. cf. CA Barton, *The Sorrows of the Ancient Romans. The Gladiator and the Monster*, Princeton: Princeton University Press, 1993, p. 96.

/ **85.** Aeschines, *Against Timarchus*, 1, p. 182: "For so stern were they [the Athenians] toward all shameful conduct, and so precious did they hold the purity of their children, that when one of the citizens found that his daughter had been seduced, and that she had failed to guard well her chastity till the time of marriage, he walled her up in an empty house with a horse, which he knew would surely kill her, if she were shut in there with him. And to this day the foundations of that house stand in your city, and that spot is called 'the place of the horse and the maid'."

/ **86.** Once in the house, the woman becomes the protector of the hearth, or *hestia* in Greek, and thus associated with the stability of the house. In *Phaedrus* 247a, Plato explains that while all other gods follow Zeus as he flies across the sky in his winged chariot, Hestia alone abides at home in the house of heaven.

/ **87.** de Coulanges, F, *The Ancient City*, Garden City, NY: Doubleday, nd, pp. 44–48.

/ **88.** Koolhaas, R, "Typical Plan" in *S,M,L,XL*, ed, R Koolhaas and B Mau, Köln: Benedikt

Taschen Verlag, 1997, p. 344; R Koolhaas, "Imagining Nothingness", *S,M,L,XL*, p. 199; originally published as R Koolhaas, "To imagine nothingness" in *L'architecture d'aujourd'hui*, no 238, April 1985, p. LXVII.

/ **89.** Tschumi, B, *Architecture and Disjunction*, Cambridge, MA: MIT, 1994, p. 122. This is one of his famous *Advertisements for Architecture*, stating that "To really appreciate architecture, you may even need to commit a murder. Architecture is defined by the actions it witnesses as much as by the enclosure of its walls. Murder in the Street differs from the Murder in the Cathedral in the same way as love in the street differs from the Street of Love." However, Clement of Alexandria would have none of this. He writes: "a murder does not become a sacrifice by being committed in a particular spot. You are not to call it a sacred sacrifice, if one slays a man either at the altar or on the highway to Artemis or Zeus, any more than if he slew him for anger or covetousness—other demons very like the former; but a sacrifice of this kind is murder and human butchery." Clement of Alexandria, *Stromata*, III, 40, p. 99.

/ **90.** Bataille, G, "Architecture" in *Rethinking Architecture*, N Leach, ed, London: Routledge, 1997, p. 21. D Hollier, *Against Architecture: The Writings of Georges Bataille*, trans B Wing, Cambridge, MA: MIT Press, 1995, p. 53.

/ **91.** Bataille, G, *The Accursed Share*, vol I, trans R Hurley, New York: Zone, 1991, pp. 55, 58 *et passim*. Carrasco, Davíd.

/ **92.** Seneca, LA, *Ad Lucilium epistulae morales*, § 90.

EX UNO LAPIDE

THE MYTH OF THE MONOLITHIC BUILDING IN ANTIQUITY

Fabio Barry

No body of theoretical writing now survives from antiquity that attests to the classical origins of a *longue durée* in architectural theory: *ex uno lapide* or, in Greek, *ἐξ ἑνὸς λίθου*. The phrase translates literally as "out of one stone", but is better rendered "all of a piece" because at heart it expressed the desire to fashion buildings that were as seamlessly perfect as any organic product of nature, from a flower to a new-born baby. Any such ambition, of course, immediately confronted a paradox: buildings neither grow nor are they born whole. Construction is instead the art of assembly, and any attempt to make buildings appear seamless depends on precisely that which stands in opposition to natural birth and growth, the signs and divisions of manufacture. This essay concludes, however, that human artifice embraced precisely this paradox by stressing the joint between parts, the seam.

This ambition satisfied primarily two objectives: first, the building seeks to measure up to Mother Nature, or any other engenderer larger than humankind; secondly, a new-born building is an apparition without a history, a building out of time and therefore beyond human experience. A temple that appears timeless can host eternal gods and accommodate an eternity not circumscribed by a history that is the sequence of human events. These goals were of special importance in religious construction, and would acquire supreme force in Christianity, for a unique God who—uniquely—creates everything out of nothing, and Who can only feel at home in an architecture that resembles that which He has made for himself, namely the Universe.

The desire to attain *ex uno lapide* is as old as the hills. It originates in monolithic construction, buildings created as nearly as possible out of single elements of the most massive dimensions. In a 'primitive' culture the idea of dragging bluestone menhirs from Wales to Wiltshire to make Stonehenge was hardly a time- or labour-saving strategy, but harnessed nature by moving mountains. The same holds for the labourious extraction of giant obelisks in Aswan by abrading or pummelling the bedrock. In both cases, all this labour was expended to the ends of a supernal reality. There is a general consensus that Stonehenge was some sort of observatory. Obelisks also point heavenwards because we know they were dedicated to the Sun-God Ra, that the name itself meant "finger of the sun", that they were considered solidified sunbeams, and that their fire-coloured granite even suggested that they were combusting. When Rome's largest obelisk, now at the Lateran, was rededicated by the emperor Constantius in 357, the inscription took care to observe that it was a "sizeable slice of mountain... hewn from the red quarry that has leapt up and strikes the heavens".[1]

Whether or not classical temples were descendants of the primitive hut, as Vitruvius has indelibly stamped upon our imaginations, once they had become petrified, the stones became absolutely integral to their sacralising. They allowed the temple to become a sort of sacred mountain itself, like those, in fact, with which archaic and classical Greek temples were themselves aligned, and on which the Gods dwelt.[2] Indeed, when Herod rebuilt the great Temple in Jerusalem, Josephus tells us, "persons straining to look at [it] were compelled to avert their eyes, as from solar rays. To approaching strangers it appeared from a distance like a snow-clad mountain."[3]

The act of quarrying must itself have raised the comparison, for once the blocks had been extracted the quarry (from Medieval Latin *quareria*, from Classical Latin *quadrum*, "square") was left a stepped and architectonic negative. Moreover, any number of classical theatres and amphitheatres across the Mediterranean, from Petra in Jordan (first century AD) to Sutri in Italy (late first century BC) fit the same bill and would become the stuff of legend in Medieval *mirabilia*.[4] Architecture's

Amphitheatre, Sutri, Italy, late first century BC.

claim on the mountain and the quarry will become a significant feature of Roman architecture. The middle ground between nature and architecture in this respect is "cyclopean masonry" of archaic Greece and Latium—a term already coined by antique observers who imagined that only giants were capable of such dexterity—a judicious assembly of irregular blocks coaxed into polygons that slide into unison almost, it seems, without human agency.[5] The most famous examples were at Tiryns and Mycenae (c. 1500–1100 BC) in the Peloponnese, but the same mansonry features in a number of sanctuaries throughout Lazio, like the second-century BC Temple of Juno Moneta at Segni. Such blocks form temple podia that are like middlemen between the bedrock and the orthogonal ashlar of the cella walls above.[6] The fact that this tradition continued unbroken in Latium, from the third century, or

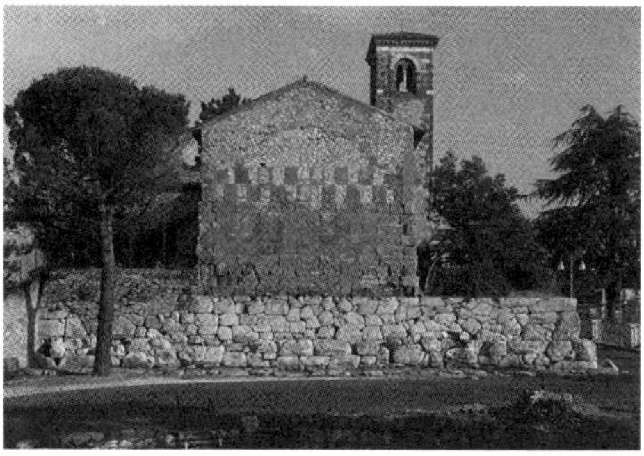

Temple of Juno Moneta, Segni, Italy, second century BC.

earlier, through to the first century AD, rules out any assumption of technological 'progression' and demonstrates that the masonry had instead an emblematic character. Livy still commends the massive masonry podium of the Capitol as the paragon of magnificence even in Augustus' newly marbled Rome.[7]

Moreover, it was said that stones were "born" in the earth, had "roots", and "grew" into the "living rock" (an expression which we still use without really knowing why).[8] Grottoes were mouths of the "living earth", in which the "living rock" was nourished by "sweet waters" from subterranean springs, and inscriptions repeat the same imagery in their man-made equivalents, nymphaea.[9] In nymphaea decked with shells and pumice the Romans feigned the aqueous concretions of nature to construct crucibles of generation and laboratories of natural art. Some ancient theories of geology taught that marbles enjoyed watery origins; that they were brews of purified earthy matter suspended in the ground water that had percolated down through the earth's crust to vast caverns, where it had been frozen or fired solid by earthly exhalations. Mountains were great reservoirs of this flux, whilst the appearance of travertine (which is, in fact, lime deposited by water) only confirmed the belief.[10] All these precepts may underlie the design of an imposing monument of engineering, the Porta Maggiore in Rome (52 AD).[11] Of course not

Porta Maggiore, Rome, 52 AD.

all roughened masonry necessarily indicates a dialectic with geology, but because the Porta Maggiore is a monumental gateway in an aqueduct (the Aqua Claudia and the Anio Vetus) there is reason to believe that its rugged faces do. Aqueducts were aerial rivers and their supports like seismic seams: or, as a late-antique poet put it, "what shall I say of the hanging streams on airy arches, where scarcely Iris [the rainbow] could raise her rainy waters? You would say rather that mountains had grown as far as the stars."[12] Because the Porta Maggiore carried the waters from springs miles distant to their outlets in the urban baths we might therefore think of it as a huge triumph of solidified water at the interface between city and country.[13] Its rustication easily presents an image of metamorphosis and its columns sprout up like palm-trees. Even the pedestrian passage between the Porta's two great arches resembles a *cuniculus* more than it does any urban feature. Only at the attic level are the crusts shorn away to reveal a smooth and incised artefact.[14]

To antique eyes the rough facades aped the architecture of nature, especially caves, as Ovid says: "not built by art: [but] nature, with her skill, had imitated art; with living pumice and light tufa she had spontaneously constructed an arch".[15] These monuments require "no embellishment, for Nature has given [them] beauty... there is no artificial splendour there; no hammer with re-echoing blow shall dress these stones, no marble workmanship take the place of the weather-worn [stone]".[16] The much later tribute to the *ruined* Theatre of Pompey that Cassiodorus (507/511 AD) puts into Theoderic's mouth might do just as well:

> It would be conceivably easier for mountains to fall than for that solidity to tremble: for that very mass is so entirely formed from vast blocks that, but for the added craftsmanship, it too might be thought the work of nature... those arched vaults, with their overhanging stonework, are so beautifully shaped with invisible jointing that you would suppose them the caverns of a lofty mountain, rather than anything man-made.[17]

Theatre of Marcellus, Rome, 44–13 BC.

Whether rough or smooth, scale was of cardinal importance in Roman architecture.[18] Temples, above all, must also satisfy *magnificence*, in the original sense of the word, a magnifying beyond normal conditions, in architectural practise both unbridled scale and unworldly splendour.[19] Thus Livy commends Antiochus because he resumed construction on the massive Temple of Zeus Olympeios in Athens (175 BC) to create, "the only one in the world that, though unfinished, was designed to conform to the greatness of the god". And Ovid says of Augustus' Temple of Mars Ultor (42–2 BC), that: "the god is as huge as the building".[20] Poets like Homer had indeed conceived the gods in monstrous proportions: thus, when Ares falls his body covers seven acres, and when he shouts he is as loud as ten thousand men.[21]

The ideal temple, was, according to Seneca, like that which God had built for mankind, "a huge mansion [...] a house in which you see, not flimsy veneers thinner than the very blade with which they are sawn, but virgin masses of the most precious stone, of a substance with such a variety of markings that you will marvel at its tiniest fragments".[22] When the rhetorician Aelius Aristeides eulogised Hadrian's massive temple at Cyzicus, 166 AD, he claimed that its marble blocks were themselves as large as temples, the temple as large as a sanctuary, and the sanctuary as large as a city.[23] These new landmarks, he says, actually altered the face of the earth. They were new mountains, or new islands.[24] Moreover, the potentially Babel-like proportions of monumental construction also suggested occupants of superhuman proportions and, because classical temples were not congregational halls but houses of the gods, their cult statues often attained colossal proportions. The most famous are Pheidias' lost statues of Athena and Zeus, in Athens and Olympia respectively, but the survival of the tradition in Rome is well illustrated by the (originally) eight metre high statue of *Fortuna Huiusce Diei*, attributed to Scopas Minor, that once dominated the eponymous temple (dedicated 101 BC).[25]

Scopas Minor (attributed), cult statue of *Fortune* from the temple of *Fortuna Huiusce Diei*, Rome (dedicated 101 BC).

Yet, just as highly prized as the scale of the god's house and the refinement of its materials, were the finishing of the masonry seams and the image of tightly-locked integrity that they presented. Following Greek practice, early shrines in tufa had been thickly coated in brilliant white stucco, some no doubt moulded to give the illusion of finely drafted ashlar, but Rome did not receive its first marble temple until 143 BC, dedicated to Jupiter Stator by Q Caecilius Metellus Macedonicus.[26]

Although this temple is long destroyed, another just as Hellenic and built only about 50 years later, the temple of Hercules Victor, still stands and offers a good example of the pristine edifice we have lost. In these new buildings masons borrowed the precision fittings of Greek architecture, finely draughted blocks whose fine joints were highlighted by channelled borders. Classical writers are not reticent about the

Temple of Hercules Victor ad Portam Trigeminam, Rome, 90/100 BC.

virtues and moral depth such coursing conjured. The ensemble of keenly draughted stone with mortar-less joints of a hair's breadth presents an image of steadfastness that matches the cohesion of the building blocks of the state itself. As Cassius Dio (c. 210/222 AD) will write, when Augustus famously said on his deathbed that he had found a Rome of brick but left one of marble, "he did not refer literally to the appearance of its buildings, but rather to the strength of the Empire".[27]

This idea became such a commonplace of rhetoric that, a century and a half after Augustus' death, when Aelius Aristeides eulogised the massive temple at Cyzicus, it was natural for him to compare well-jointed masonry to the regimen of the well-ordered city: "The temple is", he says, "a colossal mass, whose individual blocks and ornaments (*read* citizens) are in harmony with the whole (*read* the state)."[28] And we can be fairly certain that this constructional metaphor held the same importance even before Augustus was born, for late republican paintings and reliefs summarise the foundations of cities as ashlar walls carefully joined and built right under the noses of the deities whose job it was to safeguard the state in question.[29] The chain of hierarchy that unified the body public into a seamless state, as pictured in these masonry composites, can be best understood from passages in Seneca. Seneca distinguishes between continuous bodies (man), composite bodies (ships, houses), and collective ones (the army, the people, the senate), but he concludes that "we believe nothing is good, which is composed from things that are distinct".[30] His densest formulation pronounces that

> some things are continuous, others composite. A composite is [defined by] the contact between two bodies joined to each other. Continuity is the uninterrupted joining of parts to each other. Unity is continuity without the composite feature [... and] when I speak of the one [...] I am referring not to a number, but to the characteristic of a body that is cohesive by its own oneness, without any external help.[31]

According to Seneca, the acme of such cohesion is a body without contiguities or joins, that is a perfect whole. In architecture, it is obvious that this gold standard was unfeasible. So, to approach perfection, two subsidiary conceits must be enlisted. The first was *ex uno lapide* ("all of a piece") and the second, *harmonia* (literally a "good fit", and thence "harmony").[32] *Ex uno lapide* denoted the overall desired result, and *harmonia* the jointing necessary to achieve it; together they signified perfectibility through confection.

The earliest record of the critical phrase "out of one stone" is an inscription on the base of a nine metre-high colossus of Apollo on Naxos (c. 590/570 BC).[33] Thereafter, in the classical and late-antique periods, not a few authors use the phrase to celebrate the integrity of sculpture. A pair of fine odes exalts sculptors' skill in extorting effects from single but variegated marble blocks, to represent the flayed Marsyas hanging from a tree, and Daphne transforming into a laurel.[34] But, if taken literally, the late-antique poet Claudian's poem "On a Statue of a Chariot" strains all credibility:

> Who had the skill to fashion so many figures out of one block of marble [*uno de marmore*]? The chariot melts into the charioteer; the horses with one common accord obey the same reins. These are distinguishable by their various forms,

top/ Foundation of a City, frieze from the Basilica Paulli (Aemilia), Rome; Museo Nazionale Romano di Palazzo Massimo (late first century BC); **bottom/** Line drawing of the Frieze from the Basilica Paulli.

but made from one and the same material without distinction. The driver is of one piece with the car: to this are attached the steeds, each joined to, and proceeding out of, another. How admirable the artist's skill! A single block combines within itself all these bodies: one mass of marble by submitting to the chisel has grown into all these various shapes [*una silex tot membra ligat ductusque per artem / mons patiens ferri varios mutatur in artus*].[35]

However, by far the most famous example of the trope is Pliny's praise of the *Laocoön*. Some commentators use Pliny's claim as evidence that he must be describing another statue, because the object that has survived is actually assembled from seven interconnecting pieces.[36] Such empiricist critiques ignore the fact that all literary mention always concerns figure-groups and, in at least one other verifiable case, the figure-groups were *not* hewn from a single block.[37] Such critiques, in fact, fail to weigh *ex uno lapide* as an ideal, a criterion of perfection—in the sense of *perficere*, to utterly finish something and bring a concept to the ultimately unattainable state of complete realisation. Ancient artists were well aware of this inadequacy, and Apelles was only one of several to sign their paintings in the *imperfect* tense because no artwork could ever attain this telos.[38]

left/ Agesander, Athenodoros and Polydorus of Rhodes, *Laocoon*; Musei Vaticani, 42/20 BC.
right/ Plaster cast of *Laocoon*, with seven components separated, Musei Vaticani.

The recognition that through art multiplicity could sum up to a whole is evident when later critics praise marble revetment and columns that are "so polished that despite the composition of many pieces they give the illusion of being one sole piece".[39] Of course, polishable surfaces like revetment can reconcile the gap between wholeness and assembly optically, but integral to the image of *ex uno lapide* in monumental architecture was the valorisation of the perfect joins between the individual stones themselves, which were so perfectly level that they ensured a perfect fit. While the Roman feats of engineering competed with Nature they did so on their own architectonic terms, approximating the buildings to an absolute value and an order based upon a higher regularity than that of nature. Nature breeds no right angles and, to prove the point, Plutarch relates that when a Spartan king was impressed by the costly coffering of the room in which he dined, he dryly enquired whether "trees grew square in that country".[40]

The perfect fit allowed the blocks to join as one, in *symmetria*, and, indeed, the phrases "*consensus lapidum*" and "*coniunctio lapidum*" were even inscribed on monuments, like the first century Mausoleum of the Flavii (c. 150 AD)[41] and a fourth century triumphal arch, the phrasing even re-appearing in the work of Carolingian poets.[42] In Greek terminology, that which Vitruvius transmitted to Roman tradition, the word used to denote this perfected joining of masonry was *ἁρμογη* (*harmoge*), which, importantly, referred to both the body and the body politic. It signified equally the working unison of different organs of government or the organic joining of human bones.[43] Its cognate, the better-known *'Αρμονία* (*harmonia*), purveyed exactly the same virtues, and in origin it too referred to the "precision of good jointing" whether in timber or stone.[44]

In monumental masonry this concern with fine fitting, with *harmonia*, had given rise to *ἀναθύρωσις* (*anathyrosis*). In this technique, the middle of a marble block (the boss) is left proud and only a narrow channel around the edge is chiselled down to ensure the block's perfect alignment with its neighbours.[45] The bosses would be chiselled off later, when the entire wall was dressed to one flush surface, unless the wall in question was considered utilitarian, as in the famous "Wailing Wall" in Jerusalem (the retaining wall of Herod's great terrace for the great Temple). Leaving the bosses intact, then, was initially a labour-saving device and there was absolutely no need to leave such bosses proud on the facing walls on premier monuments, especially temples (like the Temple of Hercules) unless they enjoyed an emblematic value. There was even less reason to continue simulating

Cella wall, *Temple of Hercules Victor ad Portam Trigeminam.*

the technique for centuries, when the facing was just that, a slender veneer over a more pedestrian material;[46] still less reason again when that veneer was stucco and concealed real masonry in perfectly orderly coursing, as on the Mausoleum of Lucius Munatius Plancus at Gaeta.[47] Moreover, the broad channelled joints were considered so important that they were even worth miniaturising on coins.

left/ Fragment of faux-ashlar, external cladding from cella of the Temple of Venus Genetrix in the Forum Iulium (Trajanic). **top right/** Temple of Janus, Sestertius of Nero, c. 65 AD. **bottom right/** Mausoleum of Lucius Munatius Plancus at Gaeta (after 15 BC).

Such solidity was indispensable in conferring a moral depth on architecture. Men of substance should not allow walls and vaults to be concealed under skin-deep mosaic, gold-leaf or veneers of shimmering marble. As Seneca rants, "under marble and gold dwells slavery".[48] If fine joining was vital to ashlar construction by the same token it proved that no alien bond was essential to the wall's integrity. Mortar was superfluous and cramps and ties were hidden. In fact, in the eyes of Vitruvius and subsequent writers for whom buildings must appear indivisible units, the overall pattern of this joining became the very 'picture' of solidity, even eternity.[49] The obvious paradox—that one could see all the joins—only resolved itself if one regarded them as the seams of union rather than the borders of segregation, and we might better apply the term "fractionising" rather than "subdivision", because it better preserves this sense of overall cohesion.[50] Much later the same paradox will be encapsulated in a Medieval adage about the Vatican obelisk: "If it is a single stone, tell me by what art it has been raised; if many stones, tell me where are the joins."[51]

While the dominion of empire was manifested in the power to command even nature herself, the ulterior ambition was buildings that appeared almost ready-formed by nature in all its seamless perfection, with the architect or artist consequently acting only as a sort of midwife to their birth.[52] As Seneca says, "unity is... the characteristic of a body that is cohesive by its own oneness, without any external help". This idea was so rooted that there was potentially even an aural equivalent to the unity of *ex uno lapide*. For the Bible tells us that Solomon's Temple was "built of stone made ready before it was brought thither, so that there was neither hammer nor axe nor any tool of iron heard in the house while it was in building".[53] These words are normally considered a precocious episode in off-site prefabrication occasioned by the necessity that not even the sounds of labour violate the sacrality of the sanctuary. However, the same passage can also signify that the alienation of labour was the first step to erasing all the indices of facture. Josephus, in fact, goes on to specify: "with great skill the whole construction of the temple was born from stones cut fine and laid together so neatly and smoothly that to the beholder there appeared no sign of the use of mallets or other work-tools, but all the material seemed to have fitted itself together naturally without the use of these things, so that their fitting together seemed to have come about of itself rather than through the force of tools".[54]

Associated with the "you can't see the joins" *topos* in pronouncing the miraculous birth of the building is another that has been equally debased by over-repetition, namely "it didn't take very long either". When the hand is removed from the artefact's making, the whole process of its manufacture is elided, and with it the dimensions of history or human time in favour of the time-less, the undivided moment of perfect birth. It is this notion that implicitly situates the artefact in a different time-scale, in mythical time, and thence the realm of the eternal and cosmic.

These considerations, in fact, subtend the remarks of Plutarch on the Parthenon, a historian of the early second century AD writing about a building of the mid-fifth century BC. Plutarch (c. 45–125 AD) marvelled not only at the skilled precision and integrity of the Parthenon (448–432 BC), but that the whole building was "created in a short time for all time". In so saying, he did not make some banal comment about speedy execution, but rather insisted on the a-chronism of the temple's creation. As he says, five hundred years after its inauguration, the Parthenon seemed "even then and at once antique, but in the freshness of its vigour" it was also "recent and newly wrought". Moreover, its precision testified that it was in no way blunted by the ages thanks to its "bloom of perpetual newness", as though "the unfaltering breath of an ageless spirit had been infused into" it.[55] In Plutarch's view the Parthenon was truly divine like the Olympians it was "immortal and ageless for all time", or as "unaging and imperishable" as the artefacts of the divine blacksmith Hephaestus.[56] The Parthenon comes into complete being just as Athena had irrupted into the world fully formed and fully armed from the head of Zeus.

Rome was overrun by Goths in 410 AD, the last emperor was deposed in 476, the city administration broke down, the economy was devastated, buildings fell into ruin, and slowly the city started cannibalising itself for building materials. Yet the memory of the mountain, the "living rock", and the ideals of *ex uno lapide* and *harmonia* still steep the writings of Cassiodorus (480–c. 575 AD), secretary to the Ostrogoth king of Ravenna, Theoderic, in the early sixth century. Praising the city's monuments, in, remarkably, a legal document—the *Formula Addressed to the Prefect of the City on the Appointment of the Architect*—he asks:

> what should we say about the lofty columns [as slender] as rushes? Those towering heaps of buildings seem to be supported as though raised on canes and hollowed out with fluted columns in such uniformity that you would much rather believe that the buildings themselves had been poured out, you would think that what you see smoothed out of the hardest minerals was actually made from wax, [and] you would say that the joins of the marbles were generative veins, which deceive the eyes into believing that these praiseworthy things have grown miraculously.[57]

/ **1.** *CIL* (*Corpus Inscriptionum Latinarum*) 6.1163: "*haut exiguam partem montis... rursus rufis avulsa metallis emicuit pulsatque polos.*"

/ **2.** Scully, VJ, *The Earth, the Temple and the Gods: Greek Sacred Architecture*, New Haven: Yale University Press, 1962, pp. 1–8.

/ **3.** Flavius Josephus, *BJ* (*Bellum Judaicum*) 5.222–223, trans HStJ Thackeray, *Josephus in Nine Volumes*, The Loeb Classical Library, Cambridge, MA: Harvard University Press/ London: William Heinemann, 1976, vol III, p. 269. cf. Joseph., op cit. *AJ* (*Antiquitates Judaicce*) 15.11.3.

/ **4.** "*the marvelous theatre in the marble mountain at Heraclea... is carved in such a way, that all the chambers in the structure, all the seats in the cavea, and all the exit ramps and caverns were carved from a single solid stone" ("Theatrum autem admirabile in Heraclea de monte marmoreo... quod quidem ita sculptum est, ut omnes cellulae mansionum et sedilia universa per girum et exitus omnes et antra ex uno solidoque lapide sculpta sint*": Magister Gregorius, *Narratio de Mirabilibus Urbis Roma*e, c. 1200, p. 11).

/ **5.** The walls of Mycenae and Tiryns "are said to be the work of the Cyclopes": Pausanias. 2.16.5; 2.25.8., trans WHS Jones, The Loeb Classical Library, Cambridge, MA: Harvard University Press/London: William Heinemann, 1976.

/ **6.** Cifarelli, FM, *Il tempio di Giunone Moneta sull'acropoli di Segni: storia, topografia e decorazione architettonica*, Rome: L'Erma di Bretschneider, 2003, especially pp. 68–72 (dating), pp. 88–96 (construction). Alba Fucens from second century–first century BC.

/ **7.** Livy 6.4.12: "*Capitolium quoque saxo quadrato substructum est, opus vel in hac magnificentia urbis conspiciendum.*"

/ **8.** Halleux, R, "Fécondité des mines et sexualité des pierres dans l'Antiquité gréco-romaine" in *Revue belge de philologie et d'histoire*, 1970, pp. 16–25; JC Plumpe, "Vivum Saxum, Vivi Lapides. The Concept of 'Living Stone' in Classical and Christian Antiquity" in *Traditio*, 1 ,1943, pp. 1–14.

/ **9.** Pliny *HN* (*Naturalis Historia*) 36.42.154: "appellantur quidem ita erosa saxa in aedificiis, quae musaea vocant, dependentia ad imaginem specus arte reddendam", Leipzig: BG Teubner, 1897. A Rinaldi, "Saxum vivum e non-finito nelle grotte fiorentine del Cinquecento" in I Lapi Ballerini, L Medri, eds, *Artifici d'acque e giardini: la cultura delle grotte e dei ninfei in Italia e in Europa*, Atti del V Convegno Internazionale sui Parchi e Giardini Storici. Florence: Ministero per i beni e le attività Culturali, 1999, pp. 299–307; P Morel, *Les grottes maniéristes en Italie au XVIe siècle: théâtre et alchimie de la nature*, Paris: Macula, 1998; S Heidet, "Pierres ponces, concrétions calcaires.... Le décor à "rocailles" des parois et des voûtes en Italie et en Gaule à l'époque romaine" in P Chardon-Picault, ed, in *Les roches décoratives dans l'architecture antique et du Haut Moyen Âge*, Paris: CTHS, 2004, pp. 289–297.

/ **10.** Extensively discussed in F Barry, "Walking on Water: Cosmic Floors in Antiquity and the Middle Ages" in *Art Bulletin* 89, no 4, 2007, pp. 630–634.

/ **11.** Coates-Stephens, R, *Porta Maggiore. Monument and Landscape*, Rome: L'Erma di Bretschneider, 2004.

/ **12.** Rutilius Claudius Namatanius, *De Reditu Suo* 1.97–99: "*Quid loquar aerio pendentes fornice rivos, / qua vix imbriferas tolleret Iris aquas? / Hoc potius dicas crevisse in sidera montes.*" cf. Publius Papinius Statius (*Silvae* 1.5.27–28) on the Aqua Marcia: "whose vagrant water multiplies on towering masses, transmitted in the air by countless arches" ("*praecelsis quarum vaga molibus unda / crescit et innumero pendens transmittitur arcu*").

/ **13.** Conversely, for the idea of trumping nature by spanning her rivers, see FS Kleiner, "The Trophy on the Bridge and the Roman Triumph over Nature" in *L'Antiquité Classique* 60, 1991, pp. 182–192.

/ **14.** Relevantly, Festus feels it necessary to distinguish between the two possible meanings of *petra*, "rock", by comparing cliffs to voussoirs: "There are two kinds of rocks, one of which is the natural rock which juts into the sea, which Ennius remembers in Bk. 11 [*Ann.* 11.351]: "a cliff deep-falling, covered by mighty rocks", and Laevius in *The Centaurs*: "Where often I wander among the rocks." The other kind of rock is shaped by hand, as Aelius Gallus shows: "Rock is the place which right and left will complete the arch up to the level of the arch apex." ("*Petrarum genera sunt duo, quorum alterum naturale saxum prominens in mare, cuius Ennius meminit; lib. XI: 'Alte delata petrisque ingentibus tecta'*; and Laevius in *Centauris: 'Ubi ego saepe petris'; alterum manufactum, ut docet Aelius Gallus: 'petra est, qui locus Dextra ac sinistra fornicem †expleturusque† ad libramentum summi fornicis.'*") in WM Lindsay, ed, *Sexti Pompei Festi De Verborum Significatu*, Leipzig: BG Teubner, 1913, p. 226.

/ **15.** Ovid, *Metamorphoses* 3.158–160: "*arte laboratum nulla: simulaverat artem / ingenio natura suo; nam pumice vivo / et levibus tofis nativum duxerat arcum*".

/ **16.** Apollinaris Sidonius, *Carmina* 22.224–6, trans M Platnauer, The Loeb Classical Library, Cambridge, MA: Harvard University Press / London: William Heinemann, 1976: "*non eget hic cultu, dedit huic natura decorem / nil fictum placuisse placet, non pompa per artem / ulla, resultanti non comet malleus ictu / saxa, nec exesum supplebunt marmora tofum*". Sidonius describes a grotto in the villa of Pontius Leontius, whose vaulted roof the natural spring had formed out of its own rock. Cited in the same context in R Coates-Stephens, *Porta Maggiore. Monument and Landscape*, p. 46.

/ **17.** Cassiodorus, *Variae* 4.51.3–4 (Theodoric to Symmachus): "montes facilius cedere putarentur, quam soliditas illa quateretur: quando et moles ipsa sic tota de cautibus fuit, ut praeter artem additam et ipsa quoque naturalis esse crederetur... caveas illas saxis pendentibus apsidatas ita iuncturis absconditis in formas pulcherrimas convenisse, ut cryptas magis excelsi montis crederes quam aliquid fabricatum esse iudicares". Mommsen dates this letter to 507/511 AD. Cassiodorus must be referring to a rugged ruin because much of the outer circuit had already collapsed in the early fifth century (*CIL*, 6. 1191, "*theatrum Pompei, [collapso] exteriore ambitu*").

/ **18.** Delaine, J, "The Temple of Hadrian at Cyzicus and Roman Attitudes to Exceptional Construction" in *Papers of the British School at Rome* 70, 2002, pp. 205–230.

/ **19.** Livy 6.4.12, (splendours of Rome); Pliny HN, 36.21.95 (Temple of Artemis, Ephesus); Cicero, *Verres* 2.4.108 (Temple of Ceres); Tacitus, *Histories* 3.72 and 4.53 (Temple of Jupiter Optimus Maximus).

/ **20.** Livy 6.4.12: "*magnificentiae vero in deos vel Iovis Olympii templum Athenis, unum in terris pro magnitudine dei, potest testis esse*" (begun 530 BC). Ovid, *Fasti* 5.553: "*Et deus est ingens et opus.*"

/ **21.** Homer, *Illiad* 21.407, 5.895–63.

/ **22.** Seneca, LA, *De Beneficiis* 4.4.2: "*Ingens tibi domicilium... in quo vides non tenuas crustas et ipsas, quae secantur, lamna graciliores, sed integras lapidis pretiossimi moles, sed totas variae distinctaeque materiae, cuius tu parvula frusta miraris.*"

/ **23.** Aristides, P Aelius, *Orations* 27, CA Behr, ed and trans, *P. Aelius Aristides. The Complete Works*, vol II. *Orations XVII–LIII*, Leiden: Brill, 1981, pp. 101, 105.

/ **24.** Aristides, PA, *Orations* 27.

/ **25.** Marchetti-Longhi, G, "Il colossale acrolito rinvenuto nell' 'Area Sacra' del Largo Argentina" in *Atti della Pontificia Accademia Romana di Archeologia* 3, 1932–1933, pp. 133–203; HG Martin, *Römische Tempelkultbilder: eine archäologische Untersuchung zur späten Republik*, Rome: L'Erma di Bretschneider, 1987, pp. 103–111. Attributed to Skopas Minor in F Coarelli, G Sauron, "La tête Pentini. Contribution à l'approche méthodologique du néo-atticisme" in *Mélanges de l'École française de Rome. Antiquité*, 90 (2), 1978, p. 724. Statue c 8 metres high, peripteral columns 11 metres; F Coarelli, *Il Campo Marzio. Dalle origini alla fine della repubblica*, Rome: Edizioni Quasar, 1997, pp. 275–293 with bibliography.

/ **26.** For the stuccowork, see F Barry "A Whiter Shade of Pale: Relative and Absolute White in Roman Sculpture and Architecture" in *Revival and Invention: sculpture through its material histories*, S Clerbois and M Droth, eds, New York: Peter Lang, 2011, pp. 31–62.

/ **27.** Suetonius, *Augustus* 28.3; Lucius Cassius Dio 56.30.3–4. The locus classicus of this attitude to public building is Marcus Vitruvius Pollio, *De Architectura*, praef.: "I observed that you [Augustus] cared not only about the common life of all men, and the constitution of the state, but also about the provision of suitable public buildings; so that the state was not only made greater through you by its new provinces, but the majesty of the empire was also expressed through the eminent dignity of its public buildings", trans F Granger, London: Heinemann, and Cambridge, MA: Harvard University Press, 1931

/ **28.** Aristides, PA, pp. 101, 105.

/ **29.** Carettoni, G, "Il fregio figurato della Basilica Emilia" in *Rivista dell'Istituto Nazionale d'Archeologia e Storia dell'Arte* 9, 1961, pp. 16–21.

/ **30.** Seneca, LA, *Epistulae Morales* 102.6, 102.7: "*nullum bonum putamus esse, quod ex distantibus constat*".

/ **31.** Seneca, LA, *Naturales Quaestiones* 2.2.2, 4: "*aliquid continuum, aliquid commissum; et commissura est duorum coniunctorum inter se corporum tactus, continuatio est partium inter se corporum tactus, continuatio est partium inter se non intermissa inter se coniunctio. Unitas est sine commissura continuatio [...] si quando dixero unum [...] non ad numerum referre, sed ad naturam corporis nulla ope externa sed unitate cohaerentis.*" This concept is also discussed by McEwen, who cites the variants of Sextus Empiricus and Pomponius, see IK McEwen, *Vitruvius: Writing the Body of Architecture*, Cambridge, MA: The MIT Press, 2003, pp. 55–66.

/ **32.** A summary history of the phrase *ex uno lapide* from Herodotus to Master Gregorius is given in S Settis et al, *Laocoonte, fama e stile*,

Rome: Donzelli, 1999, pp. 79–81. It is fleetingly treated in I Lavin, "*Ex Uno Lapide*: The Renaissance Sculptor's *Tour de Force*" in *Il cortile delle statue. Der Statuenhof des Belvedere im Vatikan*, M Winner, ed, et al, Akten des internationalen Kongresses zu Ehren von Richard Krautheimer, Rom, 21–23 Oktober 1992, Mainz, 1998, pp. 191–210. However, Lavin argues that the antique *topos* was only "a source for admiration... without reference to any underlying matter of theory or principle" and only in the Renaissance did the "integrity of the block [become] a veritable ethical imperative, a testimony not only to the bravura of the artist but also to his personal integrity", p. 194. It has also been asserted, grammatical implausibility notwithstanding, that the phrase only means "out of one type of marble", see MA Tomei, "*I resti dell'arco di Ottaviano sul Palatino e il portico delle Danaidi*" in *Mélanges de l'Ecole française de Rome. Antiquité* 112, 2000, p. 558.

/ **33.** Gruben, G, "Naxos und Delos. Studien zur archaischen Architektur der Kykladen" in *Jahrbuch des Deutschen Archäologischen Instituts* 112, 1997, pp. 261–416, especially pp. 267–287 for the Colossus, pp. 293–300 for another roughed-out figure still in the quarries. L Giuliani, ed, "Der Koloss der Naxier" in *Meisterwerke der antiken Kunst*, Munich: CH Beck Verlag, 2005, pp. 12–27 (my thanks to Clemente Marconi for these references).

/ **34.** *Anthologia Latina* 162 (173): "Defeated Marsyas hangs from an airy branch, And natural red reveals the constriction of his chest. A skilled hand has filed the stone into various limbs. The faithful likeness of man and tree shine forth through art." ("*Aerio victus dependet Marsya ramo / nativusque probat pectora tensa rubor / docta manus varios lapidem limavit in artus / arboris atque hominis fulget ab arte fides*"). *Anth. Lat.* 161 (172R): "*On Daphne.* A skilful hand ensured that the sculpted boughs and limbs would contain an appropriate colour. The joining of skill and painterliness produce a marvellous beauty, when variegated marble depicts two entities" ("De Daphne. */ Frondibus et membris servavit dextera sollers / congruus ut sculptis posset inesse color. / Dant mirum iunctae ars et pictura decorem, / ostendit varius cum duo signa lapis*").

/ **35.** Appolinaris, S, *Carmina*, p. 87.

/ **36.** Laocoon: Pliny *HN*, 36.4.37. Seven pieces: F. Magi, "Il ripristino del Laocoonte"in *Rendiconti della Pontificia Accademia Romana di Archeologia* 11, 1960, pp. 13–22. Pliny mentions two other sculptures "ex uno lapide": *Chariot with Apollo and Diana* (*HN* 36.36); *Winged Cupids Playing with a Lioness* (*HN* 36.41).

/ **37.** Pausanias, 8.37.3: "The actual images of the goddesses, Despoine and Demeter [by Damophon, at Lykosoura], the throne on which they sit, along with the footstool under their feet, are all made out of one piece of stone. No part of the drapery, and no part of the carvings about the throne, is fastened to another stone by iron or cement, but the whole is from one block. This stone was not brought in by them, but they say that in obedience to a dream they dug up the earth within the enclosure and so found it." The statue is, in fact, a composite. The fragments are extensively studied and described in M Jost, *Sanctuaires et cultes d'Arcadie*, Paris: Librairie Philosophique J Vrin, 1985.

/ **38.** Pliny, *Praes* 26; M Baxandall, *Giotto and the Orators: Humanist Observers of Painting in Italy and the Discovery of Pictorial Composition 1350–1450*, New York: Oxford University Press, 1971, pp. 64–65.

/ **39.** Symmacus, Quintus Aurelius (*Epistulae* 1.12), before 377 AD, says of the marbles in his father's house, "the upper floor chambers are covered with a revetment so polished that despite its composition of many pieces it gives the illusion of being one sole piece. This also holds for the expensive columns which I believe, if I have good eyes, to be cut from Bithynian stone" ("*superiores conclavia crustis teguntur ea operis levitate, ut conpago solidum mentiatur. Columnas nihilo amplius mercatus es, quam si tibi muneri contigissent. Eas bithynio lapide caesas, si bene oculis utor, existimo*").

/ **40.** Plutarch, *Lycurgus* 13.5: ἐρωτῆσαι τὸν ξένον εἰ τετράγωνα παρ'αὐτοῖς τά ξύλα φύεται.

/ **41.** Mausoleum of T Flavius Secundus, Kasserine (Tunisia): *CIL*, 1552. "here on earth there remains this impressive tomb in its eternal newness, that thus the shining stones perfectly cohere, that as the steps rise from their root they have grown finer, so that every corner has been traced as if with the stuff of malleable wax.... Its impressiveness reaches into the sky, impinges on the neighboring clouds and measures the course of the sun." ("*hic tantam faciem superesse sepulchri / perpetua novitate sui, sic stare nitentes / consensus lapidum, sic de radice levatos / in melius crevisse gradus, ut et angulus omnis / sic quasi mollitae ductus sit stamine cerae... Stat sublimis honor vicinaq(ue) nubila pulsat / et solis metitur iter.*")

/ **42.** Vitruvius, 1.2.4: "*symmetria est ex ipsius operis membris conveniens consensus ex* *partibusque separatis ad universae figurae speciem ratae partis responsus.*" *Symmetria* indicates *commensurability* of parts, not our *symmetry.* "Coniunctio lapidum": inscription dating to the reign of Gratian, Valentinian II and Theodosius (379–383) on an arch (*CIL*, op. cit., 8. 14728) see C Lepelley, *Les cités de l'Afrique romaine au Bas-Empire*, 2 vols, Paris, 1979–1981, vol 2, p. 251 (where it is erroneously cited as no. 14729): "ARCUM TRIUMPHALEM FUNDITUS QUADRA[*ATIS LAPIDIBUS OLIM*] EXTRUCTUM [...] EORUNDEM LAPIDUM CONIUNCTIONIS [... *A*]D ORNAMENTUM SPLENDIDISSIMAE CIVI[*TATIS*...]. Angilbert, (790/814 AD) on Charlemagne's palace at Aachen, "saxa locat, solido coiungens marmora nexu": *Carmen de Karolo Magno III*, v 94; Jv Schlosser, ed, *Schriftquellen zur Geschichte der Karolingischen Kunst*, Vienna: Verlag von Carl Graeser, 1896, p. 25, cat. 97.

/ **43.** Polybius 6.18.1; Galen, *On the Natural Faculties* (Gal *Nat Fac*) 19.460; Joseph, *AJ* 13.11.3; JJ Pollitt, T*he Ancient View of Greek Art: Criticism, History, and Terminology*, New Haven: Yale University Press, 1974, pp. 150–51. In painting and sculpture the term also referred to the seamless meshing of one part with another.

/ **44.** Pausanias, 8.41.8, on the Temple of Apollo at Bassae; Paus. 8.8.8, on the blocks in fortifications; Diodorus Siculus 2.8.2, on the construction of a bridge, see JJ Pollitt, *The Ancient view of Greek Art*, pp. 151–54.

/ **45.** Orlandos, AK, *Les Matériaux de construction et la technique architecturale des anciens Grecs*, Paris: E de Boccard, 1966–1968, vol 2, pp. 99–100; R Martin, *Manuel d'archéologie grecque. Matériaux et techniques*, Paris: EA et J Picard, 1965, vol 1, pp. 114–199. Most scholars now use the term exclusively to denote the jointing *within* the wall, where each face was hollowed out and only the perimetral border smoothed to a flush finish; but the draughted margins of the facing ashlar accomplished the same task and go under the same name, see G Lugli, *La tecnica edilizia romana, con particolare riguardo a Roma e Lazio*, 2 vols, Rome: Giovanni Bardi, 1957, vol.1, pp. 207–208; JJ Coulton, *Greek Architects at Work. Problems of Structure and Design*, 2nd ed, London: Harper Collins, 1982, pp. 46–47.

/ **46.** The example illustrated is external cladding from cella of the Temple of Venus Genetrix in the Forum Iulium, dating to the Trajanic rebuilding, see CM Amici, *Il Foro di Cesare*, Florence: Leo S Olschki, 1991, p. 88. A good example of a brick structure disguised as a marble temple is the Capitolium at Ostia, see C Albo, "Il Capitolium di Ostia. Alcune considerazioni sulla tecnica edilizia ed ipotesi ricostruttiva" in *Mélanges de l'École française de Rome. Antiquité* 114, 2002, pp. 363–390.

/ **47.** Fellmann, R, *Das Grab des LM Plancus bei Gaeta*, Schr. Inst. Ur- u. Frühgesch. Schweiz XI, Basel, 1957.

/ **48.** Seneca, *Epist.* 90.10: "sub marmore atque auro servitus habitat." cf. *Epist.* 8.5-6; 110.14-18; 115.3-9. Cicero's indictment of Verres for corruption receives added weight from the charge that he literally "white-washed" the columns ("columnas dealbari") of the Temple of Castor and Pollux in the Forum Romanum, rather than having newly-quarried ones delivered (Cicero, *Verr.* 2.5.145, 2.5.147). In his treatise on female cosmetics Ovid also suggests that this sort of beauty is only skin-deep: "Lofty halls are plated with gold, black earth lays hidden under set marble" ("*auro sublimia tecta linuntur / Nigra sub imposito marmore terra latet*" (Ovid, *Medicamina Faciei Femineae*. 7–8). Seneca the elder also reviles "that stone which is cut to cover walls with its thin veneer" ("*ille secatur lapis et tenui fronte parietem tegit*" (Seneca the elder, *Controversiae* 2.1.12)

/ **49.** Vitruvius, 4.4.4: "if the walls [of the temple] are to be built of squared stone or marble the pieces should be of moderate and equal size [*quadrato saxo aut marmore, maxime modicis paribusque videtur esse faciundum*]... the protruding joins surrounding the vertical and bedding joints will produce a more pictorial effect in the general view [*circum coagmenta et cubilia eminentes expressiones graphicoteran efficient in aspectu delectationem*]." Of Greek masonry he says that perfect coursing bonded in depth will endure for eternity (2.8.5: "*et sic maxime ad aeternitatem firmas perficiunt virtutes*").

/ **50.** Vitruvius' conception of buildings as indivisible units is implicit in his statement that "there is no kind of material, no body, and no thing that can be produced or conceived of, which is not made up of elementary particles." (Vitruvius, 2.1).

/ **51.** "*Si lapis est unus, dic qua sit arte levatus, / Si lapides plures, dic ubi congeries*": Magister Gregorius, p. 29; S Settis *et al*, p. 80.

/ **52.** Delaine, J, *The Temple of Hadrian at Cyzicus and Roman Attitudes to Exceptional Construction*, pp. 205–230.

/ **53.** *I Kings* 6:7.

/ **54.** Joseph, *AJ* 8.69: ἡ δ'ὅλη τοῦ οἰκοδομία κατὰ πολλὴν τέχνην ἐκ λίθων ἀκροτόμων ἐγένετο συντεθέντων ἁρμονίως πάνυ καὶ λείως, ὡς μήτε σφύρας μήτε ἄλλου τινὸς ἐργαλείου τεκτονικοῦ τοῖς κατανοοῦσιν ἐργασίαν δηλοῦσθαι, ἀλλά δίχα τῆς τούτων χρήσεως πᾶσαν ἡρμόσθαι τὴν ὕλην προσφυῶς, ὡς ἑκούσιον τὴν ἁρμονίαν αὐτῆς δοκεῖν μᾶλλον ἢ τῆς τῶν ἐργαλείων ἀνάγκης.

/ **55.** Plutarch, *Pericles* 159: ἔργα πρὸς πολὺν χρόνον ἐν ὀλίγῳ γενόμενα. Κάλλει μὲν γὰρ ἕκαστον εὐθὺς ἦν τότε ἀρχαῖον, ἀκμῇ δὲ μέχρι νῦν πρόσφατόν ἐστι καὶ νεουργόν· οὕτως ἐπανθεῖ καινότης ἀεί τις ἄθικτον ὑπὸ τοῦ χρόνου διατηροῦσα τὴν ὄψιν, ὥσπερ ἀειθαλὲς πνεῦμα καὶ ψυχὴν ἀγήρω καταμεμιγμένην τῶν ἔργων ἐχόντων.

/ **56.** e.g. Homer, *Il.* 8.539, 12.323, 17.444. The golden dogs that Hephaistos fashioned to guard the palace of Alcinous are "immortal and unaging" (*Od.* 7.94): JS Clay, "Immortal and Ageless Forever" in *Classical Journal* 77, no 2, 1981–1982, pp. 112–118.

/ **57.** Cassiodorus, 7.15.3: "*quid dicamus columnarum iunceam proceritatem? moles illas sublimissimas fabricarum quasi quibusdam erectis hastilibus contineri et sub tanta aequalitate concavis canalibus excavatas, ut magis ipsas aestimes fuisse transfusas, ceris iudices factum, quod metallis durissimis videas expolitum, marmorum iuncturas venas dicas esse genitales, ubi dum falluntur oculi, laus probatur crevisse miraculis.*" I take the problematic "*concavis canalibus*", (literally "hollow/concave pipes") to indicate the scoops of fluting.

All illustrations courtesy of Fabio Barry.

MYTHS OF THE BODY IN ARCHITECTURE

AN ANTHROPOLOGICAL APPROACH

Laurent Baridon

Postmodernity has, in many ways, been characterised by the notion of the body. Even if one were to believe, with some degree of legitimacy, that new technologies will turn our organisms into cyborgs, our bodies are still subject to their changing physiology, responding to both sensuality and suffering.[1] The huge increase in studies dedicated to the relations between the biological and the political, between mankind and social structures and in particular to what links the individual to his specific context and environment that have been published since Michel Foucault's original research shows that the notion still has resonance today. Architecture, because it shelters or accommodates human beings with a view to serving them or to restricting them, is the discipline best placed to witness these corporeal connections.

An examination of the main theoretical texts of the early Italian Renaissance provides an ideal approach to the theme of the body in architecture. Because they are widely accepted as having influenced the ideas and imagination of Western architects for half a millennium, they have been the subject of numerous interpretations. Some of the most recent have emphasised the recurrence of their corporeal themes by relating them to the history of ideas,[2] of the sacred[3] and of the political.[4] These interpretations have provided a complete re-evaluation of the theoretical texts. In spite of this and in the light of the drastic evolution of technical know-how and social conditions of production in architecture since they were written, they are clearly obsolescent today. On the other hand, within the context of a reflection on the myths of architecture, an analysis of the foundational character of the relationship between the body and building is achievable not so much by looking for its relevance today, but, on the contrary, by demonstrating its antiquity and its value as an archetype.

With this objective in mind, two particularly dominant concepts can be considered representative of the topic: the body-edifice and the support-body. Both themes have several characteristics in common and on the basis of these, their connections with myths belonging to extra-European cultures merit examination. This approach allows us to confirm whether or not the notion of the body in architecture has always served, via symbolism of a sacred nature, to create a relation between the individual and society.

REPRESENTATIONS OF THE ARCHITECTURAL BODY AT THE END OF THE *QUATTROCENTO*

The pictures that illustrate the treatises of Francesco di Giorgio Martini make up the most complete group of images of the architectural body of this period, making it possible to evaluate this process of incarnation within architecture.[5] They appear in the margins of manuscripts dating from the 1480s and their content is largely inspired by the *De architectura* of Vitruvius. Francesco di Giorgio's point of view, however, requires qualification by taking into account the chronology of the texts and the evolution of the author's own thought on the subject.[6]

Francesco di Giorgio knew this essential source better than his predecessors did and he even produced a translation of the text.[7] Nevertheless his own writings remained independent from those of the Latin author, especially when dealing with subjects directly related to his own practical experience, machines and fortifications in particular. Most of the marginal drawings that are of interest come from the *De architectura*, but are not simple illustrations that might compensate for any obscurity that a text, reaching the Renaissance without its images, might entail and that are for that matter purely hypothetical. These drawings offer true explanations, if not interpretations. The importance of this "graphic mediation"[8] has already been underlined, namely by John Onians who noted that Aristotle was quoted by Francesco di Giorgio as a justification for resorting to visual stimulus and to the senses.[9] The prologue of one of his treatises stresses the importance of images and this is later confirmed by the assertion of their heuristic value and their capacity to act through the imagination rather than via the abstractions of language.[10]

Francesco di Giorgio therefore extended the analogies between body and architecture that could be found in Vitruvius and, with the use of pictures, reinforced them. These cases make the variety of possible forms perfectly clear by using examples that, unmistakably, originate in an ambition to be both thorough and experimental. They show, by means of the drawings in the different versions of his treatises, the different ways of personifying buildings, be it in their plan, their elevation or the profiles of their moldings. Bodies are depicted inserted in church plans, their heads in the main apse, male or female heads in Corinthian capitals, facial profiles in the sections of cornices and bodies in facades. To this list must also be added the young Corinthian woman who appears in columns and the female bodies depicted in Ionic columns.[11] A close examination of the pictures suggests multiple cross-references and even contaminations from one text to another. On the same folio where the original description of the orders is presented, the *marginaliae* seem to contain graphical commentaries that integrate different moments in these accounts. As a result, by explaining the text, its meaning is rendered more complex thus encouraging further interpretations. When the profiles of entablature moldings are compared to human faces, for example, it seems that the correlation between the different parts of the face and those of the cornice are at least as important as the proportions that they correspond to. Francesco di Giorgio details the different facial features by naming them, juxtaposing them, both in the text and the images. It is even possible that in some drawings the facial expression may have a meaning and give the moldings in question an expressivity linked to physiognomic criteria.[12] The anthropomorphic and zoomorphic helmets presented at the end of the codex, their grimacing features destined to scare the enemy, proceed from the same kind of ideas.[13] The church facades with a human body superimposed show how the position of the arms determines the slope of the roofs of the side-aisles as much as the proportions of the facade do.

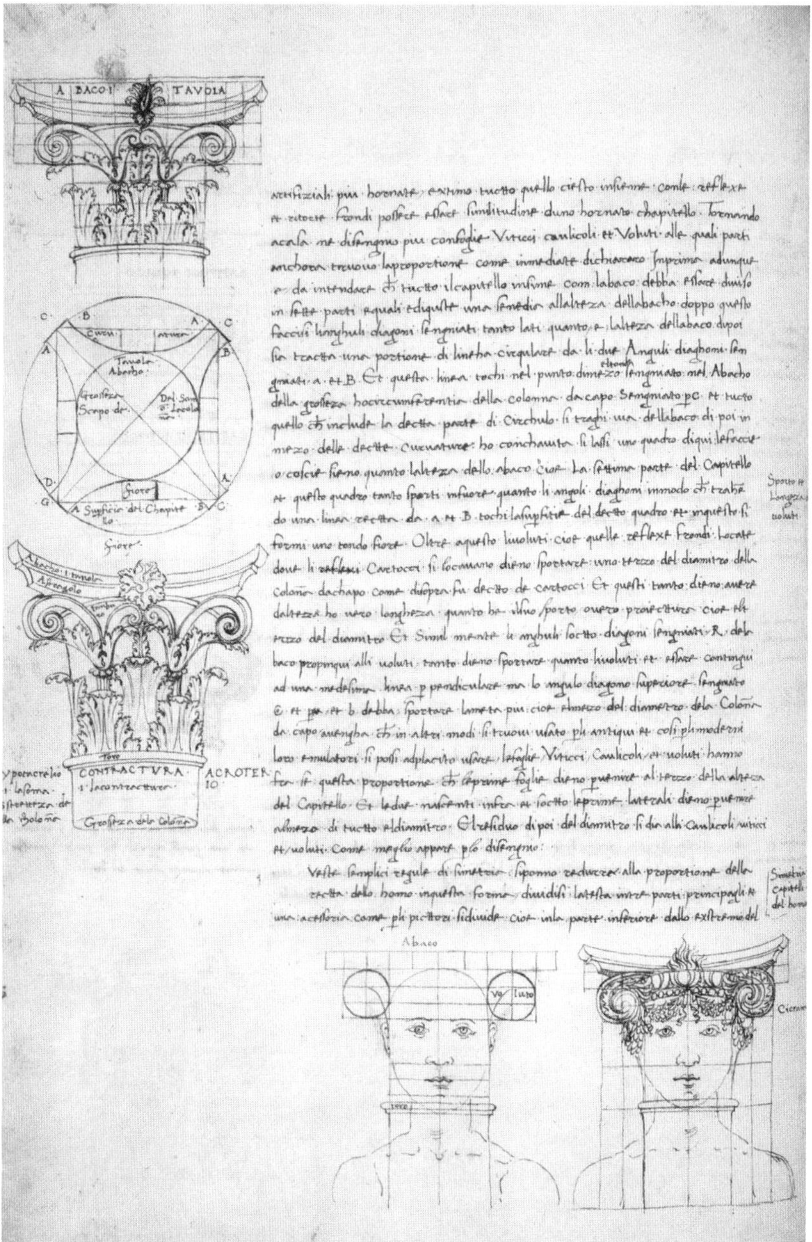

Francesco di Giorgio Martini, *Architettura civile e arte militare*, codex Magliabechiano II.I.141, f. 33v. Image courtesy of Ministero per i Beni e le Attività Culturali/Biblioteca Nazionale Centrale, Firenze. Photo Donato Pineider.

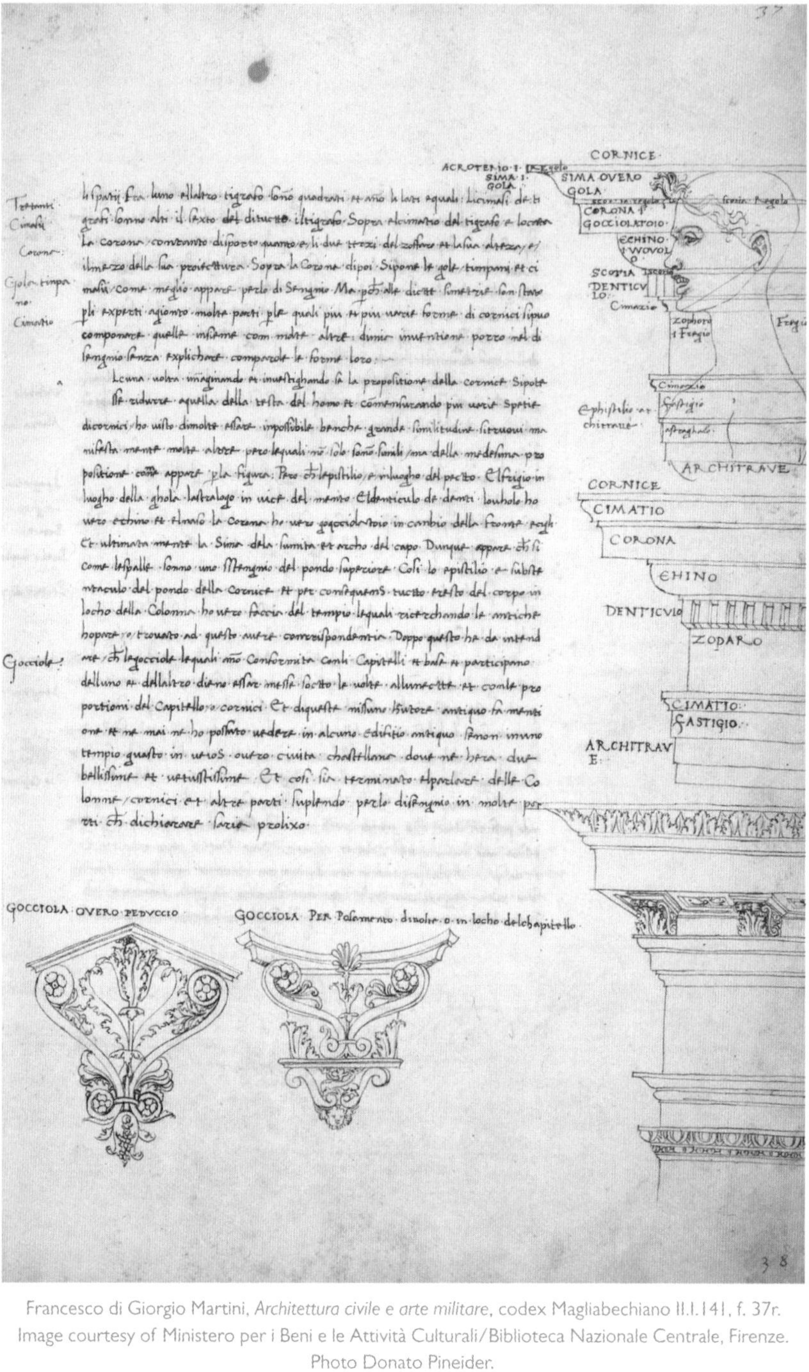

Francesco di Giorgio Martini, *Architettura civile e arte militare*, codex Magliabechiano II.I.141, f. 37r. Image courtesy of Ministero per i Beni e le Attività Culturali/Biblioteca Nazionale Centrale, Firenze. Photo Donato Pineider.

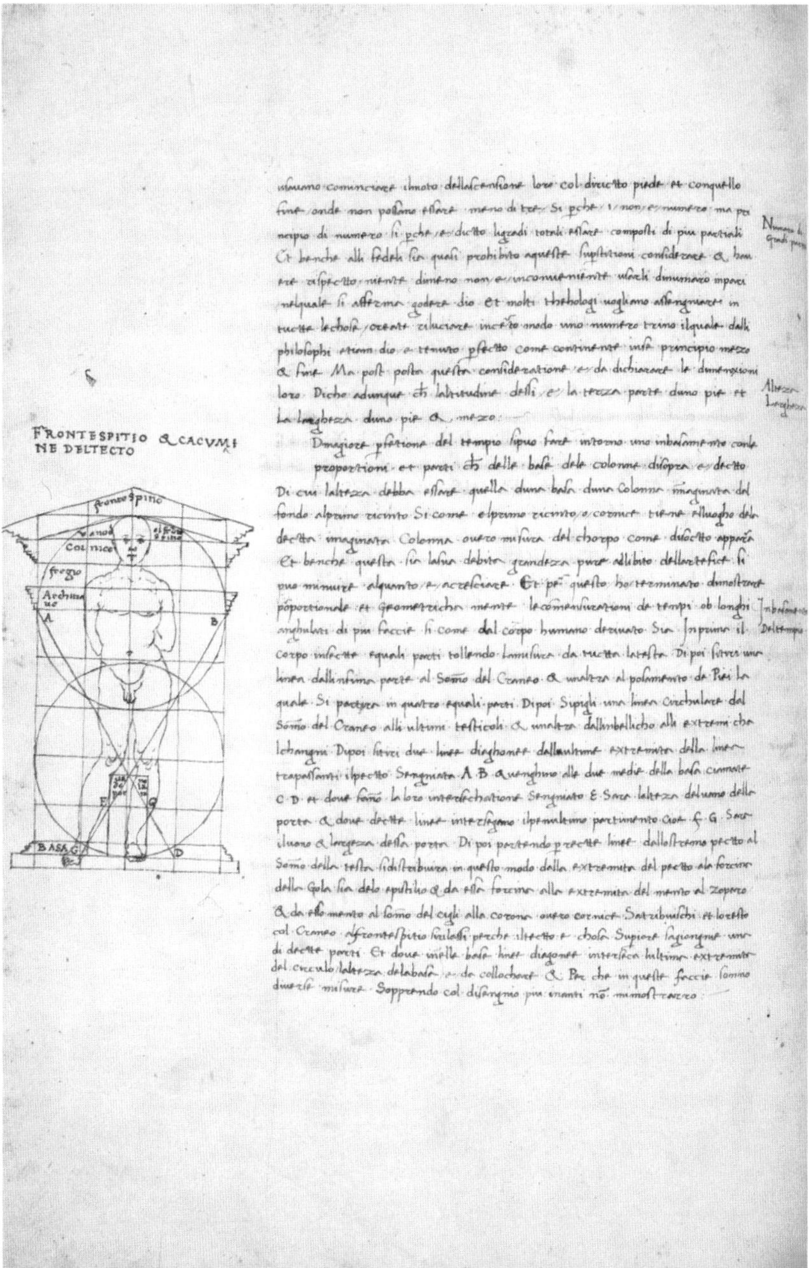

Francesco di Giorgio Martini, *Architettura civile e arte militare*, codex Magliabechiano II.I.141, f. 38v. Image courtesy of Ministero per i Beni e le Attività Culturali/Biblioteca Nazionale Centrale, Firenze. Photo Donato Pineider.

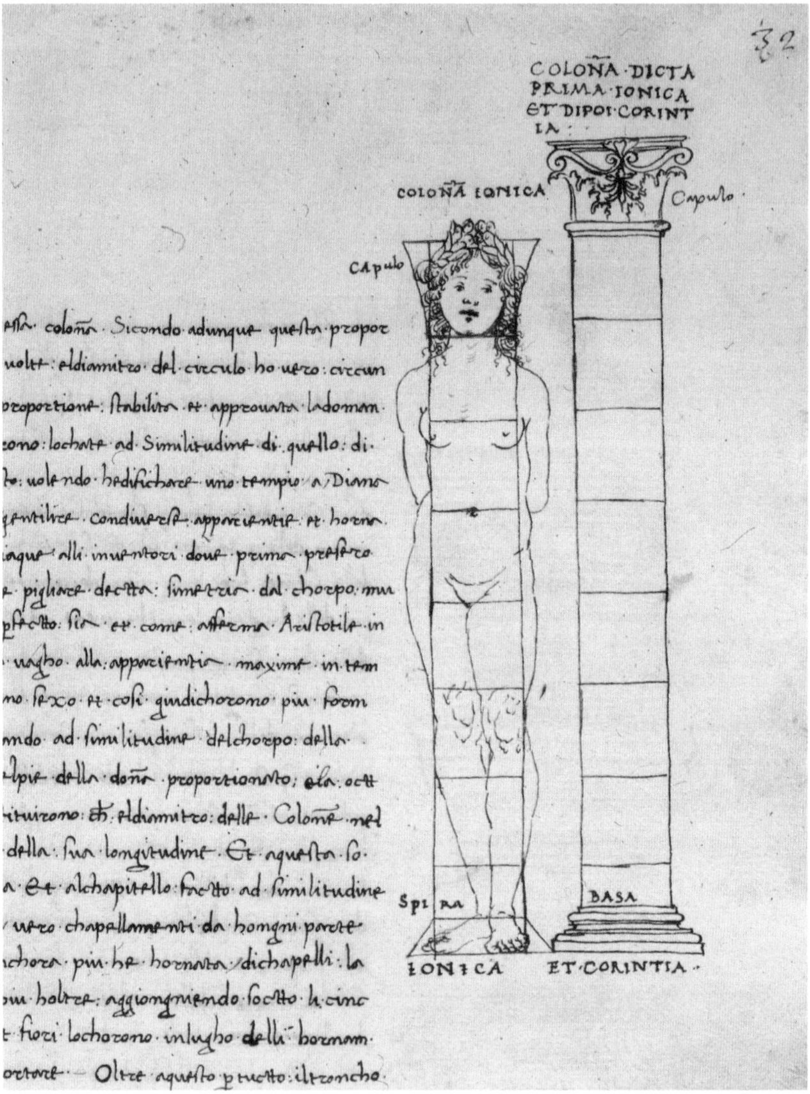

Francesco di Giorgio Martini, *Architettura civile e arte militare*, codex Magliabechiano II.I.141, f. 32r.
Image courtesy of Ministero per i Beni e le Attività Culturali/Biblioteca Nazionale Centrale, Firenze.
Photo Donato Pineider.

This relative lack of interest in proportions distinguishes Francesco di Giorgio from Vitruvius. Possibly as a result of the influence of his pictorial and sculptural practices, the representation of architecture plays a predominant role in his work. Often the human body is encased in architectural forms that are loosely proportional. The relief *La Discordia* shows this formal correspondence of the body and the supports, applied to the whole architectural framework.[14] Perspective is exploited to assign, within the space created, equal importance to these two elements.[15] The analogy column-body is also true for the figure of Christ, who, placed in front of a temple with colossal columns, is attached to a pillar of his size and proportion.[16] These images convey a Christian symbolism that corresponds to, and adapts, Vitruvius' paganism.

The physiological necessity of architecture to relate to the scale and proportion of the human body extends from the house to the city, whether fortified or not. The analogy with the body lies not so much in the proportions and the ratio between the parts and the whole, but in a particular rationale of order.[17] This can be observed in the first illustration of *Architettura ingegneria e arte militare* representing a man-fortress. Captioned "*Chorpo dela città*" and "*fighura del chorpo dov'è la circhunferentia della città e distribuitioni d'essa*", the representations of a juvenile male body and the plan of a fortified city overlap. The head, the place for decision-taking and intelligence, corresponds to the keep; the arms and legs to defense towers (*torone*); the heart to the church (*tempio*). The central square (*piazza*) is circular and centered around the navel.[18] This umbilical centre, especially since it gives access to the church, is also the meeting place of the city.

The drawings of Francesco di Giorgio that illustrate the notion of the corporeality of architecture fall under a wide variety of classifications. Vitruvian or Christian, they could be interpreted through the prism of Platonist or Aristotelian traditions, no doubt reflected in a proportional and ideal conception for the former, and a physiological and functional conception for the latter. What is most important, however, is that these drawings establish a complete and coherent network of relationships between architecture and the human body. They connect, in so doing, the orders of columns, the profiles of facades, their elevations, building plans and, finally, the city plan. The scattering of these drawings in the various works of Francesco di Giorgio and their different manuscript versions, puts their coherence into the right perspective, but the whole body of drawings is a reflection of the conclusions of his predecessors' investigations on the analogy between the body and architecture. This analogy clearly survives beyond the *Quattrocento*.[19] How Francesco di Giorgio's predecessors defined these very themes needs to be clarified, even if it cannot be examined in detail here. These propositions, in spite of their diversity, are based on the reinterpretation of two main themes that concern, on the one hand, the analogy between the body and the edifice and, on the other hand, between the body and columns themselves.

THE EDIFICE-BODY[20]

Already from the middle of the Quattrocento, in the prologue of his *De re aedificatoria*, Alberti formulates the axiom of the edifice-body when he writes: "We consider that the edifice is a form of body, which like any other consists of lineaments and matter, the one the product of thought, the other of nature; the one requiring the mind and the power of reason, the other dependent on preparation and selection [...]"[21]

This duality of the body and that of architecture is connected to the subject at hand. The question of proportions and composition would appear to emerge from the lineaments, from thought, from a certain abstraction relating to intellect, in short from Platonist idealism. The abstraction of Nature's product, on the other hand, is derived from a reworking of matter, hence materials, and relates to Aristotelian physiologism. From this point of view, one can see that numerical proportions are not the sole criteria considered and that the physiological aspect is at least as important.

The Albertian definition of beauty (*pulchritudo*) is associated with abstract and physiological notions. It is based on harmony (*concinnitas*) which, close to *proportio*, is defined as a relation between the parts and the whole: "[...] so, instead of concentrating all one's efforts on embellishing one part at the expense of others, one should make them all correspond, so that they seem to form one same, well-constituted body, and not separate and scattered members."[22]

The definition is made up of three other notions: number (*numerus*), outline (*finitio*) and distribution (*collocatio*). Alberti specifies that number derives from Nature. While trying to draw up a list of 'chosen' numbers,[23] he recommends always using an even number of supports and an odd number of openings, employing a configuration found in human beings to whom Nature gave "an even number of ears, eyes, nostrils on either side of the face, but in the middle only one large mouth".[24] The question of proportions themselves, such as mentioned by Vitruvius in the first chapter of Book III in a passage filled with neo-Platonic idealism, is moreover not covered by Alberti in the *De re aedificatoria* but in the *De statua*. With this in mind, one can see that, for Alberti, proportions are not the only acceptable criteria and that physiology is at least as central. *Concinnitas* is derived from the idea that if one removes a member or moves a member of a body, or modifies or enlarges it, one destroys its harmony and therefore its beauty:[25] "Nature does not pursue an aim more important than the absolute perfection of everything it creates. It could in no way achieve this aim without harmony, as, without the latter, the perfect accord of the parts that should be obtained would disappear."[26]

By referring to the process of the "production" of Nature, Alberti also describes the process of the elaboration of architectural form in the context of architectural creation. The latter distinguishes two essential components: the structure and the exterior: "Like everybody, the building is made of a skeleton, tendons, ligaments, as well as flesh and skin."[27] From then onwards the approach becomes pragmatic, as the aesthetic aspects are supported by the technical characteristics, differentiating structure from what is contained within. The concept of *collocatio* is for that matter explained with the help of the horse's anatomy, whose beauty allies the perfect adaptation to its use.[28]

Finally, Alberti extends the analyses of the edifice-body to the city. Before dealing with the *partitio* and developing organicist metaphors, Alberti points out that the city is like a large house and the house like a little city.[29] As for the house, the defining criteria of the city are beauty and commodity. In this manner, Alberti opens the way for the concept of the ideal city, whose form could be the body, and whose institutions obey the principles given in his other treatises. Furthermore, the hygienist principles concern a population as a whole, giving the architect, in contrast to Vitrivius, a medical and social role as well.

Filarete, from the very first pages of his treatise written in the 1460s, describes the birth of architecture and claims: "I will now show that the building is truly a living being." He points out, like Alberti, that "the building has a shape and a substance analogous to the members and the form of man". Like the author of the

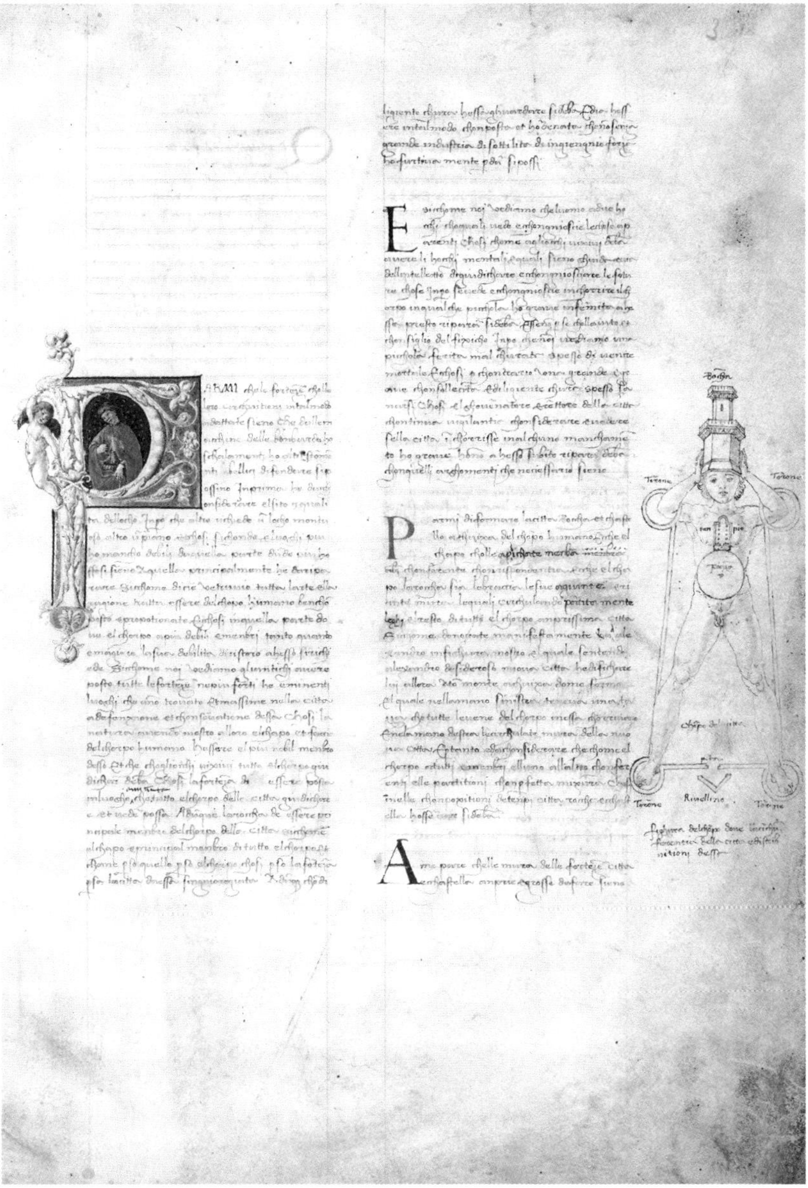

Francesco di Giorgio Martini, *Architettura ingenierare e arte militare*, codex Saluzziano 148, f. 3.
Image courtesy of Ministero per i Beni e le Attività Culturali/Biblioteca Reale, Firenze.

De re aedificatoria, he establishes a comparison between the openings of buildings and the orifices of the body, then gives numerous examples of all the expressions of this physiological connection between the body and the building. Man's fatigue and illnesses are equivalent to the dangers that threaten the building. The causes of these dangers lie in wars and the lack of upkeep. Bodies pierced by weapons are compared to walls ripped open. The architect is therefore likened to a doctor and can, like him, save buildings that have been jeopardised. Filarete, the first to indulge in the self-promotion characteristic of later theoreticians, does not hesitate to credit himself with one such work of salvation. Antique ruins are mentioned as an example of the dangers that await badly kept buildings, and this progressive disappearance is to be deplored, in the same way that one regrets the death of a famous person or a loved one.[30] Francesco di Giorgio echoes this idea which justifies the study of antique ruins.[31] The edifice-body is, for Filarete, characterised by illness and death. This analogy can seem superficial or anecdotic, but its recurrence in the text indicates a vague physiological orientation that links the building to both Aristotelian and Hippocratic ideas.

Filarete, however, does not extend his correspondence with the body to the city plan. His treatise relates the creation of a new city, Sforzinda. Its plan is centred, no doubt inspired by *The Republic* and the tale of Atlantis in the *Timaeus* of Plato, and without any physical reference to its organicism.

COLUMN-BODIES

Leon-Battista Alberti, whilst conceiving the axiom of the edifice-body, also attaches relative importance to the corporeal aspects of the architectural orders. In the *De re aedificatoria* the accounts of the origins of the orders are indeed considerably simplified compared to the *De architectura* of Vitruvius (cf. infra). When Alberti explains the ethnic origins of the Greek orders, in other words the fundamental Greekness of the origins of architecture, he dubiously interjects "that is to say, if we believe that everything came from the Greeks".[32] Besides, he suggests that the Doric order is Italian, a way of founding the Latinity of architecture, of which the "Tuscan" araeostyle portico of Poggio a Caiano could be a trace. Alberti does indeed indicate that the Tuscan order was used even before the Doric order. One must consider that this affirmation reflects the desire to promote not only the Latinity of architecture but, what is more, Florence over Rome.[33] The social and heuristic concerns, added to the general political ambitions regarding the foundation of a Latin, and more specifically Tuscan identity, led Alberti to put the importance of the Vitruvian anecdotes into another perspective.

In spite of this, the terminology applied to the support is anthropomorphic. In Book IX, the Greek terms used by Vitruvius—*entasis* for example—are abandoned in favour of Latin words. *Caput*, *venter* and *planta* designate respectively the capital, the shaft and the base of the column. It is probable, as John Onians has demonstrated that in this case it is a direct influence of the *De Etymologiae* by Isidore of Seville.[34] Likewise Alberti considered that columns were made in the image of man and specifies that the phenomenon is similar to that described by religious commentators when they point out that Noah's ark was shaped like a human body.[35] Moreover, in an attempt to limit the importance of Greece in favour of the Roman world, Alberti consciously associated Medieval Christian traditions with antique pagan traditions. Alberti therefore adapted Vitruvius' work in accordance with his view of Renaissance society, remodeling Vitruvian themes into workable concepts.

Columns are considered from a structural point of view, like a sub-category of the *paries*, the walls. The characteristics of their appearance and resistance contribute to the solidity and beauty of the edifice-body: "The one, massive, was more suited to effort and continuity: they named it Doric; the other was thin and graceful: they called it Corinthian; as for the medium one that looked as if it were made of the two others, they named it Ionic. So that's what they imagined regarding the body of the whole building."[36]

Alberti also created an analogy between the rhetorical genres and the architectural orders, relying, in order to achieve this, on his knowledge of Cicero.[37] This type of association was common in Antiquity.[38] Ethnical definitions are similarly mentioned, the tastes of the populations concerned participating in the choice of decorative elements of the different capitals.[39] Yet this effort to find other symbolic threads within the architectural orders other than those of the body did not have a great influence on Alberti's successors in the theoretical field.

Filarete expounded the axiom of the column-body at the very beginning of his treatise. He did this by synthesising the Vitruvian description of the ideal man and that of the origins of architecture. Having established that the canon of the well-proportioned man is conceived on the basis of a modular relation of 1/9th, and that the module is equivalent to the height of the head, Filarete suggested comparing the module to the height of the capital.[40] However, the desire to establish the axiom column-body as solidly as that of the edifice-body led him to suggest a genealogy based on the body of Adam. According to Filarete, the Doric order seems to have been conceived by early man in the image of Adam, if not by Adam himself in his own image. Bringing together Vitruvian thought and Christian tradition, Filarete succeeded in this way in legitimising the proportions of the oldest order. He then used Nature to explain the characters of the three orders.[41] After having ruled out the dwarves and giants, he retained three types of men, the tall, the middle-sized and the small, which he associated with the three orders. Each order of columns has a defined number of modules, that is, of *testa* or capitals, the two words being interchangeable for Filarete. Doric is *misura grande* of nine heads, Ionic, *misura picola* of seven and Corinthian, *misura mezzana* of eight.

This tripartite division of humanity is associated with several other ternary classifications.[42] Filarete remarked that there are several types of people: good-looking, less good-looking or more good-looking; rich, poor, richer; old, young, less young; etc.. He then defined three kinds of *qualità*, a central concept that identifies human and social types like architectural types.[43] Three "qualities" of houses correspond to three states of wealth in the city of Sforzinda,[44] which is built with three different dimensions of stones depending on the buildings.[45] In these triplets, the Doric always designates the male and it is the order of nobility. These equivalences between the body and social position are therefore extended to the orders.[46] Very logically, their use in sacred architecture is related to the gods concerned. Filarete agreed with Vitruvius on this point, but followed the genealogy of Alberti first explaining the Doric and the Corinthian, then finally the Ionic order. The orders are not assigned to the gods according to their gender, but according to their qualities. The Ionic order "of lower quality and lesser majesty" is attributed to Diana, Juno and Bacchus.[47] Filarete therefore reinforced the analogy between the column and the body but established a classification that corresponds to Christian symbols and social reasoning. He also elaborated on the first representations of *atlantes*, following the text of Vitruvius, but adding complex underlying symbolic meanings.[48]

VITRUVIUS' ACCOUNTS OF ORIGIN

All three Renaissance authors and architects that have been mentioned so far have drawn on the same Vitruvian source. The *De Architectura*, on the other hand, while highlighting the importance of the accounts of the origins of the three orders, addresses much less the question of the edifice-body. As we have seen, the drawings of Francesco di Giorgio, form part of a highly significant body of work concerned with the notion of corporeality. One must, however consider that Alberti extended and reinforced this paradigm, making it more effective for the building and the city. In so doing, he explains what Vitruvius had only suggested: "the architect, mastering the art of building, must have a central political role, at the sides of the prince, his commissioner".

Vitruvius first insisted on the fact that the architect must have medical knowledge in order to be capable of choosing a site for the foundation of the city, thereby protecting it. The passage from Book III that, during the Renaissance, gave rise to the drawings of the Vitruvian man set out to determine the proportions of temples, albeit not very comprehensibly. In Vitruvius' work, the accounts of the origins of the orders, whilst failing to acknowledge the importance of the emerging architect in respect of the corporeal paradigm are the most developed and the most evocative.

These accounts have been widely studied by academics who have identified very varied meanings embedded in them. They aim to establish a differentiation of genders between the three Greek orders. The Doric order is indeed described as male, the Ionic as female and the Corinthian is likewise female but refers to the anatomy of a young girl. The latter resembles the other two in its proportions, as though it were a product of both of them.[49]

The Doric column has "the proportions, the solidity and the beauty of a man's body".[50] The order was thus named with reference to Dorus, son of Hellenos and a nymph, who commissioned Juno to build a temple in the antique city of Argos. He is one of the mythical and sacred characters of ancient Greece, holder of military and political power. During the colonisation of what was to become Ionia, the Greeks, led by Dorus, built a temple dedicated to Apollo Panionios and emulated the temple of Argos. However, realising that they did not know how to define suitable proportions, they transposed vertically the size of a man's foot in order to define the module of the Doric column. As they seem to have observed that man's foot corresponds to a sixth of his height, they decided to apply the same ratio to the column. As a result, they transferred the width that they had given to the base of the shaft six times vertically, including the capital.

The story of the invention of the Ionic order is also set against the backdrop of Asia Minor. In a similar manner, Vitruvius explained how, when the Greeks later wanted to build a temple dedicated to Diana, they decided this time to refer to the female body, by using the proportions of a module of 1:8 in order to create a more slender silhouette. A base was placed under the column "after the manner of a shoe to the foot" and, on either side of the capital, volutes were placed "like graceful curling hair hanging on each side". The aspect of the frieze of ova that decorates the *cymatium* or the *echinus*, between the canal and the astragal, imitates a fringe of hair and the fluting of the column refers to the folds of the "matronal" robes. Thus Vitruvius concludes "two orders were invented, one of a masculine character, without ornament, the other bearing a character which resembled the delicacy, ornament, and proportion of a female".[51]

These male/female definitions may correspond to distinctions between Dorians and Ionians rooted in Greek mentalities at the time of the Peloponnesian wars.[52] Could one go further and envisage corporeal classifications related to ethnographical criteria? Could one consider the Doric order to be an incarnation of the Spartan strength and the Ionic order to represent the sophistication of the Ionians? No texts confirm this. Yet it is nonetheless true that Aristophanes or Thucydides attributed indolence to the Ionians and virility to the Dorians.[53] It is hard to believe that the similarity between the characteristics attributed to the populations by Greek opinion and the characteristics of the orders named after these populations is purely coincidental. Would it be pushing things too far to identify the symbolic image of naked and muscled bodies of Dorian warriors in the Doric order?[54] The heroic nudity seems to find an echo in the sobriety of the Doric order. The fact that the Greek sources used by Vitruvius are lost makes all certainty practically impossible.

The account of the invention of the Corinthian order stands out, even if it is most probably based on the same Hellenistic treatises. The relation to the body is of a different nature and there is some incoherence probably due to a simplification of the Greek legends. A young Corinthian girl who had reached marriageable age, still a virgin,[55] and who had died of sickness, was buried in a tomb on which her 'nurse' had placed a basket containing drinking vessels that she had loved.[56] She covered the basket with a tile to protect them. The root of an acanthus plant that, as it so happened, was under the basket grew, the plant surrounding and covering the basket until it reached the tile which forced the tips of its stems to fold down towards the ground and form volutes. That's when the sculptor Callimachus came across this motif and "Pleased with the form and novelty of the combination, he constructed from the hint thus afforded, columns of this species in the country about Corinth, and arranged its proportions, determining their proper measures by perfect rules."[57]

Considered to be an 'old wives' tale', this account has long been neglected by commentators.[58] It breaks away from the numerical and proportional aspects of the two former accounts dedicated to the Doric and Ionic orders and focuses on their symbolic aspects. Presumably, Vitruvius took his inspiration from Greek sources that he sums up or presents, but without repeating the original sacred connotations. Many apparently unnecessary details are a source of confusion. Why for example specify that it is about a "marriageable" girl and why point out that the basket and its objects were placed there by her nurse? One may accept the idea that the nurse may have wanted to honor the memory of the child that she had brought up, but why specify that the girl is nubile and a virgin?[59] This host of details is all the more disturbing as the basket is filled with drinking vessels, objects used in the banquets that respectable women were not supposed to participate in—let alone young ladies.[60] It is therefore difficult to understand why a nurse would have wanted to honour a loved one with objects used in banquets where the only women present were prostitutes.

However Vitruvius does not elucidate this account, strange because of its inconsistencies, no doubt due to the use of incomplete sources—unless the text was truncated by the Medieval copyists.[61] All that Vitruvius is interested in is presenting the characteristics of the Corinthian order to his readers. This order has the elegance of young ladies, and was designed by an artist whose nickname, "*Catatechnos*",[62] reflects his personal style, and the elegance and sophistication of his works.[63] The

Corinthian capital contributes to the definition of an order that is characterised by the imitation of the virginal slenderness of young ladies and is decorated in a fashion that, according to Vitruvius, expresses the elegance of their attires.[64]

This account can be interpreted in many different ways. From the point of view of an ethnical interpretation of the orders, it is interesting to observe that the Corinthian order is presented as resulting from the Doric and Ionic orders.[65] It is indeed only its capital that distinguishes it, as the entablature and the column can be found on both of the major orders. The Corinthian order could be seen to have the advantage of being neither Ionian nor Dorian, thus becoming a unifying order, Panhellenic, one might say, with reference to the Greek political ideal that was perpetually unreachable. Does its creation overlap chronologically with the Peloponnesian wars? This cannot be excluded, especially since the existence of theoretical texts promoting the Ionic versus the Doric is attested to, before the Corinthian order progressively imposed itself as a standard.[66]

Joseph Rykwert showed that this account focusing on a tomb can be associated with the funerary rites and the sacred myths of ancient Greece.[67] Present on the burial scenes that decorate *lecythi*, the acanthus symbolise death and resurrection. They can indeed be observed on the body of quite a few of these funerary vases, planted in baskets, with a shape evoking that of the Corinthian capital. In Delphi, Apollo's tripod was placed on a pedestal decorated with acanthus leaves, topped with palmettes. This clearly seems to be the formal and symbolic origin of the Corinthian column, especially since the first Corinthian columns could be found in temples, used as sacred columns or as support for the cult statue. It is interesting to note that the latter was surrounded by an Ionic colonnade decorating the *naos*, whereas the Doric order was reserved for the outside of the temple. Joseph Rykwert is no doubt also right to conclude that the "Corinthian columns probably commemorated or celebrated the afterlife and its powers: they mark the places designed for concepts of destruction and regeneration."[68]

Although he used different methods, George Hersey made interpretations that were, to a certain extent, similar. Adopting Richard Broxton Onians' system, he referred to the tropes comprised in the Greek words that can be identified directly or indirectly in Vitruvius' text in order to reveal their symbolic dimension.[69] *Κόρη* designates a young girl, but it is also the name of Persephone, queen of the shadows and the goddess who allows vegetation to come out of the earth in spring. The term *κόρηθςον* ("broom") could also appeal to the Greek reader's mind: it is a plant related to the acanthus and its close species, for example *ἀκανθίς* ("groundsel") or *ἀκανθινος* ("thistle"). The incredibly widespread use of the acanthus motif on Greek steles, and its association with motifs of loutrophoroi and canthari, confirm its funerary and sacred symbolism. In a suggestive way, the acanthus is, in the context of the Vitruvian tale, associated with the naked bodies of mermaids that seem to emerge from the plant like efflorescence.[70] However Vitruvius' text is also in line with the Apollonian classicism of the Augustan period, which employs the acanthus abundantly while attempting to rediscover its purer forms of expression.[71] This is confirmed by the fact the *De architectura* condemns decorations representing hybrid, human and animal monstrosities that appear in decorative foliage.[72]

An enquiry into the veritable sources concealed in the Vitruvian accounts[73] is secondary to the important use of myths that should be looked at in a sacred context and which establish the interaction between art and politics.[74] With this in mind, it is quite noteworthy that the Vitruvian version is very similar to other myths, which, in other cultures, determine a similar relation between the body and architecture, via the themes of the edifice-body and the column-body.

THE CORPOREAL MYTHS OF ARCHITECTURE IN NON-EUROPEAN CULTURES

The analogy between body and architecture is indeed universal. Ethnology testifies to its presence in many cultures within multiple cosmogonies. In the religions and myths of the Far East, the body is a house, a dwelling, which does not exclude the fact that it is described as the world.[75] These connections between the body, the house, society and the cosmos guarantee a harmonious existence between man and the universe, a peaceful coexistence between architecture as an artefact and its natural and cultural environments.

In the same way as for the theoreticians of the Renaissance, the anthropomorphic relation is expressed with a specific terminology that very precisely compares the body parts to those of houses and villages. For the Thai Isans, the vocabulary that reflects the organisation of the social space of the village refers to a hierarchy of the body. It translates the structural homology that this population has established between the body, social organisation, the house and rice.[76] To designate their igloo, the Inuits use words semantically close to those of the human body.[77] The Tambermas, people from the West African savanna, see their houses as being comparable to bodies and they are given precise anatomical names—head, eyes, lips, tongue, nose, stomach, penis, etc.. A gender interpretation of the architectural orders can be found in the symbolism of the traditional Kabyle house. As shown by Pierre Bourdieu, it is divided into upper and lower parts that correspond to the space for women and the space for men.[78] This separation according to gender is echoed and takes shape in the decoration. Such is also the case of the Gurensi and Igbo houses.[79]

The terminology of the body also serves to relate the house and its inhabitants to nature. The Bugis, people of the Sulawesi islands, have a very concrete expression of their relation to the cosmos. The central post of their house is considered to be the symbolic equivalent of the Cosmic Tree called *Posi'Tana* ("the Navel of the World"), described by ancient myths as having roots that plunge down to the abyss and branches that reach up to the sky. The pillar is in fact called *posi'bola* ("navel of the house"), a name that can still be found in the plug-hole of the boats of this population of fishermen: *posi'lopi* ("navel of the boat"). This umbilical post is often invested with a social function in the inauguration rites and festivities of the house—or in the building of the boat—integrating its owner into the structure of relations amongst the inhabitants of the village. Moreover each community is organised in accordance with territorial limits, with a sacred centre that used to be marked by a kind of investiture stone, also called *posi'tana*.[80]

The myths of the origins of the orders passed down by Vitruvius and taken up again in the Renaissance, contain the same references to community foundations and symbolic, social and gender criteria. Supports are frequently empowered with such values. In Kabylia, the woman is compared to the main pillar (*thigejdith*, feminine word) that crosses the space of the home; it is expected for the young bride to be "the pillar solidly planted in the middle of the house". In this same system of symbolic representation, the man is the main beam (*asalas alemmas*, masculine term), as he extends his protection to the entire house and its living spaces; when a boy is born, one wishes that "he may become the main beam of the house".

Rites that pass on myths and give form to them exemplify this anthropomorphism of the support. For the Bugis, gold or silver is buried beneath the central post (*posi'bola*). The post is also used to hang fragments of fabric, food, a sheaf of rice or a container of water in order to guarantee the security and prosperity of the inhabitants. The post is also painted with blood so that it can preserve and pass down the vital force *(sumange)* of the navel of the world, which it represents. For the Kanakas of the Grande Terre, the central post of the "Great Hut" is a very clear symbol of the authority and virile force of the chief. When the tall tree necessary for the post is felled, the witch doctor makes sure that the various protagonists of the process have no sexual relations, and that no woman even approaches the passage of the convoy bringing the tree trunk to the village. This post is indeed a "living chief", even before being erected or sculpted, since it is considered to have received in the forest the soul of a past chief. The latter will participate in establishing the authority of the chief for whom this hut was built. This rite of rebirth clearly involves replaying a primitive scene, the numerous men necessary for the transport and erection of this primordial element of the Great Hut also contributing to this rebirth. When the post is placed, all the lineages participate. The ceremony during which the tree is handed over to its owner involves the paternal lineages who participated in the initial phase of the endeavour, whereas it is the uterine uncles who have the honour of placing the post in the hole in the centre of the hut.[81] These rites are clearly powerful unifying factors for society, and the support—once erected—is a symbol of all the myths of origin that it is invested with during these ceremonies. One is reminded of the tale of the creation of the Doric order that introduces the character Dorus, tutelary and unifying figure of the Doric colony of Ionia.

The Dogon civilisation has long been the object of research that makes it possible to comprehend the different components of the myth of embodiment. The Dogon house is based on the image of man, to the extent that the plan drawn with a stick on the ground to define the outline of the walls is called "sign of the image of the man in the house that is being started" (*ginu tolo inne yala tonu*). Therefore, in the completed house, "the kitchen is the head, the two storerooms on either side of the inner room are the arms alongside the body, and the entrance represents the legs, the door being the genitalia".[82] Placed in the part of the house that corresponds to the "head", "the hearth symbolises life because there, one can find water boiling on the fire animated by the wind. The four elements symbolise man and his relation to the world: the water is his blood, the fire his flesh, the earth his bones and the air the life that he breathes."[83] The symbolism of the decoration also refers back to the anthropomorphism that we are familiar with in Western traditions.[84]

According to Ogotemmeli, interviewed by Marcel Griaule in 1948, the general anthropomorphic organisation of the Dogon house combines the male and female gender symbols. The plan of the house represents the male body, whose genitals correspond to the door in front of the entrance hall. However the grand room with a roof supported by four posts refers to the woman: "the lateral storerooms are her arms, the door communicating [with the entrance] her genitals. Rooms and storerooms expose the woman, lying on her back, arms spread, door open, ready for union." The village needs to have a similar organisation. The head corresponds to the sheltered place where the council convenes, the chest to the homes of the families, the female genitalia the oilstone and the male genitalia correspond to the altar of the village.[85]

Within the complex cosmogony of the Dogon, the construction rites of the home guarantee the fertility of the family who is going to settle there. When the roof is built, the young girls from the neighbourhood of the owner's wife are summoned and asked to pour water into the hole opened in the earth, in order to make the mortar that will cover the roof. However the mixture is then made by the young men from the neighborhood of the husband and every young girl who comes with a recipient full of water to be poured into the hole is pulled into it by the young men, not without resistance on the part of the girl and joking and teasing from the young men. In fact, the wet earth is the symbol of male semen and the resistance of the young women is that of the bride when she reaches the nuptial home. The gibes that are addressed to her are the same as those that she will hear on her wedding day, as they are meant to reduce her vital force, thereby obliging her to recover a part of it when she is with her husband.

This sort of wedding rehearsal becomes even more significant when one knows that, after the completion of the construction, it is followed by an imaginary meal, prepared by the same young women, with sand that everyone pretends to eat. The idea is to reproduce the lives of the first men before they had built houses. The completion of the house is thus an opportunity to bring the origins of the community to life again, to reactivate these founding acts and to place the newly built home into a historical cycle. This house, with a gender-oriented structure, symbol of both man and woman, is thereby a conveyor of myth. This is echoed throughout the whole house, entirely designed according to measurements with proportions that are male and female.[86]

It is clear that the rites and myths of personification and incarnation are linked to symbolic representations of gender, family and social hierarchies. Because they refer to the figure of the body, while maintaining a distinction between its divisions, they confirm the cohesion and homogeneity of the entire system. Among these phenomena, the fertility rites play an important part. This seems logical considering that what is involved is setting up a home, where a family is going to settle down, prosper and reproduce. But the impact is also more general because—like in the ceremony of the erection of the great post for the Kanakas—it is also about reviving etiological tales. The personification of the house at the moment of its construction could be compared to the restoration of the world after the original disorder and seems to serve as a guard against the possibility of future disorder.

These examples taken from ethnology confirm that to exist is to inhabit, as shown by Martin Heidegger when underlining the common roots of the German verbs "to build" and "to be". The architecture of houses is governed by a symbolic rhizome that likens it to a body, that of its inhabitants as well as that of society or the cosmos. In most cases, this bodily figure serves the purpose of ensuring the homogeneity of the entities created, whether it concerns the young bride in her patrilineal structure, the young chief in a society or the house in relation to Nature. In the case of the latter, the notion of sacred is immanent and the rites mentioned are carried out and directed by the religious authority of the place and time. His representatives often act together with the builder, unless the two characters are merged into a single person. So, for the Bugis, the presence of the *sanro* is essential for each step of the construction as well as for the anniversaries. At the inauguration, he is compared to an obstetrician who presides over a birth and "the erection of the main post (as well as the solemn closing of the plug-hole of the boat with a wooden plug) [is] likened to the cutting of the umbilical cord of a living being".[87]

Is it not this same power that the theoreticians of the Renaissance want to be invested with? Filarete considers the creation of a building to be similar to procreation, its actors being the architect and the prince, the mother and the father respectively:

> Since no-one can conceive himself without a woman, by another simile the building cannot be conceived by one man alone. As it cannot be done without a woman, so he who wishes to build needs an architect. He conceives it with him and then the architect carries it. When the architect has given birth, he becomes the mother of the building. Before the architect gives birth, he should dream about his conception, think about it, and turn it over in his mind in many ways for seven to nine months, just as a woman carries her child in her body for seven to nine months. He should also make various drawings of the conception that he has made with the patron, according to his own desires. As the woman can do nothing without the man, so the architect is the mother to carry this conception.[88]

In this context, one might suggest the following hypothesis: the Vitruvian accounts that served as a matrix for the corporeal paradigms of the Renaissance were above all valued as myths that—like all accounts of origins—have constantly been reworked, reformulated and adapted to the necessities of place and time. They share the same themes with the architectural mythologies of non-European cultures: edifice-body and support-body. Their function is to connect the inhabitant to his home, to establish systems ensuring the stability of gender-oriented structures for the couple and the family and to link the building to the community or city space. The accounts of origins, by their ancestral and sacred nature, legitimise these functions and ensure their continuity.

The body terminology leaves an imprint on the spirit and practices of builders. In the Renaissance, while artists were trying hard to redefine their status by deriving inspiration from Antiquity, the architect appeared, with Vitruvius as intercessor, like a reference figure, invested with powers legitimated by ancestral knowledge. This attempt to conceptualise the figure of the architect through the myths of the body was admittedly a relative failure. The drawings of Francesco di Giorgio were not engraved and their distribution remained limited. Instead, the theoreticians of the sixteenth century following Vignola underestimated the question of body proportions and turned their attention to other issues.

Nonetheless, the body analogy is still actively discussed in architectural debate belonging as it does to the founding myths that explain the relation between man and his environment and between the individual and society.

/ **1.** Picon, A, *La ville territoire des cyborgs*, Besançon: Les Editions de l'Imprimeur, 1998.

/ **2.** Choay, F, "La ville et le domaine bâti comme corps dans les textes des architectes théoriciens de la première Renaissance italienne" in *Nouvelle revue de psychanalyse*, n° 9 (*Le Dehors et le dedans*), Paris: Gallimard, 1974, pp. 239–251; Choay, F, *La Règle et le modèle. Sur la théorie de l'architecture et de l'urbanisme*, Paris: Editions du Seuil, 1996 [1980]; Onians, J, *Bearers of Meaning. The Classical Orders in Antiquity, Middle Ages, and the Renaissance*, Princeton: Princeton University Press, 1989.

/ **3.** Rykwert, J, *La Maison d'Adam au Paradis*, Paris: Editions du Seuil, 1976 [New York,

1972]; Rykwert, J, "Körper und Bauwerk = Body and Building" in *Daidalos*, n° 45, 15 September, 1992, pp. 100–109; Rykwert, J, *The Dancing Column: on Order in Architecture*, Cambridge, MA and London: MIT Press, 1996; Hersey, G, *The Lost Meaning of Classical Architecture. Speculations on Ornament from Vitruvius to Venturi*, Cambridge, MA and London: MIT Press, 1988; Hersey, G, *The Monumental Impulse. Architecture's biological roots*, Cambridge, MA and London: MIT Press, 1999.

/ **4.** McEwen, IK, *Vitruvius, Writing the Body of Architecture*, Cambridge, MA: MIT Press, 2003.

/ **5.** Their attribution to the author of the text has sometimes been questioned. cf. G Scaglia, "Autour de Francesco di Giorgio ingénieur et dessinateur" in *Revue de l'Art*, 1980, pp. 7–25.

/ **6.** Betts, RJ, "On the chronology of Francesco di Giorgio's Treatises: New Evidence from an unpublished manuscript" in *Journal of the Society of Architectural Historians*, XXXVI, 1977, pp. 3–14; and by the same author, *The Architectural Theories of Francesco di Giorgio*, Ph.D diss. Princeton, 1971, especially pp. 51–99 regarding the body analogy.

/ **7.** cf. Marco Biffi (dir.), *Francesco di Giorgio Martini, La traduzione del De Architectura di Vitruvio dal ms II.I.141 della Biblioteca Nazionale Centrale du Firenze*, Pisa: Scuola Normale Superiore, 2002; as well as M Mussini, *Francesco di Giorgio e Vitruvio. Le traduzioni del "De Architectura" nei codici Zichy, Spencer 129 e Maglibechiano II.I.141*, Florence: Leo Olschki, 2003, 2 volumes.

/ **8.** First by F Choay, *La Règle et le modèle*.

/ **9.** Onians, J, *Bearers of Meaning*, pp. 172–174. cf. Francesco di Giorgio Martini, *Trattati di architettura ingegneria e arte militare, a cura di Corrado Maltese*, Trascrizione di Livia Maltese Degrassi, Milan: Edizioni Il Polifilo, 1967, vol II : Architettura civile e militare, pp. 444–445.

/ **10.** di Giorgio Martini, Francesco, *La traduzione del De Architectura di Vitruvio dal ms II.I.141 della Biblioteca Nazionale Centrale du Firenze*, respectively p. 505 and p. 517.

/ **11.** di Giorgio Martini, *La traduzione del De Architectura di Vitruvio dal ms II.I.141 della Biblioteca Nazionale Centrale du Firenze*, vol I: *Architettura ingegneria e arte militare* (Codex saluzzianus 148), The man-fortress on f° 3, the men in the church plan on f° 11, the heads in the church apses on f° 12, Callimachus on f° 14 v°, the Corinthian men capitals on f° 15, the cornice profiles on f° 21, the man-church facade with spread arms on f° 21 v°. In the codex *Magliabechiano of Architettura civile e militare* (*idem.*, vol II: *Architettura civile e militare*, Codex Senese S. IV): Dinocrates on f° 27 v°; man and women columns on f° 31 v° et 32 v°; Ionic female head capital on f° 33 v°, body woman facade or window on f° 38 v°, man-church plan with apses on f° 42 v°.

/ **12.** Referring here to the profiles that Jacques-François Blondel presented in his *Cours d'architecture*, vol I, 1771, p. 259. See L Baridon and M Guédron, *Corps & arts. Physionomies et physiologies dans les arts visuels*, Paris, 1999, pp. 196–197.

/ **13.** di Giorgio Martini, Francesco, *La traduzione del De Architectura di Vitruvio dal ms II.I.141 della Biblioteca Nazionale Centrale du Firenze*, vol I: *Architettura ingegneria e arte militare* (Codex saluzzianus 148), f° 96 v and 97, pl. 178–179.

/ **14.** Bellosi, L, ed, *Francesco di Giorgio e il Rinascimento a Siena, 1450–1500*, exhibition catalogue, Siena, Church of Sant'Agostino, 25 April–31 July 1993, Milan: Electa, 1993, cat. nr 67.

/ **15.** Francesco di Giorgio collaborated with Piero della Francesca when writing his *De prospectiva pingendi*.

/ **16.** Bellosi, L, *Francesco di Giorgio e il Rinascimento a Siena*, cat. nr 72.

/ **17.** di Giorgio Martini, Francesco, *La traduzione del De Architectura di Vitruvio dal ms II.I.141 della Biblioteca Nazionale Centrale du Firenze*, vol II : Architettura civile e militare, p. 365, about a regular town plan: "La ultima, che tutte le dette partisieno correspondenti e proporzionate alla città tutta, come el membro a tutto el corpo umano."

/ **18.** di Giorgio Martini, *La traduzione del De Architectura di Vitruvio dal ms II.I.141 della Biblioteca Nazionale Centrale du Firenze*, f° 29, pl. 213.

/ **19.** For example for Michelangelo: "That's why it is certain that the members of architecture obey the same laws as human members. The man who has not been and who is not a good master sculptor, and in particular, anatomist, cannot know." (Michelangelo, "Lettre au cardinal Rodolfo Pio da Carpi, Rome, 1560" in *Lettres de Michel-Ange traduites en français intégralement et pour la première fois par Marie Dormoy*, Paris: Rieder & Cie, 1926, v. 1, p. 225). [Translator's note: the English version has been translated from the French text].

/ **20.** This expression comes from: F Choay, *La Règle et le modèle*.

/ **21.** Alberti, LB, *L'art d'édifier*, translation, introduction and notes by P Caye et F Choay, Paris: Éditions du Seuil, 2004, Prologue, p. 51. [Translator's note: the English version is trans from the French text.]

/ **22.** Alberti, LB, *L'art d'édifier*, I, 9, p. 80.

/ **23.** 3, 5, 7, 9, 40 (Alberti, *L'art d'édifier*, IX, 5, pp. 441–442)

/ **24.** Alberti, LB, *L'art d'édifier*, p. 441.

/ **25.** Alberti, LB, *L'art d'édifier*, II, 1 and IX, 5.

/ **26.** Alberti, LB, *L'art d'édifier* IX, 5, p. 440.

/ **27.** Quoted by F Choay, *La Règle et le modèle*, p. 137.

/ **28.** Alberti, LB, *L'art d'édifier*, VI, 3, pp. 281–282.

/ **29.** Alberti, LB, *L'art d'édifier*, I, 9, p. 70: "If, according to the philosopher's maxim, the city is like a very big house, and if conversely the house is like a very small city, why would their members not in turn be considered to be little dwellings?"

/ **30.** We have used the edition directed by Anna Maria Finoli and Liliana Grassi: Filarete, *Trattato di architettura*, Milano: Il Profilo, 1972, 2 vol. The references refer to the folios of the Codex Magliabechianus of the Biblioteca Nazionale di Firenze, considered to be a copy of the original by Filarete, now lost, and to the page numbers of this edition. Here, cf. Filarete, *Trattato di architettura*, L. I, f° 7 r°, pp. 36–37.

/ **31.** At the end of the Codex Saluzziano 148 of Torino, the folios 71 to 95 collated, with little text, antique buildings or their reconstitutions, with the objective, according to Francesco di Giorgio, of safeguarding them before they disappear (Francesco di Giorgio Martini, *La traduzione del De Architectura di Vitruvio dal ms II.I.141 della Biblioteca Nazionale Centrale du Firenze*, vol. I: *Architettura ingegneria e arte militare*, pl. 130–176).

/ **32.** Alberti, LB, *L'art d'édifier*, VII, 6, p. 334.

/ **33.** Onians, J, *Bearers of Meaning*, p. 150 and LB Alberti, *L'art d'édifier*, VI, 3 and VII, 3, amongst others.

/ **34.** Onians, J, *Bearers of Meaning*, p. 149.

/ **35.** Alberti, LB, *L'art d'édifier*, IX, 7, p. 450.

/ **36.** Alberti, LB, *L'art d'édifier*, IX, 5, p. 441.

/ **37.** cf. J Onians, *Bearers of Meaning*, pp. 153–155; and Y Pauwels, *L'architecture au temps de la Pléiade*, Paris: Gérard Montfort, 2002.

/ **38.** Dionysus of Halicarnassus, *Commentaries on the Attic Orators*, 3, 3, 6: "It would not be unfounded, it seems to me, to compare the eloquence of Isocrates to the art of Polykleitos or Phidias, regarding gravity, majesty and dignity, and that of Lysias to the art of Calamis or Callimachus, as concerns force and grace". Quoted by: A Rouveret, *Histoire et imaginaire de la peinture ancienne (Ve siècle av. J.-C.–Ier siècle ap. J.-C.)*, Rome: Ecole française de Rome, 1989, p. 445. [Translator's note: the English version is translated from the French text]

/ **39.** Alberti, LB, *L'art d'édifier*, VII, 6, f° 117 v°.

/ **40.** cf. Filarete, *Trattato di architettura*, L. I, f° 3 v° and 4 r°, pp. 19–21.

/ **41.** Filarete, *Trattato di architettura*, f° 3 r°, pp. 15–16.

/ **42.** Filarete, *Trattato di architettura*, f° 5 v°-6 r°, pp. 26–28.

/ **43.** Onians, J, *Bearers of Meaning*, especially p. 167.

/ **44.** Filarete, *Trattato di architettura*, L. VI, f° 40 v°, pp. 158–159; and L. XI, f° 84 r°, pp. 322–324 ff.

/ **45.** Filarete, *Trattato di architettura*, L. IV, f° 22 r°, pp. 90–91.

/ **46.** Filarete, *Trattato di architettura*, L. VIII, f° 56 v°, pp. 232–233: "Sono, come ho detto, più maniere di colonne, ma tre sono le principali; come che ho detto che sono di più qualità d'uomini, come de' gentili, i quali apresso e' signori sono per sostegno e per ornamento; gli altri mezzani sono ancora utilità e adornamento, ma non sono però in adornamento quanto i gentili; gli altri più infimi sono a utilità e necessità e servitudine del signore; e a bellezza di vista non sono tanto quanto gli altri due superiori; gli altri, secondo accaderà di fare, intenderete [...]".

/ **47.** Filarete, *Trattato di architettura*, f° 48 r°, pp. 186–187. The Doric for Hercules and Hera, Minerva and Mars; the Corinthian for Venus, Proserpina, Flora and Ceres. The Ionic "più infimi, cioè di più bassa qualità e di meno pompa che gli altri, e questo dedicavano a Diani, a Giuno, e a Bacco e altri idei simili".

/ **48.** Filarete, *Trattato di architettura*, L. XVIII, f° 150 r°, p. 557 ("[...] el quale era retto pure da colonne a guisa di figure fatte, a similitudine di certi popoli che si ribellorono e poi per forza furono suggiugati, e così per loro più vilipendi furono fatti a loro simulacri a quella similitudine, e ancora per più segno di servitute fu fatta une figura a similitudine d'uomo e di femina, come dire moglie e marito; e sotto questo teto stavano a vedere uomini da bene e donne, a luoghi a luoghi spartiti").

/ **49.** "Thus, from the two orders, by the interposition of a capital, a third order arises" (Vitruvius, *De architectura*, IV, 1, 3).

/ **50.** Vitruvius, *De architectura*, IV, 1, 6.

/ **51.** Vitruvius, *De architectura*, IV, 1, 7.

/ **52.** Vitruvius, *De architectura*, p. 15 ff.

/ **53.** Onians, J, *Bearers of Meaning*, p. 16.

/ **54.** As does G Hersey, *The Lost Meaning*, pp. 53–59.

/ **55.** Vitruvius, *De architectura*, IV, 1, 9. "Virgo civis Corinthia iam matura nuptiis implicata morbo decessit".

/ **56.** Vitruvius, *De architectura*, They are indeed vessels used for drinking wine: "Post sepulcram eius, quibus ea virgo viva poculis delectabatur [...]."

/ **57.** Vitruvius, *De architectura*, IV, 1, 9–10.

/ **58.** Philandrier, for example, does not mention it.

/ **59.** It is however true that the Odysseus introduces the wet nurse of Ulysses when he returns to his palace in Ithaca, having reached a mature age.

/ **60.** Most translators are uncomfortable with this word and have replaced it with vaguer terms. This is the case of the French translation used by the author [translators' note: used in the original French version of the text]; cf Vitruvius, *De l'architecture*, Paris: Les Belles Lettres, 1992, Bk IV, the note 9.4 p. 76 discusses this question.

/ **61.** Vitruvius cites his sources and says how much he owes them in the preface of Bk VII, paragraphs 10 and ff.

/ **62.** The reconstructed Greek term, *catatexitechnos*, means "too meticulous". See Vitruvius, *De l'architecture*, pp. 78–79, note 10.2 for an analysis of the different versions of the term in the antique sources. Also G Hersey, *The Lost Meaning*, pp. 64–65, who points out that the tropes of Callimachus suggest *κάλλος* ("beauty") and, even better, *καλλίμαχη* ("beauty competition"). Callimachus' name leads to the idea of an artist fighting to create beauty with an elegance that corresponds to the Corinthian capital.

/ **63.** "*Subtilitatem*": Vitruvius also uses this term to characterise the slenderness of young girls' waistlines, whereas for the Ionic order he uses the term "*gracilitatem*".

/ **64.** Vitruvius, *De l'architecture*, IV, 1, 7–8.

/ **65.** Vitruvius, *De l'architecture*, IV, 1, 3: he points out that from the two former orders a third is produced by the introduction of a new capital.

/ **66.** Pythios is supposedly the author of one of these treatises entitled Commentaries. See S Kostof, "The practice of Architecture in the Ancient World: Egypt and Greece" in S Kostof, ed, *The Architect: Chapters in the History of the Profession*, Berkeley, Los Angeles, London: University of California Press, 2000 [1977], p. 17.

/ **67.** Rykwert, J, *The Dancing Column*, chapter X: "The Corinthian Girl", pp. 317–349.

/ **68.** Rykwert, J, *The Dancing Column*, p. 349.

/ **69.** Hersey, G, *The Lost Meaning*, pp. 64–67.

/ **70.** Stele of Diogenes, Piraeus Museum, 349, Attic stele. Reproduced in D. Woysch-Meautis, "La représentation des animaux et des êtres fabuleux sur les monuments funéraires grecs de l'époque archaïque à la fin du IVe siècle av. J.-C." in *Cahiers d'archéologie romande*, nr 21, Lausanne, 1982, cat. nr 373, description p. 135.

/ **71.** See G Sauron, "La promotion apollinienne de l'acanthe et la définition d'une esthétique classique à l'époque d'Auguste" in *L'Acanthe dans la sculpture monumentale de l'Antiquité à la Renaissance, actes du colloque tenu du 1er au 5 octobre 1990 à la Sorbonne*, Paris, 1993,especially p. 81.

/ **72.** Vitruvius, *De l'architecture*, VII, 5, 3.

/ **73.** Pierre Gros reckons that, as far as the etiological tale of the Corinthian capital is concerned, it is probably taken from the epigones of Pythios and Hermogenes, often quoted by Vitruvius. See P Gros, "Situation stylistique et chronologique du chapiteau corinthien de Vitruve" in *L'Acanthe*, p. 35.

/ **74.** On the political determinations of the Vitruvian accounts, see IK McEwen, *Vitruvius, Writing the Body of Architecture*.

/ **75.** RA Stein, on the basis of research by Marcel Granet, showed how, in the religions and myths of the Far East, "the closest habitat of man, his own body, was also conceived both as the world and a house." (see RA Stein, *Le Monde en petit*, Paris: Flammarion, 1987, p. 9). cf. also, by the same author "L'Habitat, le Monde et le corps humain en Extrême-Orient et en Haute-Asie" in *Journal Asiatique*, 1957, pp. 38–74.

/ **76.** Formoso, B, "From the Human Body to the Humanized Space. The System of Reference and Representation of Space in Two Villages of Northeast Thailand" in *Journal of the Siam Society*, vol. 78, n° 1, 1990, pp. 67–83.

/ **77.** Therrien, M, "La maison de neige (Illuvigaq), une métaphore du corps humain" in *Inter-Nord. Revue Internationale d'Études Arctiques et Nordiques*, n° 6, 1982, pp. 121–126.

/ **78.** Bordieu, P, *Le Sens pratique*, Paris: Les éditions de Minuit, 1980, pp. 442–461.

/ **79.** Smith, FT, "Compound Entryway Decoration. Male Space and Female Creativity" in *African Arts*, vol. 19, n°3, 1986, pp. 52–59.

/ **80.** Pelras, C, "La maison Bugis (Célèbes, Indonésie) : structure, symbolisme et aspects rituels" in *Maison d'Eurasie. Architecture, symbolisme et signification sociale*, Paris: L'Harmattan, Société des Etudes franco-asiatiques, 1996, pp. 289–290.

/ **81.** Boulay, R, *La maison kanak. Contributions de Alban Bensa et Alain Saussol, dessins de Christian Seignobos*, Marseille: Éditions Parenthèses, Agence pour le développement de la culture kanak, Éditions de l'Orstom, 1990, pp. 65–76.

/ **82.** See G Calame-Griaule, referring to the works of Marcel Griaule, "Notes sur l'habitation du plateau central nigérien" in *Bulletin de l'IFAN*, série B, XVII, n° 1–2, 1955, p. 481.

/ **83.** Calame-Griaule, G, *Bulletin de l'IFAN*, p. 480.

/ **84.** Preston Blier, S, "Houses are Human: Architectural Self-images of Africa's Tamberma" in *Journal of the Society of Architectural Historians*, XLII, 4, December 1983, pp. 371 ff.

/ **85.** Griaule, M, *Dieu d'eau. Entretiens avec Ogotemmêli*, Paris: Fayard, 1966 [1948], p. 90.

/ **86.** "The ordinary house measures eight strides by six, that is two times four, number of the woman, by two times three, number of the man. The inner room or "stomach of the room" (*de bere*) measures four strides by four, as it is the realm of the woman." (G Calame-Griaule, "Notes sur l'habitation du plateau central nigérien" in *Bulletin de l'IFAN*, pp. 482 ff.). This is also true for the attics, those for men being distinct from those for women.

/ **87.** Pelras, C, "La maison Bugis (Célèbes, Indonésie) : structure, symbolisme et aspects rituels" in *Maison d'Eurasie*, p. 291.

/ **88.** Filarete, *Trattato d'architettura (1461–63); Treatise on Architecture*, translated, with an introduction and notes by JR Spencer, 2 vols, New Haven, Yale University Press, 1965: "*— [...] tu m'hai detto che lo edificio si rasomiglia a l'uomo ; adunque se così è, è bisono generare e poi partorire come l'uomo. — Proprio così : l'edificio prima si genera, per similitudine lo portrai intendere, e così nasce sì come la madre partrorisce il figliulo in capo di nove mesi, o alcuna volta di sette mesi, e con buono ordine e sollecitudine farlo crescere. — Dimmi, questo generamento in che modo egli è ? — Il generare dello edificio si è in questa forma : che sì come niuno per sé solo non può generare senza la donna un altro, così eziando a similitudine la edificio per uno solo non può essere creato, e come senza la donna non si può fare , così colui che vuole edificare bisogna che abbia l'architetto e insieme collui ingenerarlo, e poi l'architetto partorirlo e poi, partorirlo che l'ha, l'architetto viene a essere la madre d'esso edificio.*"

FROM ATLAS TO THE CARYATID ORDER

ANTHROPOMORPHIC SUPPORTS AND IMMENSENESS OF THE WORLD

Pascal Julien

Atlantes and caryatids, figures sculpted on innumerable monuments, are not simply expressions of poetic or ornamental license. These intriguing statues are intimately related to the myth of Atlas, who bore the world on his shoulders, and are important elements that participate in the foundation of architectural anthropomorphism. This myth refers back to the Greek theme that takes man as the central point of reference, a theme that was theorised by Roman architects, and, subsequently, from the fifteenth century onwards, so often discussed in connection with the notion of proportion. The theory of the column orders that consequently developed went through several transformations linked to this principle of dimension, and also experienced an application as unusual as it was explicit. Indeed, during the Renaissance, alongside the Doric, Ionic, Corinthian, Tuscan and Composite orders, the mythical figure of Atlas engendered the Caryatid order, which aimed at rationalising the use of captive figures, trapped between the roles of support and decoration.[1]

If, etymologically, myth is a narrative, it is not simply an abstract discourse, peopled with extraordinary creatures. It can also take shape in pure form to record a social use or as a reflection on the human condition. Myth then becomes "the story chosen by history".[2] In a similar way, the figures erected and inserted in architecture clearly constitute a message in stone reaching to the deepest cultural foundations, a form of myth that has for thousands of years delivered its discourse through the medium of images. This message talks of the relationship between the terrestrial and the celestial worlds, the story of the soul striving to ascend, as much by force as by the imagination and despite natural constraints, above an elusive and tragic world. This language, all force and invention, operates its distortion by means of a "rationale of ambiguity" which defines, albeit in a formal context, "an architecture of the spirit".[3]

The Caryatid order has in so many countries fascinated theoreticians and the greatest artists. It underwent, as a result, several mutations, even generating its own specific discourses that brought about the resurgence or emergence of other myths. It has constantly been used to record in stone the demiurgic quest for the unity of the body with invented forms, creating figures captured between *firmitas* and *venustas*, between solidity and beauty, like a principle of harmony, of durability and of liberty, in the face of the immenseness of the world.

MAN AND FORM: ATLAS THE MIGHTY, HERMES THE AGILE

In architecture, as in sculpture, to contemplate the human body as a means of conceiving an ideal form can be linked to the myths of the divine creation of man. This idea has however undergone a particular adaptation with the theme of Atlas, be it in the relation of the body to the phenomenon of support or as a result of a concern for the vitality of the figure that has been transformed to stone. To this Titan, the Renaissance added another god, Hermes, in order to create a motif that carried deeper meaning. This complex evolution took place over centuries and can here only be retraced in broad outline, following, rather than its own particular course, a specific discourse.

Atlas, the brother of Prometheus, was condemned by Zeus to support throughout eternity "with his untiring head and hands" the crushing weight of the world or of the celestial vault, or both, depending on the author.[4] Likewise he had, according to certain sources, tragic relationships with the mythical Heroes: with Hercules, who tricked him in order to seize the golden apples from the Garden of the Hesperides, or with Perseus, who petrified him by showing him the head of Medusa. This impressive Atlas, whom Homer already considered as the guardian of the columns of the skies, fits perfectly with the notion of anthropomorphic support. Most ancient examples of this architectural element have been widely studied, from the Egyptian colossi to the telamons of the temple of Zeus in Agrigento. Feminine versions of these supports were fused as early as the archaic period with column shafts, namely in the treasury of Siphnos, in Delphi (530 BC), before developing as classical models on the Acropolis of Athens, with such famous statues as those on the southern porch of the Erechtheion (421–406 BC). Vitruvius determined the names of this statuary

Southern porch of the Erechtheion, 421–406 BC, Acropolis, Athens. Photo Jens Bruenslow.

type by reporting, in his *De Architectura* (c. 25 BC), the distortion of a historical event that turned these masculine figures into "Persians"—supposedly captive Persians—sculpted by the Greeks to celebrate the victory of Plateia, in 479 BC. He also called the feminine figures "caryatids", invoking a legendary link with the women of Caria, in Laconia, who danced with a basket on their heads and who, brought as captives to Athens after a conflict, had seemingly been turned into statues as an eternal punishment.[5] If these "historicised" explanations are only pure fiction, for Vitruvius they did however correspond to contemporary usage. The most famous example is that of the renowned *Kneeling Barbarians*, polychrome marble atlantes that possibly supported a colossal bronze tripod, celebrating the pacification of the

East by Augustus (c. 20 BC).[6] Despite their erroneous characterisation, it is important to value these interpretations associated with the notion of servitude, because they were reproduced and commented upon until the Age of the Enlightenment.

The direct theme of the Titan Atlas persisted throughout the Middle Ages, yet the use of standing atlantes, like those of the facade of the cathedral of Orvieto, was incredibly rare. Much more frequent, if not commonplace, was the use of multiple consoles decorated with small kneeling figures. Generally placed at the base of vaults, these bowed atlantes supported arches, ogees or transverse arches with their mass and their arms often raised. In a similar way, the correspondence between the column and the human body, exposed by Vitruvius, remained integral to Western thinking, reappearing in a spectacular way in the twelfth and thirteenth centuries in France on several church and cathedral portals, from Chartres to Reims, from Senlis to Toulouse, where they took the form of statues that were as much columns as they were caryatids. However this phenomenon remained relatively limited and it was in Italy from the *Quattrocento* onwards, that this anthropomorphism regained all its vigour, as a result of the renewed study and application of the Vitruvian texts.[7]

The notion of the body-column, was consequently greatly developed, coinciding with the renewal of the theme of atlantes and caryatids, considered as metaphorical and compelling models. However, before attempting to understand their gradual classification into an order, one must recall the overall approach of the Renaissance with regards to ancient mythology. In fact, at this time, several myths were superimposed on that of Atlas, enhancing these figurative supports, and it would be necessary to understand how Atlas, restrained between the sky and the earth, came to merge formally with his grandson Hermes, mediator between Olympus and mankind.

God of travelers, a mobile and active messenger, Hermes has figured in some magnificent statuary representations. But his role as mediator between the sky and the earth, along with his capacity to occupy various places and routes also immortalised him in solid form, to the extent that he was frequently represented not in the form of a perfect human body, but as a simple quadrangular pillar, equipped with a phallus and topped by a bearded head. Having appeared so in Athens around the end of the sixth century BC, then multiplied, scattered along paths, positioned on crossroads, thresholds and portals, he was called upon to mark and fertilise the area that he was given control of. God of eloquence and of good counsel, he sometimes also carried moral maxims, making him a cultural mediator.[8]

These Hermaic pillars, with their rigid and smooth lower section, underwent numerous divine and profane adaptations and, from the Greek period onwards, this statuary type was topped with various heads which celebrated other gods, as well as important personalities. From the royal period onwards, the Romans took up this device to represent one of their oldest gods, Terminus, and to mark off the limits of a territory. They also transformed this formal type for other purposes, namely as supports. Made of marble, granite or porphyry, these *termes*—the name has been preserved in the French language—are abundantly evident from the first century onwards, sporting faces of Hercules, Dionysus, satyrs or other maenads, when they were used to support porticoes or, more frequently, basins and marble tables.[9]

During the sixteenth century, at the time of the cultural and formal revival of Antiquity, these figures, omnipresent in painting and statuary, were re-used to invade gardens and architecture. It is the very particular expression, taken from models from Antiquity, of the body imprisoned by Nature which it escapes thanks only to its divine nature, together with the great symbolism attributed to the theme, that was the reason for its exceptional success. Consequently, many fusions and adaptations that accentuated the most spectacular contrasts appeared. Powerful and muscled Titans saw the lower part of their bodies, the most animal, captured in solid form, whereas with their raised arms, they tried both to support their burden and protect themselves from it. Placed half-way between gods and men, Atlas and Hermes thereby found themselves progressively associated in a same statuary type.

This fusion gave birth to prolific metamorphoses and all kinds of often extraordinary figures then appeared, with a more or less human bust and the rest of their body reduced to a stone sheath, sometimes with the feet sticking out. This sheath, too, evolved and was travestied. The myths of Atlas, the strong support, and that of Hermes, the agile courier, were thus closely mingled in an equal expression of strength and hospitality.

CREATION OF AN ORDER AND THE DISORDER OF BODIES

The incarnation of a god cast in stone, or a Titan, was not just an anecdotal phenomenon, linked to a passionate observation of the ancient world. In the course of the sixteenth century, while the Greek and Roman orders had become the guiding principle of every monument and every reflection upon architecture, a real passion for the use of this new formal type, based on its qualities as a direct expression of the body, emerged.[10] Sometimes called the "Persian order", more often the "Caryatid order", for both the male and female types, it served as an ostentatious classical reference in keeping with Vitruvius' text. On the other hand, enriched as it was by the marvelous and monster-ridden world of fables, it also served as a model of inventiveness, subject to all types of license and all manner

Cesare Cesariano, "Caryatum Porticus", 1521, in Vitruvius, *De architectura libri decem*.

of extravagance. The oblivion into which it has today fallen contrasts strangely with the role that has constantly been accorded to it, as much in the writings of scholars as in a wide variety of works.

At first, it was the reiteration of the commentary of Vitruvius concerning these supports and the first illustrations of his treatise that served as a theoretical and practical source. An engraving of the *De architectura* edited in Venice by Fra Giocondo in 1511 already offered a surprising interpretation of the facade of the Erechtheion of Athens, adapted to the female *Caryatids* and the male *Persians* alike. Reproduced and made more elaborate in several plates by Cesare Cesariano in 1521 (*Vitruvius: De architectura libri decem*), who accentuated the theme of the enslaved barbarians, this presentation in the frontal form of a gallery was later translated, amended and perfected many times. The famous *Gallery of the Caryatids*, engraved by Marcantonio Raimondi, was based on a probable model by Raphael. More widespread in its use, this motif was similarly catalogued in a series of prints like those of Jacques Prévost, in 1535, Agostino Musi in 1536 or Giulio Bonasone in 1548. Already several of these figures, although designed after antique models, gave way to beautiful extravagances and were widely spread, as can be seen in several monuments of Aragon.

In France, it seems that it is Primaticcio who, inspired by Giulio Romano, brought acclaim to terms and caryatids by placing them between 1533 and 1540—sheathed and with feet—in the stuccos of the castle of Fontainebleau, to satisfy the cultural aspirations of Francis 1st. These unbridled decorations and these schools of thought inspired by Raphael as well as Michelangelo, in turn generated numerous prints and interpretations by the engravers and painters of the "School of Fontainebleau". However, it was quite logically the quest for a pure and mastered classicism, proclaimed by the French artists at the end of the reign, that sparked off one of the most famous revivals of the Vitruvian and even Greek model, the one engraved by Jean Goujon to illustrate the first book of *L'architecture ou Art de bien bastir de Marc Vitruve Pollion*, published by Jean Martin in 1547.

Goujon sculpted his most accomplished version of this Caryatid order in 1550, at the Louvre palace, for the portico of the Lower Hall, known as the Ballroom. His four magnificently draped statues, supporting a gallery, were the most beautiful echo of the Erechtheion, thanks to a first-hand knowledge of the Roman copies of the Greek model. In accordance with the idea of enslavement that had imposed

Jean Goujon, *Ballroom Portico*, 1550, Louvre palace, Paris. Photo Pascal Julien.

itself on this type of figure, Goujon represented them in their historical state, with their arms foreshortened, thereby strongly accentuating the impression of heaviness and servitude. However, with their full and sensual forms, the perfection of their faces, the grace of their attitudes and delicacy of their drapery, he deliberately accentuated the *venustas*, the beauty of these magnificent female figures adapted to architecture. Often represented in engravings and held up as an example, they themselves became a model destined to travel down through the ages.

The Caryatid order therefore developed following two main forms, as figures or as terms, the two being sometimes used in tandem.[11] The series of prints and treatises which were published were therefore, in all countries, the source of countless adaptations, both in the domain of facade elevations or interior decorations, be it for portals, windows or chimneys. Painting was not left out, nor was tapestry, carpentry or the craft of goldsmiths. Atlantes and caryatids fascinated writers in equal measure and in fact became, in the course of the century, one of the main ornaments of book frontispieces, where they served as frames. It is probable, in this very particular context of written works, that it is the theme of Hermes, considered to be the god of eloquence and truth, the progenitor of literature that was used as an adornment as well as a moral introduction to the title of the books.[12] Erasmus gave an explicit formulation of this by having himself portrayed by Holbein the Younger framed by a portico supported by two sheathed terms, with his hand placed on a bust of the god Terminus, in keeping with his motto *Cedo nulli*. This motto refers to the god who refused to succumb to the Roman God Jupiter. It recalls the idea of force, strength and resistance expressed by the atlantes, an idea that Vitruvius had already expressed under the name of *firmitas*, or solidity, as one of the three principles of architecture, along with *venustas* and *utilitas*.

This "perpetual firmness" advocated by Alberti, this "force" required by Philbert de l'Orme or this "durability" recommended by Palladio were specifically portrayed by the atlante and its relation to Atlas, symbol of eternal support, a mythical dimension familiar to most architects. Many texts, as well as many engravings testify to this. Amongst the latter, those of the *Vitruvius Teutsch* by Walther Ryff in 1548, stand out most clearly. Here, a series of seven oneiric terms—highly inspired by Raimondi—end with the figure of Atlas himself supporting the globe. This link is even more clearly expressed in *The First and Chief Grovnds of Architectvre* by John Shute. The work published in 1563, is a paraphrase of Vitruvius' text and is enhanced with superb images of the classical orders.[13] For the Tuscan order, Shute places the column in parallel with a tall statue of Atlas, in his legendary royal appearance, supporting the same entablature. Furthermore, to accentuate the meaning of this comparison, he represents the episode of Hercules leaving Atlas on the pedestal of the column after having by trickery given him back the weight of the world.[14] In the same way, the Doric order is compared with a statue of Hercules similarly placed as a support in order to emphasise his force. This distinction clearly refers to the *firmitas*, but likewise eloquently evokes the relation to the body and its correspondence to the unity of the column.

Philibert de l'Orme conveyed this close link by specifying, in book VII of his *Premier tome de l'architecture*, in 1567: "*Je n'oublieray pas de vous advertir qu'au lieu des colomnes, vous pouvez aussi mettre des figures qui representeront hommes ou femmes, ainsi que iadis feirent les Grecs [...] Il ne fault aussi omettre, que plusieurs au lieu des colomnes ont appliqué des Termes, les autres des Satyres, comme vous en voyez un à la figure cy devant, qui pourra servir à la ieunesse apprenant à protraire [dessiner].*"[15]

(I won't forget to inform you that instead of columns, you can also place figures that represent men or women, like the Greeks used to do [...]. One must not forget that many, instead of columns, used Terms, others satyrs, like the one that you can see on the figure opposite, that may be used by young people learning to portray.)

He thereby confirmed and illustrated the classification of anthropomorphic supports into classical models and invented models, into statues and terms, the latter often thought of at the time as descended from Roman art. The "figure opposite" was, moreover, the drawing of one of the famous *Della Valle Satyrs*, two marble sculptures from the second century, whose bronze casts made in Rome in 1540, were used as chimney jambs for the ballroom of Fontainebleau. This resort to hybridisation of all kinds only became more marked with time and, little by little, fable gave way to imagination. This division and mutation took place as a result of creativity, a creativity above all based on the use of the human figure, whether complete or incomplete, realistic or imaginary, but remaining always credible in whatever metamorphosis it was to undergo.

Since the publication of the first engraved series, like Musi's, the most restrained terms were placed alongside the most liberated figures, whether they be tree-like or covered with scales. This theme of monstrous figures, ever present in Western art, came close in this specific case to the chimerical exuberance of Roman grotesques. Moreover there are no decorations of this type that do not provide examples of some inventive terms. In fact, many a model of the caryatid order can be considered as the sumptuous metamorphosis of these grotesque "figures of the imagination".[16]

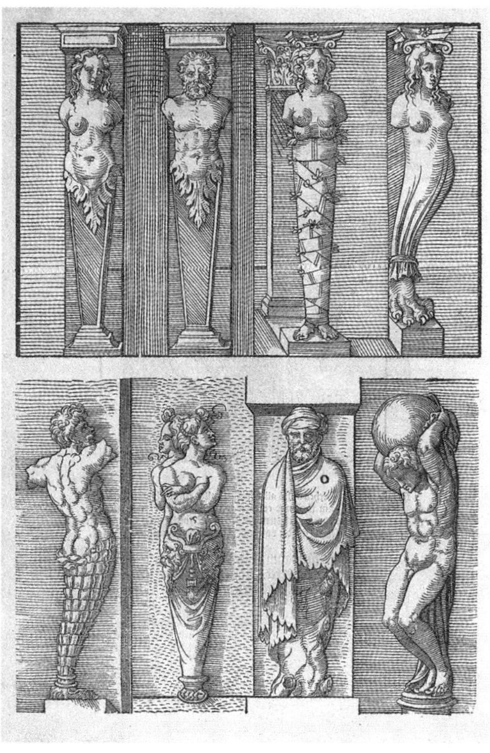

Woodcut by Peter Flotner from Walther Ryff, *Vitruvius Teutsch*, Nuremberg, 1548.

The adaptation of this burlesque poetry and eulogy of the paradoxical enjoyed a spectacular success and saw some incredible applications in the second half of the sixteenth century in France. Fantasy and profusion invaded not only architectural monuments, but all of the arts too and one would have difficulty classifying so numerous and varied an array of harpies, griffins, chimeras, sphinxes, satyrs, or other mermaids and indefinable unrestrained terms, whose prolific metamorphoses were studied by Jacques Thirion, in particular in the field of furniture.[17]

Even before artists like Vredeman de Vries or Crispin de Passe exploited the theme in their work, one of the main authors of this lavish inventiveness was the architect and engineer Jacques Androuet du Cerceau (c. 1510–1585), who enriched the second half of the century with his dream-like creations. Thanks to his excellent mastering of the art of enhancement through engraving, he came up, between 1550 and 1570, with several variations of extraordinary terms, elegantly mixing plant and floral themes, animal and human figures, adding fish fins, birds' wings, claws, over-a bundant trophies, graceful faces and grimacing masks, appealing bosoms and muscular busts. He presented them in isolation or in a series, or inserted them into sumptuous fittings like luxurious fireplaces. Several of his models echoed and magnified themes already enriched by other myths, like those that told of mermaids, wavering between bird and fish, sensual women with provocatively beautiful busts, attractive and engaging, but whose legs, coiled in spirals or hidden in a sheath of scales, warned against the dangerous paths of their damnable voluptuousness.

His art, however, was not just a simply symbolic and attractive decor; he also conceived caryatids and monumental terms adapted to grand facades, like those for the castle of Verneuil or the castle of Charleval. In his conception, these tall figures engaged in an aesthetic of the sublime, elevating exuberance to the level of a colossus.

The models offered by Du Cerceau enriched all of those already used, and this dynamic inventiveness generated, in other hands, ideas so spectacular and sometimes so hermetic that they, in turn, gave birth to many a myth, centred around their own creators. This was the case of the famous Hugues Sambin, who, although we only know for certain about a scarce number of his works, is considered to be one of the most prolific originators of French "mannerism".[18] Sambin engraved and published a series entitled *Œuvre de la diversité des termes* (Study on the diversity of terms) which has been linked to dozens of pieces of furniture that enthusiastic biographers and unscrupulous antique dealers would attribute to him. In spite of this, his role as the creator of models appears to be relatively limited, and his prints are far from having conveyed their original meaning, which is not purely ornamental. This is also the case for the engravings of terms of one of his contemporaries, Joseph Boillot, about whom much has been written. In fact, a very thorough study of his work has brought to light not only his literary, hieroglyphic and political influence, but also his architectural or ornamentalist claims.[19]

Up to the seventeenth century, Du Cerceau inspired many creators who adapted and developed his models in a variety of forms. A prodigious repertoire of humorous and eccentric terms invaded buildings as well as the decorative arts, in particular paneling and fireplaces. It was even used in church furniture: organs, pulpits, stalls or lecterns, up to the Holy of Holies on tabernacles. Architecture books echoed this exuberance, like the peculiar *Architectura von Außtheilung, Symmetria und Proportion der Fünff Seulen* by the German author Wendel Dietterlin, in 1598. Faced with such abundance and vitality, one might question the reasons for this

Stalls, possibly inspired by Du Cerceau. Photo Pascal Julien.

obsession, that seems to have been driven by the ever-renewing desire to reinsert man in the monumental and the decorative. At the same time, this obsession emphasised the myth of his central role in the three kingdoms, animal, vegetal and mineral, that alternately invade his being and modify his body.

It would be tedious, yet revealing, to draw up the list of the many treatises and architecture books that in the seventeenth and eighteenth centuries turned this order, without always accepting it as such, into a theoretical reference, whether it was to approve or to question its relevance. Its use is nearly always explained, often commented upon and its representations are placed on independent plates or sometimes even inserted between the Greek and Roman orders. With time, however, many authors gradually favoured the most classical expressions and the hybrid exuberances became rarer. Roland Fréart de Chambray, in his *Parallèle de l'architecture antique avec la moderne*, in 1650, entitled two of his chapters *De l'ordre des caryatides* and *De l'ordre persique*, whereas Juan Caramuel de Lobkowitz, in his *Architectura civil recta, y obliqua*, in 1678, suggested a "paranymph and atlante" order and Guarino Guarini, in his *Architettura civile*, 1683, published in 1737, presented the "caryatidic" order. From then on, all show full-length figures or, sometimes, rare terms with meticulously portrayed anatomies.

In most countries, these supports progressively became more sober and more rational in the course of time. They did however preserve their human or semi-human appearance above all, and were everywhere an important object of study and debate.

THE IMMENSITY OF THE BODY

The important role attached to this remarkable order in fact resulted from a combination of a practical reality and a theoretical issue: on the one hand, it had sustained famous adaptations—some discussed, others respected—and on the other hand it always referred to an essential notion of the body, in a perpetual interrogation on man as measure of all things. It was moreover this philosophical dimension that, from an ethical point of view, ended up sealing the fate of these figures.

If Vitruvius, in his literary synthesis of antique knowledge, provided architecture with the elements of classification that travelled down the ages, his treatise lay a foundation in two ways: on the one hand unifying and modeling a Western monumental spirit, and on the other hand enriching several myths, foremost that of the human body as ideal module, as source of all *symmetri* and *proportio* that found, in the column, its most accomplished expression.[20] This notion, which has been discussed at great length, has rarely been addressed in connection with the relation between structure and sculpture, or between building and statuary. It would be legitimate therefore to question the relation between architectural anthropomorphism and the famous formula of Protagoras developed by Vitruvius, "man as measure of all things".

Indeed, the body became, in this context, the standard of a system of measurements that it fully enhances. It is, however, a submissive body, imprisoned, encircled in the erect column. This body aspires to become an unchained and dynamic creation in the stone of the statue-support, but it remains, tragically, the incarnation of a submission to the forces that enslave it. The atlas, like the caryatid, is therefore an expression of constraint. Yet it is equally a symbol of a resistance to the immensity of a world in which man must respect the place that he has been assigned. Atlantes and caryatids certainly concur with the Platonic conceptions of the soul inseparable from the body and the aspiration of man to a perfection of being. These statues are not only an internalisation of this ambition, but they also express the idea of human nature condemned to remain subjugated to the nature of the world that encompasses it. It is then understandable that a myth like that of Atlas may have been taken up by Christian art in its various sculpted expressions. It provides a vision of man rejected by God and existing in an animate world, adapting to it or trying to overcome it without however ever having to free himself from it or being able to extract himself from it. Only the power of art could provide an escape.

As far as statuary was concerned, the Renaissance developed a certain fascination for the difficult task of carving gigantic works and, better still, from a single block.[21] The atlas adapted entirely to this hunger for technical feats. The perfect command of its raw elements became the expression of a nature sublimated and dominated. The sense of myth was thereby renewed, the body becoming not only the representation of a submission, but also the sculpted expression of the dexterous conquest of the sculptor's craftsmanship over the unformed. No-one has expressed this ambition better than Michelangelo. Several of his *Slaves* or *Prisoners* destined to support the tomb of Julius II show his desire for complete bodies skillfully encompassing the wholeness of matter.[22]. This drive found its moment of maximum expression in the famous *Atlas* of the *Accademia* of Florence that illustrates at its best the strange relation, created by the sculptor, between body and stone. It is as if, instead of bringing out the forms of the body, he had, like Perseus before him, wanted to eternally immortalise the flesh of his atlas, once nothing would work to set it free.

Moreover, this dialogue with substance has itself become mythical. The definition of the *non finito*, opened the way for many a modern interpretation. These fascinating and terrifying images that Michelangelo has bequeathed us in unrefined stone, accentuating the torment of the figures, fully illustrate the idea that "every myth is a condensed human drama".[23] The eternal suffering of Atlas was thereby ritualised in the form of strong and harrowing figures for we must remember that in ancient mythology, although Hercules delivered Prometheus, brother of Atlas, from his torment, he did nothing for Atlas himself, who was as a result forever condemned to suffer the burden of the world.

This fact is far from insignificant. The metaphor adds another dimension to the notion of force: that of endurance. In concrete terms, it explains the presence of a cushion on so many engraved figures and statues offering a variation of the Caryatid order where the weight carried by the head is cushioned. This cushion is a tangible expression and a confirmation of the correspondence of the order to myth: when

Hercules took the place of Atlas so that the latter could go and fetch the golden apples in the Garden of the Hesperides, he was almost destined to keep his burden for eternity. It is thanks only to his cunning that he managed to escape from it, by asking the giant to lift up the mass of the world in order to to protect his head with a cushion. This detail is a constant reminder of the original myth and, even if the meaning may have been lost, the symbolism has endured: that of a fateful subjection of man to the burden of existence, despite the multifarious partial improvements to his state.

Amongst all the applications of the Caryatid order, if there is one model whose importance and legacy must be underlined, it is precisely the model created by Michelangelo. Whilst the elegant feminine figures of Jean Goujon in the Louvre were the basis for a classical norm of sober unreality, countless hybrid terms brought together extravagance and coherence as if questioning the order of the world. The very masculine and muscular slaves of the tomb of Julius II were widely echoed and sublimated in their tragic honesty. It is possible to follow their multiple interpretations in painting as in sculpture, up to the version put forward by Pierre Puget in 1656 for the portal of the Town Hall of Toulon. There, the sculptor combined force, grace and torment in equal refinement and while anchoring the work of his glorious predecessor he even surpassed it. There were of course earlier attempts, both in Italy and in Provence, to achieve this, but it was Puget who managed to balance body and form very precisely, the weight of the world on human nature: moderation and immoderation here reach a fine equilibrium thanks solely to the skill of the artist. This model was in turn taken up again indefinitely and Atlas was once more magnified by the power of suffering: suspended, his muscular arms raised in desperation, yet weighed down by the load and subjugated to eternal frustration. Amongst countless examples, the portal of the Episcopal Seminary of Mdina in Malta (today the Cathedral Museum) built in 1734–1742 can be cited. Two monumental terms frame the entrance and, although proudly depicted upright, they struggle under the weight of a balcony above.[24] The mythical Vitruvian theme of the enslaved figures still had

left/ Pierre Puget, *Portal*, 1656, Town Hall, Toulon. Photo Pascal Julien.
right/ *Portal*, 1734–1742, Episcopal Seminary, Mdina. Photo Guillaume Dreyfuss.

a bright future, also thanks to the astonishing sacred expressions of angel atlantes; however it did not last indefinitely. Its deepest meaning having been perfectly understood, it could no longer accord with the conquest of rationalism or the progress of human thought, especially concerning the relation between man and the world. Indeed, as from the seventeenth century, but especially in the course of the eighteenth century, several objections were raised, criticising not only the lack of adequacy between a necessary *firmitas* and such "ornaments", but also and above all rejecting these figures, obvious representations of a condemnation and even demeaning of the human being.

Voltaire, who denounced the tradition that required prisoners to be placed around equestrian statues to symbolise the nations subjugated by triumphant kings, inspired Bouchardon in 1750 to replace this type of captive with four Virtues derived from the classical caryatids of the Erechtheion, to adorn the pedestal of the equestrian statue of Louis XV in Paris. By leaving the bodies of his statues free, the sculptor conformed to the precepts expressed from 1714 onwards by Sébastien Leclerc, one of the defenders of anthropomorphic supports, who wrote: "one no longer depicts Caryatids with images of slavery and servitude, like in the past, these characters are disgraceful and too offensive to the fair sex, one only uses them in buildings as noble symbols, like for Prudence, Wisdom, Justice, Temperance, etc.".[25] Blondel, in 1752, went one step further, considering that such figures, both masculine and feminine, were contrary to good taste, propriety and nature. Furthermore, as they were still often used in churches, namely in stalls and organ cases, he added "it is even more incorrect to place angels instead of columns, this servile situation not being suitable for celestial spirits".[26]

It is hardly necessary to repeat the examples that underline to what extent, in the Age of the Enlightenment, the Caryatid order became inappropriate, in thought as in "good architecture". However it still subsisted especially in Northern and Eastern Europe, where it found spectacular architectonic uses. In France, however, its fate was sealed and one can only mention a late, very significant and extraordinary use, put forward by the architect Lequeu in 1789, with his *Ordre symbolique de la Sale des Etats d'un Palais national*. Adopting the most questionable motifs derived from the myth, he conceived a term prototype: royally dressed, decorated with the Order of Saint Michael, resigned, eyes and arms lowered, hands joined and chained to the column which acts as a sheath, in order to depict "some, fugitive aristocratic Lords, the others their subordinate accomplices, all criminals of treason against the nation, chained up". Political power was thereby mythicised; Louis XVI replaced Atlas and supported solely with his head, which was at this time still in place, the weight of a crumbling world.

Through its multiple facets, complex evolution and metamorphosis, the myth of Atlas resembles a constantly changing allegory, a language offering physical and moral truths that, for some, seem obvious and for others escape understanding. This is especially the case since these truths were conceived in a process of constant distortion, expressing values as contradictory as they are complementary. The resulting figures were always used with a will to improve and embellish by recalling various symbols as well as resorting to elegant formal aesthetics.

In the final third of the nineteenth century, the caryatid order reappeared in France with a vengeance. It adorned the most beautiful architecture of the vast urban transformations that were taking place at that time. It ennobled the facades integrating all of the cultural values of these supports, with the more classical full-length models, and the invented sheathed ones, often inspired by the sixteenth century.[27] However in this eclecticism of pomp, the most quoted model was that of Michelangelo re-interpreted by Puget. This model offered particularly dynamic and expressive sculpted forms. The order then disappeared again, reappearing only episodically. On the facade of the *Team Disney Building*, in Burbank, California, in 1991, Michael Graves cast the seven dwarfs of Snow White in the form of immense atlantes, paradoxically investing them with the comic role of Titans of Modernity in pursuit of new mythologies.

Conversely, returning to the beginnings of this architectural element, it would be imperative to retrace one's steps to the origins of Malta, the mythical Atlantis, where ancient accounts report that on the portals of certain megalithic temples, giant figures supporting lintels existed.[28] It is therefore possible that, on this island, at the heart of the Mediterranean, one of the founding myths of architecture may have undergone some of its first metamorphoses, in a *firmitas* that was already seeking the lure of *venustas*.

/ **1.** This article is dedicated to the memory of the art historian Jacques Thirion who had a passion for the caryatid order and was one of the rare authors to study its "various figures".

/ **2.** Barthes, R, *Mythologies*, Paris: Seuil, 1957, p. 182.

/ **3.** Vernant, JP, "Lectures et problèmes du mythe" in *Mythe et société en Grèce ancienne*, Paris: La Découverte, 2004 (1st edition: 1974), pp. 244–250. Regarding figurative distortions see S Georgoudi and JP Vernant, *Mythes grecs au figuré, de l'antiquité au baroque*, Paris: Gallimard, 1996.

/ **4.** Hesiod, *Theogony*, p. 519.

/ **5.** Vitruvius, *De architectura*, 1, 1, 5. The first French version of this text is explicit: *A l'occasion de quoy, ceulx qui pour le temps d'adonc estoient Architectes, meirent en leurs edifices publiques les images de ces dames comme destinees a supporter le faix, afin que la punition du forfaict des Caryens, feust congneue, et serveist d'exemple a toute la posterité.* ("On this occasion, those who at that time were architects, placed in their public buildings the images of these ladies as if they were destined to support a burden, so that the punishment of the forfeit of the Carians be known and be an example for posterity") J Martin, *Architecture ou Art de bien bastir de Marc Vitruve Pollion Autheur romain antique*, Paris, 1547, p. 1.

/ **6.** *I marmi colorati della Roma imperiale*, exhibition held at the Mercati di Traiano, Rome, 28/9/2002–19/1/2003, catalogue, Roma, 2003, pp. 82–88, 423–436. The theme of enslaved barbarians was often repeated, especially in the form of atlantes that marked the rhythm of the attic of the facade of the Basilica Ulpia (106–113) on the forum of Trajan. ibid., pp. 125–133.

/ **7.** There were however many other spectacular adaptations, amongst which the angels of the *Well of Moses* of the Chartreuse de Champmol (1395) or the weepers of the tomb of Philippe Pot (Louvre, c. 1480).

/ **8.** Frontisi-Ducroux, F, "Les limites de l'anthropomorphisme : Hermès et Dionysos" in *Corps des dieux*, Paris: Gallimard, 1986, pp. 256–286.

/ **9.** In 1789, Johann Joachim Winckelmann wrote "I call caryatids all the figures of women and men that support an element of architecture, although I do know that one calls the latter Atlas or Atlante." He thereby recalled that an age-long erudition had presided over complex definitions, divergences and correspondences established between multiple anthropomorphic supports, whether they be feminine or masculine, called atlantes, Persians, telamones, caryatids, herms, terms or other canephora figures. JJ Winckelmann, *Histoire de l'art chez les anciens*, Paris, 1789, vol. 3, p. 169.

/ **10.** Thirion, J, "Termes et cariatides" in *Le mobilier du Moyen Âge et de la Renaissance en France*, Dijon: Editions Faton, 1998, pp. 177–195.

/ **11.** As did the sculptor Esteban Jamete in Spain from Ubeda to Cuenca or Siguenza, between 1540 and 1560. A Turcat, *Esteban Jamete sculpteur français de la Renaissance en Espagne, condamné par l'Inquisition*, Paris: Picard, 1994. For a study of this topic concerning Spanish art see JA Ramírez, *Edificios-cuerpo*, Madrid: Ediciones Siruela, 2003.

/ **12.** This correspondence between *termes* and Mercury was perfectly established, and its explanation was still being provided in the *Encyclopaedia* of Diderot and d'Alembert in the eighteenth century, under the word *term*: "*ces* termes *représentoient véritablement Mercure, que les latins appelloient* Mercurius quadrifons, *parce qu'ils prétendoient que ce dieu avoit enseigné aux hommes les lettres, la musique, la lutte & la géométrie*" ("these *terms* really represented Mercury, whom the Latins called *Mercurius quadrifons*, because they claimed that this god had taught literature, music, wrestling and geometry to men").

/ **13.** Shute, J, *The First and Chief Grounds of Architecture*, London, 1563.

/ **14.** One of the legends of Atlas, that related to his petrifaction by Perseus, presents him as king of the kingdom of Hesperia; Ovid, *Metamorphoses*, IV, pp. 634–665.

/ **15.** de L'Orme, P, *Le premier tome de l'architecture de Philibert de L'Orme*, Paris, 1567, edition JM Pérouse de Montclos, Paris: Laget, 1988, ff. 221–222.

/ **16.** Morel, P, *Les grotesques, les figures de l'imaginaire dans la peinture italienne de la fin de la Renaissance*, Paris: Flammarion, 1997.

/ **17.** Thirion, J, *Le mobilier du Moyen Âge et de la Renaissance en France*, pp. 177–195.

/ **18.** Sambin was a practical pretext. Werner Szambien thus considered that if the rigor of Vignola had imposed itself in France in the seventeenth century, it was because, formerly, architecture had been "too inventive", especially with the use of terms, use that he confined to the sole propositions of Sambin and Boillot (W Szambien, *Symétrie, goût, caractère, Théorie et terminologie de l'architecture à l'âge classique, 1550–1800*, Paris: Picard, 1986, p. 38). Jacques Thirion attempted to correct this mythical perception of Sambin (J Thirion, "Les termes de Sambin. Mythe et réalité" in *Hommage à Hubert Landais*, Paris: s. l. Blanchard, 1987, pp. 151–159), still observed today (A Erlande-Brandenbourg (dir.), *Hugues Sambin, un créateur au XVIe siècle (vers 1520–1601)*, Paris: Editions de la Réunion des Musées Nationaux, 2001).

/ **19.** Boillot, J, *Nouveaux pourtraictz et figures de termes pour user en l'architecture : Composez et enrichiz de diversité d'Animaux, representez au vray selon l'Antipathie et contrarieté naturelle de chacun d'iceulx*, Langres, 1592. I Bouvrande, "Les termes zoomorphes de Joseph Boillot, étude sur le langage hiéroglyphique à la fin du XVIe siècle", in *Albertiana*, V, 2002, pp. 165–187.

/ **20.** Regarding the writings of Vitruvius, see P Gros, *Vitruve et la tradition des traités d'architecture, fabrica et ratiocinatio*, Collection de l'Ecole française de Rome, 366, Roma, 2006. Concerning the question of the body and the column, see J Rykwert, *The Dancing Column: on order in architecture*, Cambridge, MA and London: MIT Press, 1996.

/ **21.** Regarding the relation between unity of the column, unity of the body and statues made of one block see P Julien, *De carrières en palais*, Manosque: Le bec en l'air, 2006, pp. 59–62.

/ **22.** Hall, J, *Michelangelo and the Reinvention of the Human Body*, London: Chatto & Windus, 2005.

/ **23.** Bachelard, G, preface of the book by P Diel, *Le symbolisme dans la mythologie grecque. Etude psychoalytique*, Paris: Payot, 1952, p. 5.

/ **24.** It is a possible work of the architect Andrea Belli (1703–1772), see L Mahoney, *5000 Years of Architecture in Malta*, Valletta Publishing, Malta, 1996, pp. 176–177.

/ **25.** Leclerc, S, *Traité d'architecture avec des remarques et des observations utiles pour les jeunes gens qui veulent s'appliquer à ce bel art*, Paris, 1714, p. 106.

/ **26.** Blondel, JF, "Des Cariatides et des Termes", in *Architecture Françoise*, Paris, 1752, I, pp. 74–75.

/ **27.** For a photographic anthology of this theme see J Nebout, *Les cariatides de Paris*, Paris: Hervas, 1992.

/ **28.** There is, namely, a description from the sixteenth century written during the works of the citadel of Rabat, in Gozo.

DISCOVERING ATLANTIS

THE PERSONAL ADVENTURE OF GEORGES GROGNET

Albert Ganado

George Grognet, *Self-portrait*, NLM Libr.615, p. 4. Image courtesy of the National Library of Malta. Photo Guillaume Dreyfuss.

Who was Georges Grognet (Grongnet, Grugnett, Greugnett) de Vassé? The architect historian, Leonard Mahoney, summarised him in a few words: "Architect, archaeologist, and author of scientific, literary and artistic works, a gifted man, but often regarded by his contemporaries as a dreamer."[1] Georges was born in Valletta on 19 February, 1774, to Jean-Baptiste Grognet de Vassé who was descended from a French noble family which left France in the late sixteenth century when King Louis XIV completely revoked the Edict of Nantes concerning the Huguenots.[2] His mother was Marie-Amélie Marchesi daughter of Chevalier Giuseppe Isidoro Marchesi (or Marchese), a member of a notable Provençal family of St Tropez which had been established in Malta since the beginning of the seventeenth century. Chev Marchesi was married to a French lady, Donna Saverina Marmier de Salins, and had two beautiful daughters Marcelle and Marie-Amélie, one of whom, so idle tongues say, was the principal attraction that enticed the French painter Antoine de Favray to our island shores. The said Marchesi was a good friend of Henry Benedict Stuart, of royal blood, Cardinal of York, who was Rector of the Seminary at Frascati.[3] That is where Georges Grognet, Marchesi's grandson, was sent to continue his studies in 1788 when he was 14 years old.[4] He harboured a great passion for mathematics, with which he combined the study of architecture and civil engineering.[5] Georges Grognet could speak fluently both Italian and French, apart from his native language, and he was well-versed in Greek and Latin, in addition to some Oriental languages.[6]

He served for 13 years under Napoleon in the Civil and Military Department of Engineers in various countries including Egypt, where he constructed some forts for the French Army. When Napoleon's fortunes were on the wane, Georges went back to Rome where he continued his studies between 1810 and 1814. He made the acquaintance of Marquis Agricol de Fortia d'Urban, *Membre de plusieurs Académies en France, en Italie, et en Allemagne*, a renowned writer and archaeologist. Through him he became a member of the Roman *Accademia Archeologica del Campidoglio*. Realising perhaps that Grognet was, in the words of Mahoney, "a very ambitious man whose aim in life was the pursuit of personal greatness", the Academicians entrusted him with the task of discovering and describing the lost continent of

Arms of M Le Marquis de Fortia in Marquis de Fortia, *Pièces relatives à la Pierre Atlantico-Phénicienne de Malte*, 1826–1832. Image courtesy of the author. Photo Guillaume Dreyfuss.

Atlantis, the mysterious, antediluvian world, the first home of civilisation shrouded in the mists of antiquity.[7] Georges Grognet fell for the idea which he pursued throughout his whole life with dedication, determination and scholarship, but also with more than a pinch of fantasy and manipulation.

Grognet came back to Malta on 4 August 1815 when the Napoleonic wars were over, after an absence of 27 years.[8] Although his life in Malta during his next ten years has not so far been recorded, it appears that he frequented the company of Dr Cleardo Naudi, agent for the British and Foreign Bible Society.[9] It was at Naudi's house that he met the Reverend Joseph Wolff in 1821.[10] He was at the time "a complete atheist". He declared to Wolff that he did not believe in any divine revelation, that the Bible was an imposture and that the world of Christianity was an imposture of the priests. At one stage, in order to prove a point, Grognet quoted from the Bible. Wolff rejoined: "you nevertheless would prove your infidelity by the authority of the Bible. I must, therefore, draw this conclusion, that you are an impostor."

Throughout this period Grognet was almost certainly immersed in his quest of the unknown. His dream of discovering Atlantis led him to proclaim in 1826 that a large stone in a perfect state of conservation with an inscription in the Atlantic-Phoenician alphabet had been unearthed at Città Notabile, as the old capital city of Mdina was known.

Grognet had in his possession a letter dated 7 May 1826 signed by Don Giuseppe Felice Galea addressed to him from Città Vecchia (or Notabile) informing him that during deep excavations carried out in the foundations of the yard of his house a large stone had been found, covered with what looked like a Phoenician script.[11] The priest who wrote this letter declared that he was donating this stone to Grognet, for him to discover the significance of the mysterious script: *io ve ne faccio un Dono, affinchè poi spiegandola, mi direte il significato, che quei caratteri racchiudono.*[12]

The script covered three sides of the stone, while on the fourth side there was an inscription in Latin in the name of the consul Tiberius Sempronius Longus dated 218 BC, which read as follows: *T. Sempron. cos. hoc. magni. Athlantis. et. soubmersae. athlantidis. reliquiom. vedit. eidemq. servari. coeravit. an. ur. DXXXVI. olymp. CXL. an. III.* [13]

Marquis de Fortia some years later rendered it in French as hereunder: *Le consul Tiberius Sempronius a vu ce reste du grand Athlas, et de l'Athlantide submergée, et il a eu soin que ce reste fût conservé, l'an de Rome 536, an 3 de l'olympiade 140.*[14]

He remarked that this Latin inscription was in perfect harmony with history and chronology. Indeed, Titus Livius wrote that Sempronius Longus had conquered Malta from the Carthaginians in 218 BC. The third year of Olympiad 140 started 2 July 218 BC and ended on 19 July 217 BC. It was in the said first six months that Malta was taken, the year of Rome 536.[15] The Latin inscription of the stone gave the same dates.

The script, considered to be in Phoenician language, was said to have been shown to a professor of the Chaldee language who deciphered the name of Athlas in large characters, the two signs of Bélier and Cancer, the seven letters which denoted the seven stars which made up the constellation of the Pléiades, and which formed the sacred name of Jéhovah.[16] The vertical characters were difficult to explain, but they were very similar to those on a bilingual inscription found in Cyrene in Africa in 1819.[17]

This bilingual inscription, in Greek and Phoenician, together with a smaller inscription in Greek, was discovered by the renowned orientalist Louis-Domeny de Rienzi who was in Malta in 1822. Before leaving Malta to return to Greece, where he had become the general in command of the artillery at the Acropolis in Athens, he entrusted the stone to *M Georges Grognet, architecte et ingénieur-géographe*, whom he had met in Rome. De Rienzi also deposited with Grognet a precious Greek manuscript on papyrus which he had discovered in Djerba (Zerbi) in 1817 when he was in the company of a Greek savant who had become famous under the name of Ariston de Samos.[18]

Grognet transcribed the inscriptions engraved on the Malta stone and he sent them triumphantly to his old Parisian friend Marquis de Fortia together with a copy of the priest's letter of 7 May 1826 announcing the amazing discovery. Beneath his signature *George Grongnet* (sic), he wrote thus at the bottom of the copy: *L'original de Cette Lettre est gardè* (sic) *par moi soigneusement, comme un Écrit qui forme époque, et qui me Constate la pleine proprietè* (sic) *d'un aussi rare monument.*[19] Together with the Phoenician inscription, Grognet sent his version of the Phoenician alphabet worked out on the basis of the characters used on the stone.[20] Probably at de Fortia's

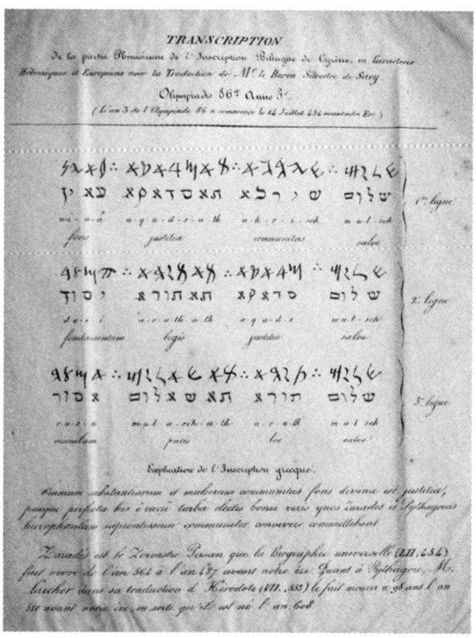

TRANSCRIPTION

de la partie Phénicienne de l'Inscription Bilingue de Cyrène, en Caractères Hébraïques et Européens avec la Traduction de Mr. le Baron Silvestre de Sacy

Olympiade 86e Anné 3e.

1re ligne

2e ligne

3e ligne

Explication de l'Inscription grecque.

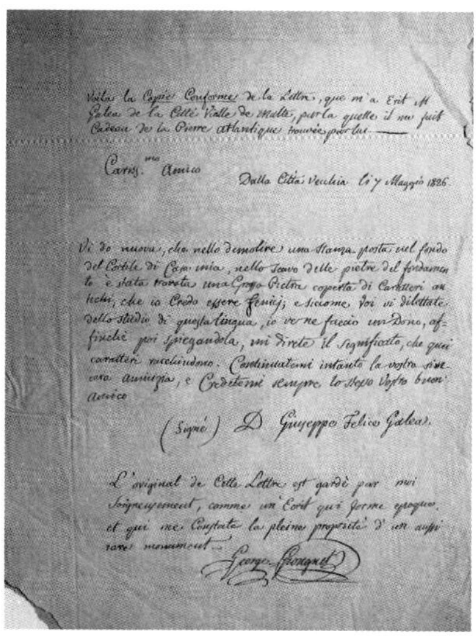

Voilà la Copie Conforme de la Lettre, que m'a Ecrit M Galea de la Cité Vielle de Malte, par la quelle il me fait Cadeau de la Pierre Atlantique trouvée par lui —

Cariss.mo Amico

Dalla Città Vecchia li 7 Maggio 1826.

Vi do nuova, che nello demolire una Stanza posta nel fondo del Cortile di Casa mia, nello scavo delle pietre del fondamento è stata trovata una Grossa Pietra coperta di Caratteri antichi, che io Credo essere Fenicj; e siccome Voi vi dilettate dello studio di questa lingua, io ve ne faccio un Dono, affinchè poi spiegandola, mi direte il significato, che quei caratteri racchiudono. Continuatemi intanto la vostra sincera amicizia, e Credetemi sempre lo stesso Vostro buon amico

(Signé) D. Giuseppe Felice Galea.

L'original de Cette Lettre est gardè par moi Soigneusement, comme un Ecrit qui forme epoque, et qui me Constate la pleine proprietè d'un aussi rare monument —

George Grongnet

"Transcription de la partie Phénicienne de l'Inscription Bilingue de Cyrène" (left) and copy of the letter by Don Giuseppe Felice Galea to Grognet dated 7 May 1826 (right) in Marquis de Fortia, *Pièces relatives à la Pierre Atlantico-Phénicienne de Malte*, 1826–1832. Images courtesy of the author. Photos Alberto Favaro.

request, who wished to have corroboration of Grognet's story, Don Giuseppe Felice Galea wrote to him a letter on 30 August 1827 from his native Città Senglea confirming his casual discovery and informing him that he had presented the stone to Grognet as a gift.[21]

Faced with such evidence and having complete trust in Grognet's ability and honesty, the Marquis De Fortia must have felt really excited and elated at the good fortune of being the one to divulge to the cultured world the fantastic news of the discovery in Malta of an antediluvian monument inscribed with the alphabet of Phoenicia and the lost continent of Atlantis, attested to as such by a Roman Consul in 218 BC.

He therefore proceeded to have the inscription lithographed in Paris, together with a separate lithograph of the Phoenician alphabet, based on the drawings made by Grognet. The latter is a simple rectangular lithograph, 195 x 138 mm, entitled *Alphabet Phoenicien tiré de la Pierre Atlantique.*[22] But the inscription itself was beautifully lithographed, as sharp and decorative as a copper engraving, which made de Fortia exclaim that it could be considered *le chef-d'œuvre de la lithographie de M Engelmann.*[23] Apart from being one of the pioneers of the novel process of lithography, invented in 1798 by the Bavarian Aloys Senefelder (1771–1834), Godefroy Engelmann (1788–1839) introduced lithography into France and invented chromolithography.

"Inscription Atlantico Phoenicienne trouvée à Médine", 1826, in Marquis de Fortia, *Pièces relatives à la Pierre Atlantico-Phénicienne de Malte*, 1826–1832. Image courtesy of the author. Photo Alberto Favaro.

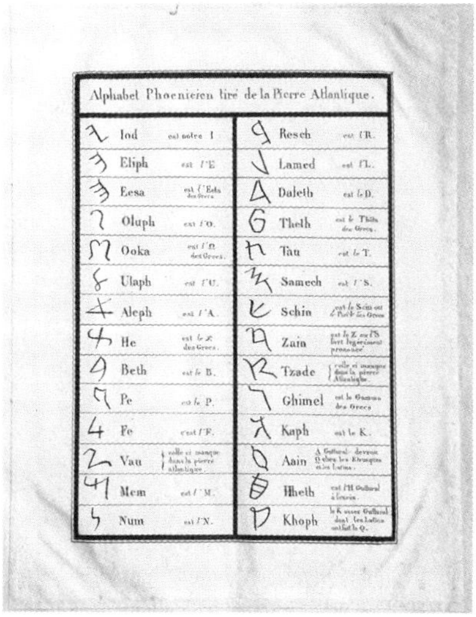

Alphabet Phoenicien tiré de la Pierre Atlantique.			
Iod	est notre I	Resch	est l'R.
Eliph	est l'E	Lamed	est l'L.
Eesa	est l'Eda des Grecs	Daleth	est le D.
Oluph	est l'O.	Theth	est le Thêta des Grecs.
Ooka	est l'Ω des Grecs.	Tau	est le T.
Ulaph	est l'U.	Samech	est l'S.
Aleph	est l'A.	Schin	est le Scin ou le Pi... des Grecs
He	est le Χ des Grecs.	Zain	est le Z ou l'S fort légèrement prononcé
Beth	est le B.	Tzade	[illegible]
Pe	est le P.	Ghimel	est le Gamma des Grecs
Fe	c'est l'F.	Kaph	est le K.
Vau	[illegible]	Aain	[illegible]
Mem	est l'M.	Hheth	[illegible]
Num	est l'N.	Khoph	[illegible]

"*Alphabet Phoenicien tiré de la Pierre Atlantique*", in Marquis de Fortia, *Pièces relatives à la Pierre Atlantico-Phénicienne de Malte*, 1826–1832. Image courtesy of the author. Photo Alberto Favaro.

Faithful to Grognet's drawing, the lithograph, (300 x 200 mm on a sheet 360 x 260 mm) is entitled and dedicated as follows:

> *Inscription Athlantico-Phoenicienne trouvée à Médine / Ancienne Capitale de l'Isle de Malte l'an 1826. / Dediée au très savant Monsieur le Marquis Agricol de Fortia d'Urban. / Membre de plusieurs Académies en France, en Italie, et en Allemagne*
> *Dessinée dans une / Echelle réduite au quart / de sa longueur (sic) naturelle / ce qui fait le seizième de / la superficie de la pierre / par George Grongnet / A.I. (Architect Ingénieur).*

A scale bar of 60 cm equivalent to 150 mm is drawn along the bottom of the lithographic print. At top left the dimensions of the stone are given: 96 cm in length, 65 cm wide at the base, and 16 cm thick.

The legend, in two irregular columns at the sides of the inscription, affirms, in typical Grognet style, that the true position of Atlantis was finally solved, that it was submerged in the year 2298 BC at the time of the deluge, and that the Maltese islands were the ancient summits of the famous Mount Atlas. The legend reads as follows:

> *Cette précieuse découverte détermine enfin au juste la véritable position de l'ancienne Athlantide qui s'étendait de puis le Golphe de la grande Syrte jusqu'entre le Cap Bon d'Afrique, et le Cap Maretimo de Sicile, étant / les Isles de Malte, et du Goze les anciens sommets du fameux Mont Athlas qui s'élevait presque au milieu de l'Athlantide submergée l'an avant l'Ere Chrétienne 2298 Epoque du Déluge D'Oggyges.*[24]

With all the essential material in hand, at a sitting of 7 January 1828, the Marquis laid before the Asiatic Society the documentation concerning the Malta stone he had referred to at the previous sitting of 3 December. He distributed various copies of the lithograph reproducing the inscription, hoping that his hearers would have better success than himself in deciphering it.[25] At the next sitting of 4 February, the Marquis read to his audience the letters he had received from Grognet and

Father Galea, in order, apparently, to allay certain doubts that had already started creeping in on the authenticity of the stone.[26]

Indeed, he told his audience that many important people, apart from himself, knew Grognet in Rome, such as, Chevalier de Gregory, a colleague, General Miollis, who was at the time the governor of Rome, Count Camille de Tournon, prefect of Rome, and then (in 1828) *pair de France*. He could also mention many persons living in Paris, among whom *Mgr le duc d'Orléans, notre président.*

He added that although the inscription had excited curiosity all round he had expected a more favourable reaction. M le baron Silvestre de Sacy who was presiding the sitting had not contested its existence; had he done so it would have been easy for me, said the Marquis, to prove it to him by means of the letters I had caused to be lithographed. De Sacy had rightly remarked that the defects in the translation made by the "Maltese professor" [Giuseppe] Cannolo, proved that the text of the inscription had not been composed by him or by Grognet; but he added that the copy itself (of the inscription) might be imperfect and it was therefore prudent to wait the arrival in Paris of the stone itself and draw up a report on it worthy of the Asiatic Society.

M le baron Silvestre de Sacy. Image courtesy of the author. Photo Guillaume Dreyfuss.

De Fortia pointed out that Phoenician inscriptions were common to Malta and he referred to what the savant Monsieur Hamaker had stated in 1827 that Malta figured among the places where monuments had been found of which he would furnish an explanation.[27] Besides, Abbé Barthelémy and Canon Pérez Bayer had given explanations of inscriptions discovered in Malta.[28] Malta had been completely Phoenician and it still conserved the language if only partly, mixed with Arabic and Italian.

De Fortia then passed on to say that the Atlantico-Phoenician inscription had been copied with great care, and he was in possession of a second copy, similar to the first, accompanied by a translation made by Cannolo.[29]

I have already mentioned a stone discovered in Africa in 1819 with a carved inscription in Greek and Phoenician. It was discovered in Cyrene (Cyrenaica) by de

Rienzi, a native of the Département de Vaucluse in Provence, who had travelled widely in Greece and Africa with the Greek savant Ariston de Samos. In 1821 de Rienzi was in Malta. The Greek part of the inscription was translated for him by M Pezzali, a Greek merchant from Parga. The Phoenician was translated by Cannolo.[30]

In 1825 this bilingual inscription was published at Halle in Germany by Wilhelm Gesenius (1786–1842)[31] with an explanation which de Fortia found clearly defective.[32] In 1828 a much better translation was given by M Hamaker in *Miscellanea Phoenicia* published in Leyden together with a lithograph of the inscription. De Fortia, however, found the translation given to him by Baron de Sacy to be more exact.[33]

De Fortia decided to have the inscription printed on a broadsheet and he had it lithographed in Paris on 30 April 1829 with a write-up contributed by Grognet and a note of his own at the end. On a large sheet measuring 46 x 35 cm, the inscription takes about three-fourths of the left part of the sheet, while the text is printed on the right. Here is the whole text:

> *Inscription bilingue ou Phoenico-Grecque Trouvée à Cyrène En 1819*
>
> *Ce Calque exactement fait, est de grandeur naturelle. Cette pierre avec une autre plus petite, mais qui est écrite toute en Grec m'ont été laissées en Dépot par Monsieur Domeny de Rienzi en 1822 avant qu'il repartit de Malte pour le Levant. Les mots Phoeniciens de cette inscription ont été traduits par Mr. Cannolo, et les mots grecs par Mr. Pezzali très exactement. La pierre sur la quelle cette Inscription est gravée, ressemble beaucoup à la pierre de Malte. Le Char de Ceres, ainsi que le Serpent en Cercle, et l'Oeuf Orphique, décèlent assez les anciens Mystères quand même le contenu ne le prouverait pas clairement. G.ge Grongnet*
>
> *Cette inscription a déjà été publiée par Guillaume Gésénius, a Halle en 1825, avec une explication qui m'a paru pouvoir être contestée. Le Marquis de Fortia*
>
> *Paris 30 Avil* (sic) *1829.*[34]

"*Inscription bilingue ou Phoenico-Grecque Trouvée à Cyrène En 1819*", 1829, in Marquis de Fortia, *Pièces relatives à la Pierre Atlantico-Phénicienne de Malte*, 1826–1832. Image courtesy of the author. Photo Alberto Favaro.

It is not the least surprising that Grognet noted that the bilingual inscription was very much alike that on the Malta stone. One is justified in assuming that it was the inscription found in 1819 which served partly as the source and the basis of inspiration for the fabrication of the Atlantico-Phoenician alphabet and its accompanying symbols and motifs.

It is also important to notice in this context the transcription made by de Sacy of the bilingual inscription, which was also lithographed. This is the title: *Transcription de la partie Phoenicienne de l'Inscription Bilingue de Cyrène, en Caractères Hébraïques et Européens avec la Traduction de M.r le Baron Silvestre de Sacy Olympiadis 86.aAnno 30. (L'an 3 de l'Olympiade 86 a commencé le 14 juillet 434 avant notre Ere).*[35] As in this bilingual inscription, the Latin inscription by the consul Tiberius Sempronius Longus on the Malta stone ended with the words *l'an de Rome 536, an 3 de l'olympiade de 140.* This Latin inscription, De Fortia pointed out in one of his papers published in 1830, was in perfect harmony with history and with chronology.[36] Grognet was no fool. He would not be caught out on a simple error of chronology and history, or through some detail of the inscription, parts of which in any case no one was able to decipher. Eventually, it was the stone itself that gave him away.

The news of Grognet's discovery travelled far and wide. De Fortia sent copies of the inscription to many savants in Germany, the Low Countries, England, Italy and Russia. As was to be expected it created great excitement throughout Italy where scholars concentrated all their efforts to try and solve the riddle of the inscription. From Florence, Federico Marini wrote a letter to Marquis de Fortia on 27 November 1828 stating that the famous polyglot Mezzofanti and Monsieur Valeriani in Bologna, Monsieur Lanzi in Rome and several important persons, both male and female, were discussing only the Atlantic stone.[37] The initial admiration and study were however followed by frustration and then incredulity.

De Fortia hastened to reply (7 December 1828) that once the inscription was antediluvian, it was easy to understand the difficulty in interpreting it. Furthermore, Grognet could not be suspected of having fabricated this Atlantico-Phoenicia monument, Fr Galea was a respectable priest, M d'Aiguillé, chancellor of the French consulate in Malta, told him in Paris that the discovery was incontrovertible and the French consul in Malta (M Duval) was of the same opinion. A French merchant who was in Malta at the time assured him that some Arab medals had been found with the stone which made the Marquis think it was the Arabs who had hidden the stone. He had had the inscription lithographed once again in its full size and Marini could find all that had been printed or lithographed on the subject at the bookshop of M Dondey-Dupré, rue de Richelieu, no 47 bis, apart, of course, from the Marquis himself at no 12 rue de La Rochefoucauld.[38]

In another publication dated 17 April 1829 it was recorded that, before sending the stone to France, Grognet had taken all the opportune precautions to establish in an authentic manner its nature and origin. He had engaged the Maltese sculptor Sigismondo Dimech (wrongly printed Diméol), who declared on 18 January 1829 before Notary Ignazio Molinos that the stone was very ancient and that by reason of its nature and the place where it was discovered it could have resisted the elements over many centuries. The notarial act was legalised on 28 January 1829 by the French Consul in Malta, Alexandre Duval, and it was carried to Paris by the chancellor M d'Aiguillé. On the 10 March 1829 it was in the possession of Marquis de Fortia.

This publication added that in Malta the stone had attracted the attention and excited the admiration of cultured persons, including M de Ribeaupierre, Strafford

Canning, all the English officers of the army and navy, and several foreign scholars who had seen it.[39] This seems to be a clear indication that Grognet was quite keen on showing off his "discovery".

In 1830 the first proper guide book was published in Malta by a Sienese writer Giuseppe Periccioúli Borzesi.[40] He wrote that in front of the Auberge de Provence (today the Museum of Archaeology in Republic Street, Valletta) there was the study of Grognet, adding that: "This very capable engineer preserves in lithography the form of a stone which is said to be antediluvian, found in Città Vecchia, and which he afterwards sent to Paris for trial of its antiquity." A Latin translation of the Atlantico-Phoenician inscription on the stone was then given, obviously supplied by Grognet himself, as no savant in Europe had yet succeeded to decipher it. On a human note the writer described Grognet as "a person of very agreeable manners, and the traveller will feel much pleased with his company and conversation".[41]

Not long after, probably in 1832, a second edition of the guide book contained a dissertation as an appendix entitled: *Che Malta, Comino e Gozo siano gli avanzi della antica Atlantide.* After quoting classics, which sited the old continent of Atlantis in the Mediterranean Sea, the writer stated that the stone discovered in 1826 was a precious monument, which placed the seal for ever on this vexed question. There can be no doubt that this unsigned dissertation was written (or at least inspired) by Grognet. Indeed, when he referred to the Latin translation of the inscription published in the first edition of the guide book, he added in a footnote that the interpretation made by the learned Baron Saci (*sic*) was not yet in hand, but he was informed it was only slightly different from that in the guide book, most probably it was Grognet, and not Borzesi, who was in constant correspondence with Baron de Sacy.[42] It is extremely likely that this second edition of the guide book was published at the instance of Grognet to enable him to publish the said dissertation to vindicate his stance on Atlantis and to prove that when it was completely submerged nothing remained except the summit of the mountain, namely, the Maltese islands.

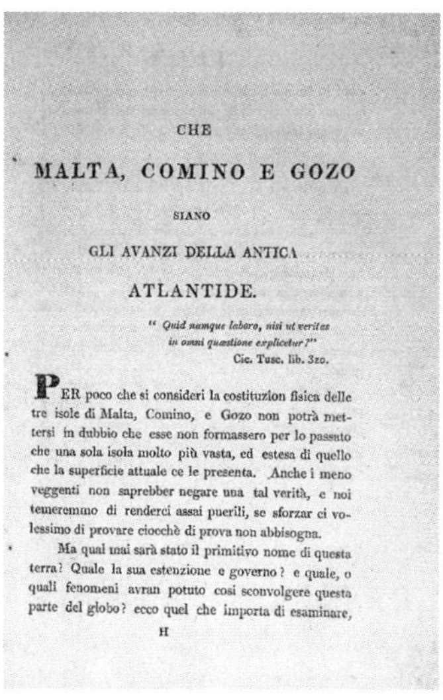

CHE

MALTA, COMINO E GOZO

SIANO

GLI AVANZI DELLA ANTICA

ATLANTIDE.

" *Quid namque laboro, nisi ut veritas in omni quæstione explicetur?*"
Cic. Tusc. lib. 3zo.

PER poco che si consideri la costituzion fisica delle tre isole di Malta, Comino, e Gozo non potrà mettersi in dubbio che esse non formassero per lo passato che una sola isola molto più vasta, ed estesa di quello che la superficie attuale ce le presenta. Anche i meno veggenti non saprebber negare una tal verità, e noi temeremmo di renderci assai puerili, se sforzar ci volessimo di provare ciocchè di prova non abbisogna.

Ma qual mai sarà stato il primitivo nome di questa terra? Quale la sua estenzione e governo? e quale, o quali fenomeni avran potuto così sconvolgere questa parte del globo? ecco quel che importa di esaminare,

H

"*Che Malta, Comino e Gozo siano gli avanzi della antica Atlantide*" in G Pericciuoli Borzesi, The historical guide of the Island of Malta and its Dependencies, Government Press, Malta, second edition c.1832. Image courtesy of the author. Photo Alberto Favaro.

In December 1831 De Fortia wrote to de Rienzi who had just returned from the East Indies and sent him through M Carmoli, a member of the Asiatic Society, eight different items, which included lithographs and printed papers on the Atlantic inscription. He confessed that up to the present he had no reason to doubt the truth of what Grognet had told him, but he wanted to know what de Rienzi had to tell him in this regard, after weighing all the circumstances and communicating with Grognet. He also brought up the subject of the manuscript on papyrus dealing with the history of Libya written by Eumalos of Cyrene (c. 330 BC) which de Rienzi had discovered at Djerba and had shown to Grognet in Malta in 1821.[43]

On 7 September 1832, de Rienzi sent a lengthy reply which was published in Paris in the same year.[44] He said he would not enter into details on the papyrus of Eumalos, for that is another story.[45] In regard to the lithograph of the bilingual inscription of Cyrene he thought it was pretty exact, but he wanted to make sure it was in order, without any interpolations or alterations. As he had left the original on deposit in 1822 with Grognet, "*homme fort instruit, mais d'une imagination fort déréglée*" (a very learned man but with a very disordered imagination), he had written twice to him, but had received no reply. De Rienzi forwarded to the Marquis a third letter to be passed on to Grognet, but he felt sure Grognet would not reply, in the same way he failed to reply to the other two letters. He had also failed to reply to a recent letter sent to him by the Marquis informing him of a conversation he had with de Rienzi regarding the fabrications de Rienzi was accusing him of. De Rienzi hoped that the publicity given to this story would at least serve to block the audacity of Grognet and prevent him from troubling any further the scholarly world with new mystifications.

De Rienzi wrote that, in one of the letters Grognet had addressed to the Marquis, "*l'habile M Grognet*" had expressed his belief that De Rienzi had perished in Oceania, and this thought had undoubtedly encouraged him to fabricate his story—"*son roman*". If Grognet were to return to him the text of the sixth book of Eumalos and the bilingual inscription he had deposited with him, he would pass them on to the Marquis in the interest of truth and to the satisfaction of the scholarly world de Fortia had so much at heart.

As to the 'famous' antique inscription allegedly found in Malta in 1826, notwithstanding the strange attestation of the consul Tiberius, de Rienzi could not refrain from pointing out how difficult it was for the stone to have survived for 4,130 years from the deluge of Ogygès, once it started deteriorating considerably after only three years in the possession of the Marquis himself. Besides, he believed in antediluvian fossils but not in antediluvian inscriptions.

In short, he considered Grognet to have played the unhappy role of a lesser Annius of Viterbo, who had fabricated books he had ascribed to the ancients, or of Sir John Mandeville who had publicly professed to have seen things that never existed, or even better the role of Antiphanes Bergoeus whose falsehoods had become proverbial. Scholars will surely be able to call an impudent forger and a clever impostor: a Grognet.[46]

De Rienzi ended his reply by asking the Marquis to forgive the sincere and somewhat crude thoughts he had entertained on a compatriot of the Marquis. Actually he was being very lenient as Grognet's conduct merited all his indignation, but love of the truth must be the guiding pen of a philosopher. He exhorted the Marquis to continue his scholarly lucubration, to distrust Grognet, to have the courage to continue researching and to connect the shreds of antiquity, in the hope that the history of past times would at last come to enlighten modern times.[47]

De Rienzi did not mince his words, which Marquis de Fortia must have felt as a dagger to his heart; he was the victim of Grognet in the same way OG Tychsen, the Rostock professor, had become the victim of Abate Giuseppe Vella four decades before.[48] Whether he replied to de Rienzi's libel is not known, but he closed his personal volume on *La Pierre Atlantique* with that document, thus laying a tombstone on the sad Grognet affair. Sad as it is, even for us Maltese, a historian cannot hide the truth. De Rienzi was proven right when at a later stage Grognet confessed he had fabricated the inscriptions on the Malta stone. He said he did so to create interest in the study of archaeology, especially concerning the real site of Atlantis.[49] If he wanted to create a tornado over the heads of European scholars he certainly succeeded, but it was eventually to engulf him.

This is the negative side of a man full of imagination and enthusiasm, but misdirected when dealing with a particular theme which became a fixed idea. His genius, however, bore fruit in other directions, which, so to say, redeemed his failing and whitewashed his past.

To start with, he was a man of great foresight. About 40 years before the opening of the Suez Canal, he wrote about the possibility of joining the Red Sea to the Mediterranean through a connecting canal. He also propounded the possibility that England could be joined to the Continent by means of an undersea tunnel. Bizarre as they may have been considered at the time, both dreams came true as one of his biographers had occasion to write: he was certainly a man of versatile talent. Another biographer wrote that Grognet was always preparing various highly impracticable schemes, such as, the enlarging of Valletta by filling in the Jews' Sallyport basin.[50]

Yet, among his intellectual pursuits, he deepened his research to prove his pet theory on Atlantis. In 1854 he published a preliminary treatise on the subject entitled *Epilogo dell'Atlantide—Compendio, ossia epilogo anticipato di un opera estesa sulla precisa situazione della famosa somersa Isola Atlantide, da Platone, e da altri antichi ricordata, e descritta, e della quale le Isole di Malta, Gozo e Comino sono certissimi resti: saggio archeologico, fisico, e filosoficao dell'Ingenere Architetto Giorgio Grognet.* To the long title he added his own attributes as follows: *Socio non residente dell'Accademia Celtica di Parigi, dell'Accademia Archeologica del Campidoglio di Roma, cioè in tempo della sua erezione, vale a dire nel 1810, e di altre scientifiche, e letterarie di Europa.*[51] The price of the book was 4s.2d. (just over 20c) obtainable from the printing press of FW Franz, Strada Forni 98, Valletta, or from the author himself at 14 Strada Alessandro (later renamed Strada Santa Margherita), Cospicua.[52]

His treatise was accompanied by a map (35 x 51.5 cm) entitled *Carta Idro-Geografica, ed Archeologica-Fisica*, made in 1840, purporting to show the site of Atlantis and other particulars connected therewith. Grognet was very adept at mapmaking. When he was serving Republican France he drew for the French government a plan of the harbour of Malta in 1800 with all its fortifications. It is entitled: *Plan Générale des Villes et Forts de Malte avec les Batteries Ennemies*, signed *George Grognet Maltais.* It is a highly detailed 'spy' map (75 x 125 cm) with a key to 179 place names, a decorative border and an emblem of the French Republic. After he came to Malta he drew another coloured plan of the harbour (50.5 x 71 cm) which is unsigned but which clearly follows the pattern of the signed 1800 map and all its details, with the introduction of the necessary changes. It is entitled: *Plan Général de la Ville Capitale de Malte* and has a key to 123 place names. The cropped watermark reads: CDMEA... 18... The map is undated; it was probably made around 1820 or 1830.[53] The

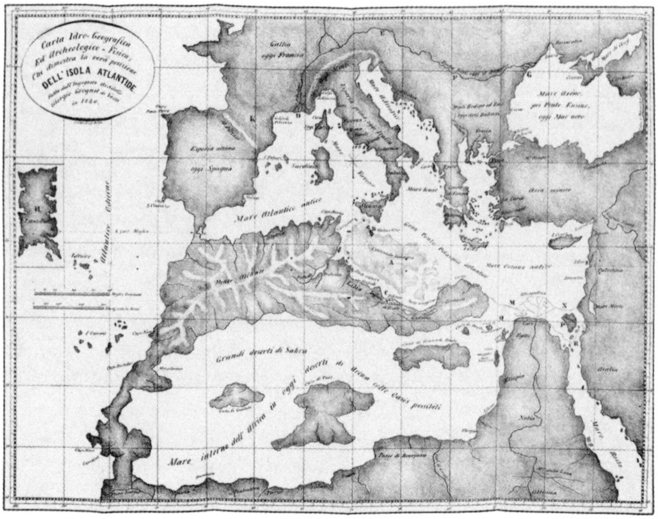

"Carta Idro-Geografica, ed Archeologica-Fisica", 1840, in Georges Grognet, *Epilogo dell'Atlantide*, 1854. Image courtesy of the National Library of Malta.

1854 treatise was a synopsis of the profound study on Atlantis which had dominated most of his life and which he had intended to publish. The manuscript, embellished with maps concerning Atlantis and many beautiful drawings, is preserved at the National Library in Valletta (Libr. Mss. 614 and 615). For the compilation of this *magnum opus* he researched 965 different authors extant in 17 libraries in Italy, France and Malta.[54] He was also planning to publish other books on civil and military architecture.

Grognet's crowning glory, however, is the construction of the imposing parish church at Mosta, which has a dome the third largest in the world. He conceived the idea of building a church modelled on the Pantheon perhaps even before he came back to Malta. The first stone was laid on 30 May 1833 but the church was completed when Grognet was an old, sick, man; he passed away on 5 September 1862 at the age of 88, comforted by the rites of Holy Mother Church. Leonard Mahoney wrote that in designing his church Grognet "had a chance to show his erudition and knowledge of scientific methods of calculation as against old methods based on experience and tradition".[55] His dome not only stood the test of time, but it remained completely indifferent when it was pierced by a 1,100-pound bomb on 9 April 1942, during the period of the worst assaults by German aircraft in World War Two. Both this bomb, and others that fell on other parts of the church, failed to explode.

Grognet's stone of antiquity has long since melted away and disappeared in the mists of time, but his Malta-stone sacred temple of religious worship will live forever.

1. Mahoney, L, *5000 years of architecture in Malta*, Malta: Valletta Publishing, 1996; pp. 318–319.

2. Schembri, CJ, "George Grongnet de Vassé—A great architect of Mosta Rotunda fame" in *Times of Malta*, 6 September 1962, p. 11. The present writer has taken the date of 19 February from the Parish records of the Collegiate Church of St Paul in Valletta, which date contradicts that shown on fig. 1.

3. Sammut, E, "A link with the Stuarts-In the margin of XVIII century art history" in *Times of Malta*, 13 July 1946, p. 5. Edward Sammut, "First centenary of Mosta Church—Grognet and his "Pantheon"" in *Times of Malta*, 22 August 1957, p. 5.

/ **4.** Galea, F, *Malta fdal Atlantis*, Zejtun: Palprint Press, 2002, p. 191.

/ **5.** Schembri, CJ, *Times of Malta*, p. 11.

/ **6.** Galea, F, *Malta fdal Atlantis*, p. 194, Mahoney, *5000 years of architecture in Malta*, pp. 318–319, Schembri, *Times of Malta*, p. 11. The quote regarding marquis de Fortia was taken from the lithograph of the Atlantico-Phoenician inscription described in fn. 23.

/ **7.** Schembri, CJ, *Times of Malta*, p. 11.

/ **8.** He came from Messina on board the *Madonna del Carmine*, described as a *Sciabecco Inglese*, after a voyage of three days (Register of Arrivals and Departures). cf. also A Camilleri, "Giorgio Grognet (1774–1862)—A national monument to an outstanding patriot" in *The Times* (Malta), 15 August 2000, p. 19.

/ **9.** Cleardo Naudi was born in Valletta on 3 June 1781 of Giovanni Battista Naudi and Maria Antonia daughter of Melchiorre Mamo. He was baptised on 4 June at St Paul's Collegiate Church and given the names *Antonius Cleardus Dominicus*. He received holy confirmation from the hands of the Archbishop Vincenzo Labini on 19 December 1787. On 15 October 1796 he was received into the Order of St John as *Cappellano d'Obbedienza*. He was devoted to his studies, graduated as a medical doctor in Naples, and attended three hospitals in London for over two years. He was appointed lecturer of Chemistry at the University of Malta on 1 June 1805 at 25 *scudi* (£25.15s. 0d. per annum) per month, and later one of the Presidents of the Maltese hospitals at 35 *scudi* per month. He translated works for the Protestant Bible and Missionary Societies and eventually in 1823 or 1824 formally became a Methodist. However, on 10 November 1827 he signed a solemn abjuration of his errors in abandoning the Roman Catholic faith in which he had been brought up. He died in the Catholic Church on 30 July 1837 assisted by the parish priest of Ħal Għaxaq, where his family originated from. He was survived by his wife and two children, to whom the government gave a gratuity of £100 in April 1839.

/ **10.** cf. *Travels and Adventures of the Rev. Joseph Wolff*, Macmillan and Co Ltd, ed, Edinburgh: R&R Clark Ltd, 1861, pp. 104–105.

/ **11.** Don Giuseppe Felice Galea was born in Senglea of Gioacchino and Filippa Galea. He was a Canon of the Cathedral Chapter. He died on 6 September 1849.

/ **12.** When Grognet copied the priest's letter to marquis de Fortia, he wrote: *Voila la Copie Conforme de la Lettre, que m'a Ecrit (*sic*) M. Galea de la Citté Vieille de Malte, par la quelle il me fait cadeau de la Pierre Atlantique trouvée par lui.* This copy is extant in a volume of manuscript and printed documents 1826–1832 assembled by the marquis de Fortia, with a manuscript title *Pièces relatives à la Pierre Atlantico-Phénicienne de Malte* and with a manuscript index. The volume measures 36.5x25 cm and smaller documents were inlaid on large paper to bring them to the size of the volume. This practice was also followed in the sixteenth century in Venice and Rome by publishers who assembled factice atlases, so-called "Lafreri Atlases", consisting of maps of varying sizes taken from stock available from time to time. This volume is in the present writer's collection. It was acquired by him in Paris in the 1970s.

/ **13.** Le marquis de Fortia, *Discours prononcé à la Société Asiatique, par M le Marquis de Fortia d'Urban le 7 Janvier 1828.* Extract from *Annales de la Littérature et des Arts*, 379e livraison, tome XXX, Paris: Trouvé et Compagnie, 1828, 1, fn. 1. (Copy in de Fortia's volume referred to in the previous footnote. It is listed no 4 in the index of contents. The volume has no pagination, and it has several blank pages).

/ **14.** Le marquis de Fortia, *Mémoire sur la langue phénicienne*, Paris: H Fournier, 1830, p. 47. (Copy in de Fortia's volume, index item no 10).

/ **15.** Le marquis de Fortia, *Mémoire sur la langue phénicienne*, also de Fortia, *Discours*, pp. 1–2.

/ **16.** Chaldean is the Aramaic vernacular that was the original language of some parts of the Bible and that superseded Hebrew among the Jews of Palestine and Babylon.

/ **17.** de Fortia, *Discours*, p. 5; (Second) *Discours composé pour la Société Asiatique, par M Le Marquis De Fortia D'Urban, séance du 4 Février 1828.* Extract from *Annales de la Littérature et des Arts*, 384e livraison, tome XXX, Paris: Trouvé et Compagnie, 1828, p. 12, fn. 3. (Copy in de Fortia's volume, index item no. 5). See also p. 5 of *Archéologie* mentioned in fn. 23.

/ **18.** de Rienzi, LD, *Questions importantes de manuscrits et inscriptions antiques. Réponses à M Le Marquis de Fortia d'Urban*, Paris 1832, p. 5. (Copy in de Fortia's volume, index item no 15). Also de Fortia, *Discours* 7.1. 1828, p. 5.

/ **19.** Copy of Grognet's letter in de Fortia's volume, index item no 3. Translation—The original of this letter is jealously preserved by me as a document which brings an epoch to an end and which proves my sole ownership of such a rare monument.

/ **20.** cf. infra.

/ **21.** Copy of Galea's letter dated 30 August 1827 to de Fortia. Index item no 3.

/ **22.** de Fortia's volume, index item no 2. No watermark or chainlines, but the paper is inlaid to bring it to the size of the volume. A reproduction of this lithograph was published in *Melita Historica*, 2004, XIV, I, p. 78, Malta 2005: Albert Ganado, "Bibliographical notes on Melitensia-2", pp. 67–93.

/ **23.** *M Grongnet, possesseur de l'inscription, en adressa d'abord une copie réduite à M de Fortia, qui desira en avoir une copie calquée sur la pierre, de manière à présenter aux yeux l'inscription telle qu'elle existe. Ce travail fut opéré; M de Fortia le fit lithographier : on peut le regarder comme le chef-d'œuvre de la lithographie de M Engelmann.* "Inscription Athlantico-Phénicienne" in *Archéologie*, Paris: Trouvé et Compagnie, 1829, p. 5. (Copy in de Fortia's volume, index item no 7).

/ **24.** This lithograph is bound immediately after the index, listed no 1 in the index. The paper is very clearly watermarked: *A COURTALIN.* No chain lines.

/ **25.** de Fortia, *Discours* 7.1.1828, pp. 1, 7.

/ **26.** de Fortia, *Discours* 4.2.1828, p. 1.

/ **27.** Extract of Henricus Hamaker's Prospectus of his "Dissertation sur les Antiquités phéniciennes" in *Journal général de littérature étrangère*, October 1827, p. 319.

/ **28.** In 1764 Jean-Jacques Barthélemy (1716–1795) recorded his considerations on some Phoenician monuments and the alphabets arising therefrom. Francisco Pérez Bayer, a Spanish scholar, dignitary canon of the church in Valencia, wrote a dissertation on the alphabet and language of the Phoenicians and their colonies. He had examined many medals and coins of Phoenician colonies in Sicily, Malta, and other places (de Fortia, *Mémoire*. pp. 26–29).

/ **29.** de Fortia, *Discours* 4.2.1828, pp. 12, 15. Giuseppe Cannolo was a knife grinder by profession, but he became well-versed in oriental and other languages. He was entrusted by the Church Missionary Society in Malta to translate into Maltese the Gospel of St John; it was printed in London in 1822 by R Watts: *Il Vangelo di Nostro Signore Gesù Cristo, secondo San Giovanni; tradotto in lingua italiana e maltese, seconda la volgata.* He made other translations of the Bible for the said Protestant society, but he remained always in the Catholic Church; indeed, he was in many respects a zealous Roman Catholic. He also wrote a Maltese grammar which seems to have been lost. Cannolo was born in Valletta of Gio Batta and Maria Cannolo. He was baptised at the Dominican parish church on 3 March, 1756, and named Giuseppe, Paolo, Calcedonio. He married Maria Antonia Azzopardi in the parish church of St Paul on 22 January 1809. In 1836, on the occasion of the election held by the *Comitato Generale Maltese* on a national scale, he signed as "Giuseppe Cannolo"; his name should not be spelt with one "n". When the Lutheran priest Christoph Friedrich Schlienz came to Malta on 22 February 1837, he described Cannolo as "an old man..., self-taught, and who, if not by the solidity, yet by the extensiveness of his oriental learning, excels almost all his countrymen". He wrote Maltese as it was spoken. (CF Schlienz, *Views on the improvement of the Maltese Language and its use for the purposes of education and literature*, Malta, 1838, pp. 38 and 46). As from 1808 he lived in a room at 130 (not 30) Strada Stretta (today's Strait Street), Valletta, leased by the Government at 12 *scudi* yearly. He died on 23 December 1845.

/ **30.** de Fortia, *Discours* 7.1.1828, pp. 5–6, and Grognet's text on the lithograph of the inscription, given further on.

/ **31.** In the same year when he was appointed Professor of Theology at Halle, Gesenius composed an early work on the Maltese language, published in 1810 at Leipzig (xvi, 78 pp.). This famous Hebrew scholar was the first to determine correctly that Maltese was an Arabic dialect, and that it was not derived from the Phoenician language later influenced by Arabic, as Michele Antonio Vassalli (1764–1829) argued in 1791, and after him Jo. Joachim Bellermann in 1809 in *Phoeniciae Linguae vestigiorum in Melitensi Specimen I.* The notion that Maltese was Arabic, however, goes much further back. Indeed, the Maltese historiographer Giovanni Francesco Abela (*Malta Illustrata*, Malta: Paolo Bonacota, 1647, pp. 257–258) had written that Maltese was very similar to Chaldee and Hebrew because it was the same as Arabic (*é il medesimo con l'Arabico*). Both Grognet and de Fortia, however, like many other subsequent writers, stuck to Vassalli's theory.

/ **32.** *Archéologie*, p. 5; de Fortia, *Mémoire*, p. 48; de Rienzi, *Questions*, p. 5.

/ **33.** *Je croix celle que m'a donnée M. Le baron Silvestre de Sacy plus exacte*, de Fortia, *Mémoire*, p. 48. Hamaker's *Miscellanea Phoenicia, sive commentarii de rebus phoenicum* (x + 368 pp) was published by Luchtmans.

/ **34.** The lithograph of this bilingual inscription is index item no 8, bound in de Fortia's volume after the pamphlet *Archéologie*. The paper's watermark is the number 52 and the chainlines are 25 mm wide. The paper is slightly thinner than that of the Atlantico-Phoenician inscription lithograph.

/ **35.** The lithograph with de Sacy's translation is index item no 9, bound after that with the bilingual inscription. It measures 25x21 cm, but it has been cropped; what remains is a flower with five petals in the form of a fleur-de-lis. No chainlines.

/ **36.** de Fortia, *Mémoire*, 47.

/ **37.** In his letter Marini was referring to Giuseppe Mezzofanti (1774–1849), who took sacred orders in 1797, became Librarian at the Vatican in 1833 and Cardinal in 1838. The mention of Monsieur Valeriani might refer to the scholar Domenico Valeriani.

/ **38.** "Extrait d'une lettre de M. Frédéric Marini, adressée à M Le Marquis De Fortia d'Urban, Florence, 27 novembre 1828" in *Annales de la Littérature et des Arts*, 430e livraison, tome XXXIV, Paris: Trouvé et Compagnie, [1829 ?], pp. 1–2, pp. 5–7. Also *Archéologie*, p. 3.

/ **39.** *Archéologie*, p. 4.

/ **40.** Pericciuoli Borzesi, G, *The historical guide of the Island of Malta and its Dependencies*, Malta: Government Press, 1830.

/ **41.** Pericciuoli Borzesi, G,*The historical guide of the Island of Malta and its Dependencies*, pp. 48–50

/ **42.** Pericciuoli Borzesi, G, 2nd edn; Appendix, 7, fn. 1. cf. Ganado, 73–79, for references to Grognet's Atlantis in the guide book. The Rev. GN Godwin (*A guide to the Maltese Islands*, Malta: Paolo Bonavia, 1880, II) thought the Appendix was written by Borzesi simply because it was published in his guide book.

/ **43.** *Copie d'une lettre de Mr le Marquis de Fortia à Mr Domeny de Rienzi*. Ms. Index item no 11.

/ **44.** de Rienzi, *Questions*, quoted in fn.18.

/ **45.** There is a quote from Eumalos in the dissertation on Atlantis published in Pericciuoli Borzesi's guide book, 2nd edn., p. 13, fn.1.

/ **46.** *Les savans pourront bientôt dire d'un fabricateur impudent et d'un adroit imposteur: il "Grognète"*. Annius of Viterbo, or Giovanni Nanni (1432–1502) was a celebrated Dominican friar. Sir John Mandeville was probably a pseudonym for Jean de Bourgogne (c. 1300–1372), a knight, born and bred in England, of the town of St Albans. His "Travels", for the most part fictitious, were written in Latin and translated in ten languages; some 300 manuscript accounts are said to have survived.

/ **47.** de Rienzi, *Questions*, pp. 3, 5–8. De Rienzi was an orientalist scholar and traveller who amassed a huge collection of antiquities of all kinds from Eastern Europe, Asia, Africa, the two Americas and Oceania. But what he had collected during twenty years was lost when he was robbed during his travels in the East. However, by 1832, 97 precious objects of antiquity passed into the hands of the French government to be distributed among various museums (*Questions*, p. 7, fn. 3).

/ **48.** Dessoulavy, CL, "Vassalli and the Vella case" in *Journal of Maltese Studies—Essays on Mikiel Anton Vassalli*, O. Friggieri, ed, nos 23–24, 1993, pp. 31–33, reproduced from *The Sundial*, ii, March 1936; pp. 404–407.

/ **49.** Aquilina, J, "Gallery of distinguished Maltese—Giorgio Grognet de Vassé (1774–1862)" in *Times of Malta*, 24 January 1978, p. 5.

/ **50.** *L'Arte*, I, 4 (7 Gennaio 1863), p. 4; EB Vella, *Storja tal-Mosta bil-Knisja taghha*, Malta: Empire Press, 1930, p. 208; E Sammut, *Times of Malta*, 22.8.1957.

/ **51.** In this book he published a Sonetto by Giuseppe Pericciuoli Borzesi, *In lode delle Isole di Malta, quale certo superstite frammento della già sommersa isola Atlantide*. This shows the close association that existed between the author of the guide book and Grognet.

/ **52.** This information was given on the original cover of the book still preserved in a copy in the present writer's collection. Very often these covers were removed when the books were bound.

/ **53.** This map belonged to the present writer's collection; it now forms part of the Albert Ganado Map Collection at the Museum of Fine Arts, Valletta, Malta. Other maps by Grognet extant in Malta are: the entrance to a fortification at La Spezia (Italy) dated 1810; two celestial planispheres; geological map of Malta; Malta from the sea; copy of a chart made by the Venetian navigator Andrea Bianco in 1436.

/ **54.** This is the manuscript title of Grognet's treatise: *L'Atlantide ossia che la famosa Isola Atlantide da Platone, e da altri antichi, e moderni ricordata, non è da ricercarsi altrove, se non nella situazione delle isole di Malta, Comino e Gozzo, della quale sono i resti. Saggio Archeologico—Fisico—e Filosofico dell'Ingegnere Architetto Giorgio Grognet di Vassé... In cui si da un altro saggio sulla Lingua Fenico-Atlanta, i di cui preziosi resti solamente si rimangono nella lingua maltese ; il che forma la seconda parte del presente Trattato. Originale autografo terminato in Malta nell'anno MDCCCLIIII doppo 48 anni di studio.*

/ **55.** Mahoney, L, *5000 years of architecture in Malta*, pp. 318–319.

FUNCTIONS, ORIGINS AND ORNAMENT ACCORDING TO LOUIS SULLIVAN

Claude Massu

In his book *The Autobiography of an Idea*, 1924, the architect Louis Henry Sullivan fiercely condemned the spectacle of the World's Columbian Exhibition of 1893 in Chicago.[1] In his eyes, this event represented all the flaws, all the confusion and the lack of perspective that the architecture of the United States in his day suffered from. It was the anti-model above all else and, according to Sullivan, this peculiar situation was simply the symptom of a far more widespread problem, that of a disconnection between architecture and the reality of American life at the end of the nineteenth century. When speaking about this subject in his *Kindergarten Chats*, 1901–1902, Sullivan resorted to medical vocabulary, using terms such as virus and pathology.[2]

In every architectural theory, there is in principle a diagnosis of what is in existence, a denunciation, a rejection. On the basis of this observation a reasoned solution can be proposed. That is exactly what Louis Sullivan set out to do in his written work when, from 1900 onwards, commissions became rarer and he was faced with a period of forced leisure that he could use for writing.

Influenced by Mr Clopet, the mathematics teacher whom he met in Paris during his brief time at the Ecole des Beaux-Arts, Sullivan defined his way of thinking as following scientific methods, yet that does not mean that it lacked all mythical dimension. In fact, in his quest for a rehabilitated architecture, Sullivan developed a mythical discourse that was very powerful, with which he later influenced future generations and in particular the questions that preoccupied the modernist historians who succeeded him.

FUNCTIONALISMS

In his analysis, Sullivan essentially turned to the natural sciences: biology, paleontology, botany, zoology. He believed that the regeneration of architecture implied the study and understanding of Nature's processes. This is why natural sciences were so important for Sullivan, as they provided him with explanations on the way that Nature functioned.

The sale of Louis Sullivan's library has made it possible to identify better the intellectual sources of the architect's theories, and in particular of the main thrust of Louis Sullivan's theory that was based on the idea of functionalism. For Sullivan, as he underlined in his article published in 1896 *The Tall Office Building Artistically Considered*, all reality is considered in terms of the relationship between form and function: "It is the pervading law of all things organic and inorganic, of all things physical and metaphysical, of all things human and all things superhuman, of all true manifestations of the head, of the heart, of the soul, that life is recognisable in its expression, that form ever follows function. This is the law."[3]

Function is everything, and all function aspires to find the appropriate form. "Form Follows Function" is one of the most famous expressions, but also one of the most misinterpreted, in the history of contemporary architecture. The phrase is taken from the writings of the American sculptor and theoretician Horatio Greenough. It is the famous axiom on which the intellectual autobiography of Sullivan *The Autobiography of an Idea*, focuses. Beneath the striking effect of the expression, enhanced by the alliterations, is concealed a complex, contradictory and somewhat mythical line of thought. Functionalist thinking allowed Sullivan to break away from ordinary rules, conventions, traditions, even superstitions and to establish architecture on a new basis.

Contrary to the position later defended in the 1920s and 1930s by the members of the International Congress of Modern Architecture (CIAM) and the architects of the Modern Movement, according to Louis Sullivan, functions were not of a technical or a sociological nature. Their meaning is biological. Form depends on a process of internal evolution. "The pressure we call Function: the resultant, Form."[4]

Functions are complex and varied in nature. They can be subjective and derive from the creative spirit of the architect when he follows his most primal and most noble instincts, those governed by emotion and intuition rather than by reason. They can be shared. In this latter case, it is society as a whole that is the function, the vital principle that aspires to find a form. Society is often considered as an organism and the role of the architect is then to bring form to this spirit, to this energy.

This is where it becomes clear that numerous themes taken from the poetry of Walt Whitman have contributed to Sullivan's ideas. Walt Whitman, the author of *Leaves of Grass*, had nine editions of his book published between 1855 and 1892 that is during Sullivan's lifetime. He contrasted European feudalism and American democracy and Louis Sullivan adopted this dialectic developed by Whitman amongst other ideas, in his *Democratic Vistas* published in 1871. Here he describes the originality of the American nation which lies in the realisation of a democratic civilisation based on a community of equal, free and enterprising individuals. For Sullivan, the existing forms of architectural eclecticism in America brought to the United States an art of building that was fundamentally authoritarian and foreign to its native culture. Organic architecture, on the other hand, aims to bring life and manifest a continually evolving democracy. It is a political function that aspires to find its form: "a certain function, an aspirant democracy, is seeking a certain form of expression, democratic architecture—& will surely find it".[5] The heroic nature of Sullivan's self-professed mission is to express, through architecture, the forces operating in contemporary society.

In this approach to the social and political role of the artist, Sullivan also draws on literary knowledge including authors both American (Ralph Waldo Emerson and the Transcendentalists) and European. The writings of Hippolyte Taine, in particular his *Philosophie de l'Art*, 1882, from which he understood the importance of the cultural context in the analysis of architecture, profoundly influenced Louis Sullivan's thinking.

SCIENTIFIC KNOWLEDGE IN THE NINETEENTH CENTURY AND ARCHITECTURAL FUNCTIONALISM

Architecture has to adapt to the functions of the present. The key word is adaptation. The law of evolution also applies to architecture or, in any case, should apply to it: "In Darwin he found much food. The Theory of Evolution seemed stupendous."[6] The natural sciences of the nineteenth century are the great models and the great references of the architectural theory of Louis Sullivan, as illustrated in the enthusiasm expressed in this extract from *The Autobiography of an Idea*.

Functions exist but they can be concealed or misinterpreted. Sullivan supported the idea that the external aspect of things reflects internal qualities and functions that can be invisible to the naked eye. He claimed "the scientific method of approach to that which lay behind appearances".[7]

Sullivan was also strongly influenced by the ideas of the physiognomist Johann Kaspar Lavater (1741–1801) who stated that physical features could reveal the hidden reality of a person.[8] The outer form is the reflection and the symbol of the character of the essential nature of things and beings. This conception may have resulted in a theory of harmony and of the body/soul unity. In his autobiography, Sullivan often describes the faces of the people he met and this insistence is symptomatic.

The capacity to judge from appearances can also apply to architecture; a building can reveal the personality of its creator. In the chapter entitled "An Oasis" in his *Kindergarten Chats*, Sullivan expresses his admiration for the Marshall Field Wholesale Store by Henry Hobson Richardson, 1885: "here is a *man* for you to look at".[9] By analogy, the building identifies the creator. In the same way, Louis Sullivan recounts how he noticed a residential apartment building designed by the Furness & Hewitt agency of Philadelphia for which he was going to work. He then adds, speaking about himself: "he had an instinctive sense of physiognomy".[10] Sullivan's interest in physiognomy shows up in other pages of his autobiography.[11]

This analogy between the building and the face is informed by a relatively anthropomorphic conception of architecture that the historian Vincent Scully clearly put into perspective, for example in *Modern Architecture* or in *Architecture The Natural and the Manmade*.[12] Moreover, Louis Sullivan had worked for some time in Philadelphia for Frank Furness whose architecture displays a muscularity composed of tensions and precarious balance. The main entrance of the Auditorium Building, 1889, in Chicago illustrates this influence. Up to a point, Sullivan's architectural functionalism suggests the body/building analogy.

The writings of the paleontologist Georges Cuvier are another source of Louis Sullivan's functionalism. From the works of the founder of comparative anatomy, Sullivan adopted the functionalist theory. The function that determines the form of the animal is inside and is invisible. The forms—that is the organs—are not visible. From this point of view, Cuvier disagrees with Lavater. However Sullivan produced a kind of synthesis of the two points of view by taking external appearances to reflect internal qualities and functions that are invisible.

Another important reference in the thinking of Louis Sullivan was Herbert Spencer who Sullivan mentions in a page of his autobiography.[13] The architect pays homage to the theorist of the progression from homogeneous to heterogeneous, of the universe as living organism subject to the law of increasing complexity. For Herbert Spencer, the development of organic life and the development of social life are just the two aspects of the same process: evolution. Creativity is a natural process subject to the laws of nature.

Louis Sullivan, Auditorium Building, Chicago, 1889.

THE MYTHICAL ORIGINS OF ARCHITECTURE

Here we come to the crux of the question concerning the origins of architecture. How, according to Sullivan, did architecture originate? In chapters 37 and 38 of his *Kindergarten Chats* he considered the question. Sullivan started with what he considered to be the fundamental elements of architecture. First there is "the pier", which is the balance between an upward thrust (aspiration, life) and a downward pressure (earth, death). The pillar is, in a certain sense, metaphorically perceived as a plant, a living organism. The second vital element of architecture is "the lintel". Associated with the pier, the lintel produces the simplest and most natural form of architecture: trabeation or the post and beam system. Sullivan gave no precise example of this form which is at the origin of architecture, but one could imagine that the megalithic sites of the island of Malta or Stonehenge in England might represent for him the beginnings of architecture. One can see, in this interpretation of the origins of architecture, the influence of Hegel.

Despite its apparent simplicity, this form based on column and lintel has been subject to great variations, as illustrated in the history of architecture, and in particular in the architectural works of the Assyrians, Egyptians and Greeks. The vocabulary used by Sullivan, on the other hand, to evoke the beginnings of architecture is taken from natural sciences. The origin of architecture is a question of birth and growth. The third fundamental element of architecture is "the arch". Louis Sullivan does not give any details about the shape of this arch, not specifying whether it is a semi-circular, equilateral or corbel arch. These three elements or these

Louis Sullivan, Getty Mausoleum, Graceland Cemetery, Chicago, 1890.

three essential forms (that is, the pier, the lintel and the arch) give rise to two possible combinations: two piers plus a lintel, or the arch by itself. Such are the origins of architecture, whose place and time of emergence Sullivan admits to being unable to specify. Consequently we find ourselves in the arena of mythical representation.

What remains is to observe form with a view to identifying the function it is supposed to fulfill using the inductive method. In both cases, the primitive forms "evidently derive from the single function SPAN."[14] At the origins of architecture, there is therefore the "spanning" function. In his autobiography, when speaking of two structures under construction in his day, Sullivan in fact emphasises his fascination for bridges, "the idea of spanning a void appealed to him as masterful in thought and deed".[15] For Louis Sullivan, the origins of architecture are therefore devoid of all symbolic connotations or of practical considerations.

ORNAMENT AND THE MYTH OF THE DEMIURGIC ARCHITECT

The issue of ornament, for Sullivan, brings questions connected to his functionalist theories to the fore. Inspired by the book of Owen Jones, The *Grammar of Ornament*, 1856, among other things, Sullivan favoured a two-dimensional conception of ornament, both inside and outside his buildings. The ornaments of the inner spaces, like those for example in the Auditorium Building or in the banks designed at the end of his career, are maybe the most significant. The meaning of his ornament, however, is unclear to say the least. In an article published in 1956, Philip Johnson had already brought up the question of the role of ornament in Sullivan's work, underlining that this subject remained, and quite rightly so, an enigma.[16]

In his treatise published in 1924 entitled *A System of Architectural Ornament According with a Philosophy of Man's Powers*, Sullivan puts forward a global conception of ornament: Man is a creator and a 'master craftsman'; he is endowed with a creative power that is a natural faculty. In order to create, man must therefore be at one with the workings of nature. Sullivan classifies these creative gifts in a series of typologies. They can be physical, intellectual, emotional, moral or spiritual.

Sullivan wanted to bring life to inert matter. If the architect is a creator who works using organic processes and the building itself is a living organism, then the demiurgic aspect must be present in his conception of ornament. If one listens to the theories of the architect himself, this is perhaps the meaning that should be given to the ornament of his buildings.

Ornament is therefore for Sullivan a metaphoric representation of organic processes existing in nature, in particular in botany. He defines the germ as the source of this vital energy that will develop and finally reach its full formal expression.

As far as ornamental figures are concerned, geometric forms are receptacles of energy. Lines are lines of energy generating primary and secondary axes. Sullivan's ornament creates a burst of life, energy radiating from a centre to the periphery or from the periphery towards the centre. Balance is to be found between the axes. Life is a permanent flow that manifests itself in an infinite multitude of forms. The doctrine of parallelism completes this vitalist theory of decoration.

Sullivan did not have a rationalist or structural conception nor did he have practical experience of ornament. His ornament is not conceived as an enhancement of the structure. From this point of view, a comparison between the Wainwright Building in Saint Louis, 1890–1891, and the Guaranty Building in Buffalo, 1895–1896, is instructive since it demonstrates no new conception. In 1949, Frank Lloyd Wright in *Genius and the Mobocracy* rightly points out that Sullivan did not have the feel for the nature of materials. With Sullivan, patterns were the same whatever material was used: terracotta, bronze, cast iron. In fact, as the historian Peter Collins wrote in his book *Changing Ideals in Modern Architecture 1750–1950* Sullivan was "an ornamentalist".[17] Sullivan considered himself a follower of Ruskinian thinking, which he believed represented a kind of high point. According to Peter Collins, Louis Sullivan is "the culminator of Ruskinism".[18]

Having been long disregarded by mainstream modernism, the decorative dimension of Sullivan's architecture has now become the object of multifarious analyses and interpretations. This is the result of the book of the photographer John Szarkowski *The Idea of Louis Sullivan* that was the first in the 1950s to recognise the importance of decoration in Sullivan's work.[19] The duality of the department store Carson Pirie & Scott, 1900, divided between the decorations of the lower part and the regular organisation of the facades of the upper levels, sums up the aesthetic ambivalence of Sullivan.

Louis Sullivan, Carson Pirie & Scott building, Chicago, 1900.

LIMITS OF THE MYTH

The biological analogy that flowered in the nineteenth century was denounced by Geoffrey Scott who, in *The Architecture of Humanism*, 1914, speaks of this "fallacy" that leads to distorted views and is likened to an error.[20] This is a myth repeated by Peter Collins in *Changing Ideals in Modern Architecture 1750–1950* (it induces a historigraphic model in terms of a necessary sequence, contunuity and projection). John Summerson, in *Heavenly Mansions and Other Essays* echoes the criticism, also denouncing these founding myths of new modern architecture.[21]

What connection is there between this founding myth of architecture and the buildings built by Sullivan? Not much in fact. The so-called functionalism of some skyscrapers is still to be demonstrated. His buildings do not correspond to his theory. In the article previously quoted, Philip Johnson questions the functionalism of Louis Sullivan and expresses his skepticism in this respect. He explains that Sullivan has not always been coherent within his doctrine, in particular regarding the vertical divisions of office buildings.

In fact the architecture of Sullivan is not faithful to the principles of functionalism, but instead reinforces the myth of the so-called innovator. It can be said that Sullivan managed, whether consciously or not, to build his own myth of the artist who is misunderstood and rejected. Modernist historians reiterated the criticisms, not to say the imprecations regarding the eclectic architecture of the United States in the nineteenth century expressed by the master of Chicago. His pseudo-prophetic judgment on the 1893 Exhibition, written in 1922, left a deep impression and was more or less accepted as such until the 1960s. The writer Thomas Carlyle, apostle of the hero cult in *Heroes and Hero-Worship*, 1841, is mentioned in the autobiography of the architect.[22] Louis Sullivan was influenced by his ideas and saw himself as the solitary prophet ahead of his time. The historian Hugh Morrison, with his book *Louis Sullivan Prophet of Modern Architecture*, 1935, had confirmed this myth by granting him the prestige of academic recognition.[23]

Yet above all, Louis Sullivan put forward a mythical and romantic vision of American society which was in fact at odds with the concrete realities of economic and social demands at the turn of the twentieth century. It is strange to think that for a disciple of Ralph Waldo Emerson, Louis Sullivan took little interest in the individual house as the expression of a creative and free individuality. Likewise, he built no public or institutional buildings. Sullivan was only interested in the impersonal and anonymous general forces that propelled American society of his time, and of which the Chicago of the time presented a turbulent picture. As from 1900, Sullivan became marginalised and this ostracism seemed to prove the inappropriateness of his theories. The pragmatism of Daniel H Burnham, who adapted and acknowledged the new industrial and financial conditions of architectural and urban development, was, on the other hand, in opposition to the intransigence and bitterness of Sullivan. Wrapped up in his own preoccupations and trapped by his imprecatory views and his mythical representations, Sullivan failed to understand the new forces in the American society of his time. He could not see the tensions, the unfairness and the divisions that plagued contemporary American democracy. His vision was limited to a literary approach.

/ **1.** Sullivan, L, *The Autobiography of an Idea*, New York: Dover, 1956 (1st ed 1924), p. 317 ff.
/ **2.** Sullivan, L, *Kindergarten Chats and other writings*, New York: Wittenborn, 1947.
/ **3.** Sullivan, L, "The tall office building artistically considered" in *Lippincott's Magazine*, March 1896.
/ **4.** Sullivan, L, *Kindergarten Chats*, p. 48.
/ **5.** Sullivan, L, *Kindergarten Chats*, p. 99.
/ **6.** Sullivan, L, *The Autobiography of an Idea*, pp. 254–255.
/ **7.** Sullivan, L, *The Autobiography of an Idea*, p. 250.
/ **8.** On this subject cf. M Pollack, "Sullivan and the Orders of Architecture" in J Zukowsky, ed, *Chicago Architecture 1872–1922*, Munich: Prestel-Verlag, 1987, pp. 251–266.
/ **9.** Sullivan, L, *Kindergarten Chats*, p. 29.
/ **10.** Sullivan, L, *The Autobiography of an Idea*, p. 191.
/ **11.** Sullivan, L, *The Autobiography of an Idea*, pp. 217, 218, 291, for example.
/ **12.** See V Scully, *Modern Architecture*, Braziller, New York, 1961 and *Architecture. The Natural and the Manmade*, New York: St Martin's Press, 1991.
/ **13.** Sullivan, L, *The Autobiography of an Idea*, p. 255.
/ **14.** Sullivan, L, *Kindergarten Chats*, p. 125.
/ **15.** Sullivan, L, *The Autobiography of an Idea*, p. 249.
/ **16.** Johnson, P, "Is Sullivan the Father of Functionalism?" in *Art News*, LV, December 1956. Reproduced in P Johnson, *Writings*, New York: Oxford University Press, 1979, pp. 183–186.
/ **17.** Collins, P, *Changing Ideals in Modern Architecture 1750–1950*, Montreal: MacGill University Press, 1965, p. 116.
/ **18.** Collins, P, *Changing Ideals in Modern Architecture 1750–1950*, p. 115.
/ **19.** See J Szarkowsky, *The Idea of Louis Sullivan*, Minneapolis: University of Minnesota Press, 1956.
/ **20.** Scott, G, *The Architecture of Humanism*, New York: Norton, 1999, (1st ed 1914), pp. 127 ff.
/ **21.** See J Summerson, *Heavenly Mansions and other Essays on Architecture*, New York: Norton, 1963.
/ **22.** Sullivan, L, *The Autobiography of an Idea*, p. 209.
/ **23.** Morrison, H, *Louis Sullivan. Prophet of Modern Architecture*, New York, The Museum of Modern Art and WW Norton and Company, 1935.

All illustrations courtesy of Claude Massu.

LE CORBUSIER

TOWARDS THE ORIGINS OF ARCHITECTURE

Henry D Fernandez

Dedicated to the memory of Jerzy Soltan
(6 March 1913–16 September 2005)

Throughout his career Le Corbusier understood, as the title of one of his books suggests, every architect's need for *L'Atelier de la recherche patiente*—"a workshop for patient search", whereby designers could fully comprehend the timeless progress of art and architecture.[1] For Le Corbusier this search began when he was still the boy Charles-Edouard Jeanneret-Gris in La Chaux-de-Fonds in Switzerland. He was fascinated by nature and the idea of quixotic search and displayed a special talent for recording his observations.[2] Eventually, through a number of significant episodes, including travel far beyond his hometown, this youthful search would evolve into his passion for architecture. However, the adult Le Corbusier never relinquished his obsession with exploring and defining the intersection between man, nature and the resultant origins of architecture, which becomes apparent when examining some of the defining moments in Le Corbusier's "patient search".

On 29 July 1933, a cruise sponsored by the *Congrès Internationaux d'Architecture Moderne* left Marseille on an adventure through the Mediterranean, visiting the formal congress site at Athens and a variety of ancient sites including several Neolithic ruins at Gozo, Khirokitia, and the Cycladic Islands.[3] Le Corbusier recounts some of these excursions away from the confines of their shipboard meetings, "The respite granted to its members gives them an opportunity for personal contacts presided over by a thrilling architecture and nature, on the Acropolis in Athens, at Delphi or at Delos, at Olympia or in the Cyclades."[4] The largest national group

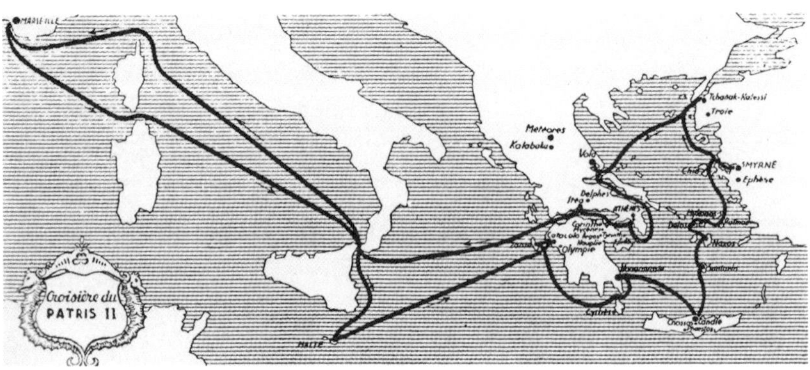

Map of the itinerary of the SS Patris II in the Mediterranean in 1933, in *Le Corbusier et la Méditerranée*, Editions Parenthèses, Marseille, 1987, p. 65.

aboard the SS *Patris II*, a converted English collier, was the Swiss delegation, which included Le Corbusier and Sigfried Giedion, the CIAM's first secretary-general.[5] On board were many of the leading figures of the Modern Movement such as László Moholy-Nagy, Walter Gropius, Richard Neutra, Alvar Aalto, Otto Neurath, Christian Zervos, Fernand Léger, as well as a few scientists and some art historians that included Sigfried's wife Carola Giedion-Welcker.[6]

left/ Le Corbusier and Gideion on the SS Patris II, 1933; **right/** Aalto, Neurath and Maholy-Nagy on the SS Patris II, 1933. Images courtesy of the gta ARCHIV, ETH Zurich.

While the *Patris II* may have been short on space, the close contact between the CIAM's participants made for an engaging meeting environment, recalled by Le Corbusier, "That cruise ship was turned into meeting rooms, committee rooms, and secretarial offices. There was only one sound: the hissing and splashing of water along the hull; there was only one atmosphere: youthfulness, trust, modesty, and professional conscience. After those two weeks of fervent work, a precious result: The Athens Charter."[7]

15 years later, in 1948, the start of this historic voyage would be recounted in Paris by Le Corbusier to one of his office colleagues, Jerzy Soltan. Soltan remembered Le Corbusier saying to him, "In the heat of the summer of 1933 we launched ourselves into the ancient waters of the Mediterranean, like Ulysses on his odyssey."[8]

Le Corbusier framed this trip, as he had other voyages in his youth, with reference to the exploits of great epic heroes in history, an interest in mythology that can be traced back to his school days in La Chaux-de-Fonds. As Paul Turner points out, "... when Jeanneret was 16, a prize-book [inscribed 1903], was given to him by the Art School—Maxime Collignon's *Mythologie figurée de la Grèce....*"[9]

Maxime Collignon's volume is a kind of text book of Greek mythology, illustrated by line-drawings, a book designed for art students, one that may have inspired the young Jeanneret to look beyond the Jura to the warmer climate of the Mediterranean.[10] As Turner points out, "he did a sketch (left in the pages of the book), which transformed a Greek coin illustrated in the work, into a decorative device picturing a pine tree, that ubiquitous Jura motif of these years...."[11] The training the 16 year old was undergoing as a designer entailed careful recording of his observations using different media, skills that Jeanneret had practised since his childhood in La Chaux-de-Fonds in Switzerland.[12] As a boy his study of nature, under the tutelage of his teacher Charles L'Eplattenier, instilled him with a profound respect and understanding of a deeper structure and order in all natural things.[13] There in the Jura Mountains he had simultaneously cultivated a serious interest in geometry and an ability to render any natural phenomena into a geometric abstraction.[14] His now famous engraved watchcase design, exhibited at the Decorative Arts Exposition at Turn in 1902 and the International Exhibition of Decorative Arts at Milan in 1906, is an example of his natural artistic gifts, talents that the teenage Jeanneret would demonstrate again in his involvement with his first architectural project, the Villa Fallet at La Chaux-de-Fonds in 1906–1907.[15] The funneling of Jeanneret's design-related interests into architecture, and his subsequent involvement in the design of the Villa Fallet was facilitated by L'Eplattenier's reconfiguration of the local Art School's curriculum. In 1905 Jeanneret's teacher instituted a programme called "*Cours Supérieur d'Art et de Décoration*", that included projects in architecture and interior design.[16] This new programme proved to be a pivotal moment in Jeanneret's career trajectory. Without it Jeanneret, like many of his fellow students, might well have stayed in La Chaux-de-Fonds for the rest of his life as a watchcase engraver.

Through L'Eplattenier's course and the professional guidance of a local supervising architect, René Chapallaz, Jeanneret was able to bring his developing sense of composition, expressed through his increasingly sophisticated command of abstraction, to fruition in the shape of a building at the Villa Fallet. Many of the details that grace the Villa Fallet attest to Jeanneret's skills in abstracting natural phenomena. One among many examples can be observed in the eave details on the west elevation of the Villa Fallet, the side exposed to the afternoon sun. Recalling the state of melting icicles on the eaves of any house on the Pouillerel Slope above the town, Jeanneret studied their jagged profile and emulated them through his transcription of an abstract pattern of icicles to the profile of the wooden eave of the Villa Fallet. With his first building experience behind him, Jeanneret would now embark on the first of his travels.

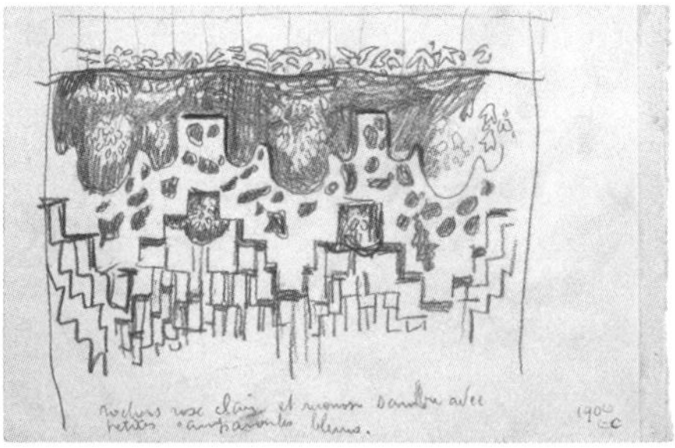

left/ Le Corbusier, *Etudes d'éléments décoratifs*, 1906. Dessin FLC 5811; **right/** Watchcase drawn and engraved by Charles-Édouard Jeanneret at the art-school. All © FLC/ADAGP.

Looking back to these early years Le Corbusier would recall the excitement of his first excursion to Italy in 1907, a trip that cast him into the "sun-drenched Mediterranean", whetting his appetite for travel, or as Soltan would remember Le Corbusier saying, "trekking through the wilderness of time, in search of the origins of architecture."[17] Throughout these travels in 1907, which included northern Italy, the young Jeanneret would perhaps unconsciously, gravitate towards buildings and situations that were familiar to him from his education, training and experience as a designer in La Chaux-de-Fonds. The Monastery of Ema at Galuzzo outside of Florence would hold a special interest for Jeanneret. Later, as Le Corbusier, he would recount how he again visited this Carthusian Monastery, a hillside building site, in 1911.[18] Fresh back from his exotic travels in 1908 Jeanneret, now a rapidly developing young architect in his home town, was acquiring the skills to transcribe his personal abstract expression and representation of Nature into a series of building designs, all on hilly terrains, which included his Villa Stotzer and Villa Jaquemet, both designed in 1908.

In May 1911 Jeanneret set off on what he would come to call his "*Voyage d'Orient*". He was accompanied by a graduate student in art history whom he had met in Berlin named August Klipstein (1885–1951), who proposed including Istanbul and Athens on their itinerary. They traveled from Italy to Istanbul, visiting many architectural wonders *en route* including one that would leave a lasting impression on Jeanneret, the Parthenon on the Acropolis at Athens.[19] Writing in his journal from Pompeii on 8 October 1911, 24 year old Jeanneret would comment on the Acropolis, "It is on the Acropolis, upon the steps of the Parthenon, and over the sea beyond, that one sees the realities of long ago."[20] On this legendary trip, the "*Voyage d'Orient*", he meticulously recorded his observations of the Acropolis and other sites in a series of drawings, about 400 photographs and six annotated sketchbooks, paying careful attention to the monuments' clear geometric shapes and overall compositions, images that would contribute to his architectural designs back home.[21] For example, due to its topographic siting, the Monastery of Ema outside of Florence held a particular attraction for Jeanneret. Like so many buildings

Le Corbusier, *Le Parthénon*, Athènes, 1911. *Carnet du Voyage d'Orient* n°3 p. 115. © FLC/ADAGP.

Charles-Édouard Jeanneret on the Acropolis, September 1911. *Photographie* L4(19)63. © FLC/ADAGP.

in La Chaux-de-Fonds, including those of his own design, they too were situated on hilly terrain. Among his surviving drawings from a trip to Italy in September 1911, is one that records a section through the hill site highlighting a typical monastic cell.[22] Emulating the sectional aspect of these monastic cells allowed Jeanneret to import an otherwise foreign idea to his hometown environment where it would be understood as something exotic and familiar at the same time. All of his early domestic designs including a house in La Chaux-de-Fonds for his parents in 1912 incorporate his predisposition towards this idea.[23]

Before leaving La Chaux-de-Fonds in 1917, he was able to crystallise his understanding of a deeper structure held within the natural world as witnessed by the clear volumetric expression of the semi-cylindrical space on the west side of the Villa Jeanneret-Perret, designed for his parents, and the similarly shaped lobes that flank the facade of the Villa Schwob, for a local prominent industrialist. Le Corbusier would continue his labours to replicate the organic order expressed in nature in his designs for the Villa Savoye during the last years of the 1920s, an architectural exploration that summed up his Purist experiments.[24] In September 1929, looking back on the first 23 years of his career Le Corbusier would comment on his work, "As I believe profoundly in our age, I continue to analyse the elements which are determining its character, and do not confine myself to trying to make its outward manifestations comprehensible. What I seek to fathom is its deeper, its constructive sense. Is not this the essence, the very purpose of architecture?"[25]

Each of these early projects leading up to the Villa Savoye allowed Jeanneret to tap into a creative element within him that had been waiting to be mined, which had lain dormant and was now fully awake. Primitive and vital, he would only truly recognise its essence in 1933 when he would visit the Neolithic sites of the Mediterranean.[26] Nonetheless, his desire to seek out, explore and express such an essence in architecture was clearly a longstanding one.

These early forays into the world of design survive as records that would serve as resources in the service of his architectural ambitions at La Chaux-de-Fonds and from 1917 onwards in his adopted home, Paris.[27] Now, 22 years later, as the internationally famous Le Corbusier, he would continue his "patient search" for the origins of architecture, a quixotic quest that would look further back, 3,000 years before the Parthenon in the Age of Pericles to a more primitive but equally complete and compelling distant past.[28] On this new venture, as he had with Klipstein on his *Voyage d'Orient*, he would be accompanied by knowledgeable companionship, this time two scholars, the Giedions.

The friendship forged during the previous decade with the Giedions would now serve to whet Le Corbusier's appetite for this knowledge of the Neolithic past. Le Corbusier's relationship with Sigfried Giedion dated back to 1923 when they met in Paris, soon after the publication of his architectural manifesto, *Vers Une Architecture*.[29] Their friendship was facilitated by their shared national homeland, Switzerland, and a deep mutual interest in an emerging Modernism that encompassed all the arts and in part drew inspiration from primitive sources. Earlier, the publication of Le Corbusier and Ozenfant's 1918 *Après Le Cubisme* and their 1920 *Le Purisme* had caught Carola Giedion-Welcker's attention. She too shared their interest in primary geometric shapes, the sphere, cube, and other prismatic forms that had distinguished the so-called primitive plastic arts for thousands of years. Six years later, in 1926, Carola Giedion-Welcker's interest in Le Corbusier's ideas concerning the plastic qualities of modern painting was expressed in her review, *Ozenfant und Jeanneret, "Moderne Malerei"*, a discourse that would be resumed aboard the SS *Patris II* and whenever it docked near Neolithic sites.[30] Throughout the 1920s the Giedions' friendship with their Swiss compatriot evolved. In 1928, the CIAM was founded in Switzerland by Madame Hélène de Mandrot, Sigfried Giedion and Le Corbusier, an organisation that sought to divert architecture from academic preoccupations. While the CIAM organisation was in the main an instrument for propagating avant-garde ideas in architecture and town planning, it also sustained a broader artistic agenda, one that was voiced by such figures as Moholy-Nagy, Walter Gropius and Carola Giedion-Welcker. When Le Corbusier, now 46, embarked on the SS *Patris II* in 1933 he was not only traveling with a distinguished group of Modernist designers and thinkers, but also with the Giedions, two scholarly friends who would prove invaluable in his search and investigation of the ancient origins of architecture.

During 1928, as construction of the Villa Stein/de Monzie at Garches came to a close and the first designs for the Villa Savoye began to emerge in his office, Le Corbusier was simultaneously investigating another direction. This new architectural investigation would employ rustic masonry in a country house outside Le Pradet, near Toulon, for Madame Hélène de Mandrot, who had hosted the first meeting of the CIAM at her Château de la Sarraz, Switzerland in June that year. While the use of bare-faced stone as a finished surface had been employed in the earliest of his houses at La Chaux-de-Fonds, his architectural investigations during the 1920s were largely distinguished by an abstract aesthetic that resulted from his experiments in Purism. In 1930–1931, soon after the completion of the Villa Savoye, this use of rough masonry would appear again in a portion of the north elevation of his Pavillon Suisse, at the Cité Unversitaire, Paris. Soltan has suggested that during this period Le Corbusier's reevaluation of architecture evolved through his reassessment of the use of materials, and his renewed appraisal of eighteenth century writings that included Laugier's ideas about the "primitive hut", and Jean-Jacques Rousseau's myth of the "Noble Savage".[31] Le Corbusier was primed to revisit the Mediterranean world again, this time in search of the most ancient of its architectural monuments.

As they steamed through the Mediterranean during the summer of 1933, Carola Giedion-Welcker's special interests in sculpture and its primitive origins engaged the attention of some of the passengers aboard the *Patris II*, especially Le Corbusier. As recorded by her husband Sigfried Giedion, the excitement of examining the ancient sites, on Gozo, one of the islands of the Maltese archipelago, Khirokitia in Cyprus and the Island of Amorgos in the Cycladic Islands, sparked many discussions about the origins of painting, sculpture and architecture.[32]

As anticipated, Gozo's Neolithic temples held a special interest for Le Corbusier and the Giedions.[33] Despite their age, dating to the fourth millennium BC, it was here that Le Corbusier encountered an exotic Neolithic architecture that was intimately familiar to him in terms of its reductive geometric shapes. Upon viewing the trilithons, at Hagar Qim, Mnajdra on Malta and Ggantija on Gozo, for the first time, Le Corbusier is reported to have remarked on these ancient doorways, "I did this; I gave life to a stone doorway [trilithon] like this one in my youth at La-Chaux-de-Fonds. The man that made this door is my brother across time."[34]

The post and lintel stone construction of a doorway on the south elevation of Jeanneret's 1908 Villa Stotzer bears a tectonic similarity to these Maltese Neolithic doorways built c. 3900 BC. One can see, then, how this life-long interest in geometry, nature, and the origins of architecture had prepared Le Corbusier to discover within the ruins on Gozo his own past, one that he would integrate into his self-fashioned mythology.[35]

left/ Le Corbusier, Villa Stotzer, door; **right/** Mnajdra Temple (Malta), Trilithon. Images courtesy of the author.

In his 1928 *Une Maison—un Palais*, Le Corbusier's commentary on the origins of the domestic dwelling, were accompanied with illustrations of Neolithic sites that included Stonehenge, Irish huts, and a plan of the Temples of Ggantija on the island of Gozo.[36] The accompanying text is infused with his ideas concerning the intersection of geometry and nature along with his interests in the Neolithic origins of architecture.

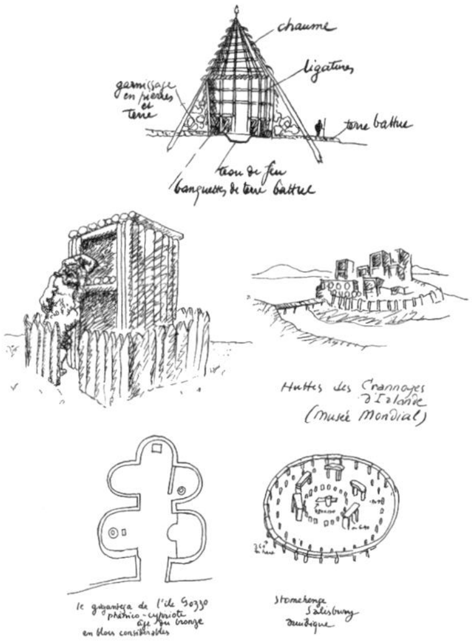

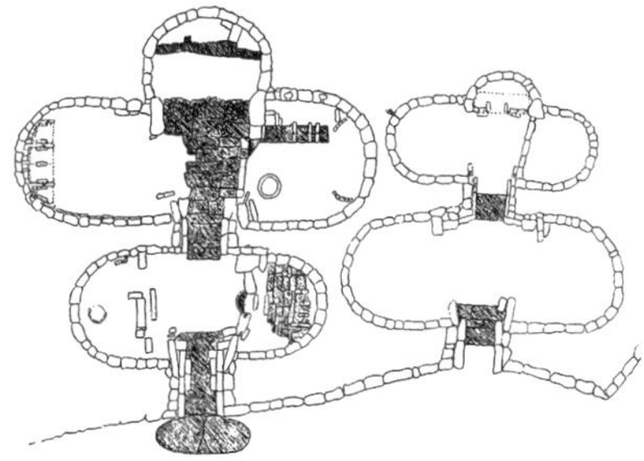

left/ Le Corbusier, *Une Maison Un Palais*, 1928, p. 39. Image courtesy of FLC; **right/** Plan of Ggantija Temple, Gozo (Malta) from Sigfried Giedion, *Architecture and the Phenomena of Transition*, Cambridge, MA: Harvard University Press, 1971, p. 30, fig. 15.

With the house across the ages we enter into architecture.
And here is the primitive house [hut]:
This is what qualifies man: a creature of geometry; he would not know how to proceed without geometry.
He is exact.
Not a piece of wood in its original form and force, not a ligature without a precise function.
Man is "economical" [*l'homme est économe*].
The house-type is a summation of such economy.
With geometry, order powerfully carries nobility and beauty.
One day, will this hut not be the Roman Pantheon, dedicated to the god?
Here is man throughout the darkest, most anguished periods of time: nature stalks him.
His house grows up to be more right and rectilinear. Each piece of his structure is an architectural power. One day, much later, he will contemplate this rustic tool, and his spirit will perceive its delectable invitations: lyricism arises in him, he will conceive a symphonic counterpoint; his brutal deeds become spiritual ones, the hovel will become the materialisation of lofty intentions and, on the Acropolis, the temple of the goddess will be above.
Overtaking the intentions of utilitarian order to attempt to think through the trouble of his still darkened conscience, to the events that dominate him, he builds, through cyclopean means, those precincts where ardent rituals are performed. He disposes altars, sacrificial tables. And this disposition is ordered by a single thought. We ourselves are taken aback today by these effective actions; for already we have arrived at great architecture.
In Celtic lands, the dolmens and menhirs of Carnac and elsewhere attest, in their gigantic dimensions, to fatal architectural faculty. *Architecturer* is to put in order; and so architecture transmits across the millennia the order of thought.

> The mountaineer builds in the high Alps,
> that is evident in the votive enclave of primitive peoples,
> the proof is everywhere in this fundamental function of order.
> And I repeat once more: in this product of order, architecture is in power,
> complete, totally, the clear and vigorous germ of that which, in later centuries,
> will form forums, vestibules, rooms, columns, pediments, domes.
> Architecture is there.
> And it is there that it is.
> And it is not there at all in those archaeological manuals that have poisoned
> the young in these last decades.[37]

For Le Corbusier, personal exploration of such places as Gozo far outweighed anything he could read in books, no matter how much he had relied in the past on the written word. But exploring Gozo and its surrounding world first-hand allowed him to make these personal connections with the past that he so greatly valued. *Ggantija*, in Maltese, means home of the race of giants. It was the island to which Odysseus sailed after escaping the home of the Cyclops. The Cyclops were mythological figures never far from Le Corbusier's mind. In the text quoted above he described the ability to design altars and sacrificial tables as created through single-minded, one eyed, "cyclopean means". And Le Corbusier, blind in one eye, strongly identified with the Cyclops.[38] In other words, Le Corbusier believed himself, or wished to present himself, as entering a world with which he was instinctively familiar, not only in terms of its architectural aesthetics, but also in terms of its mythology. In particular, the archeological exploration of this poetic text anticipated his journey to Gozo. "Cyclopean means" had a special meaning for both the architect and the island.

The *Patris II* continued on to Cyprus, on the eastern edge of the Mediterranean, 40 miles from the coast of Asia Minor. As recounted by Sigfried Giedion, at Khirokitia on the island of Cyprus, some members of the CIAM group visited a Neolithic settlement of several hundred *tholoi* or circular domed huts.[39] These Neolithic ruins, dated from c. 3700 BC, stirred a great excitement in Le Corbusier. Giedion would later write:

> The most interesting feature of the Khirokitia dwellings is their internal organisation. They had an upper floor covering half the area of the ground floor. This division is still usual in the rectangular house plans of the Greek Islands, and Le Corbusier reintroduced the age-old principle in his Pavillon de l'Esprit Nouveau, Paris, 1925. When he [Le Corbusier] visited the Greek islands in 1933, together with several friends, he took out his tape measure, and I remember his delight when he found that the floor-to-ceiling heights of the houses (226 cm) corresponded exactly to the dimension he liked to use and later incorporated in his Modular system.[40]

Similarly, Jerzy Soltan would recall many instances when dimensional and proportional aspects of the Neolithic remains at Khirokitia would come up in conversation as he worked with Le Corbusier in the development of the Modular system.[41] Soltan felt that for Le Corbusier, recording a direct relationship with these fourth millennium ruins allowed him to connect to an architectural continuum, one that included Le Corbusier as an active participant in the timeless art of architecture.

Le Corbusier, accompanied by the Giedions, also explored the Island of Amorgos in the Cycladic Islands. Le Corbusier recalled going to Minoa, the ancient capital of the island, located on a high cliff above Katapola. "While only a few ruins remained from that ancient past, I saw what I needed to see, where King Minos ruled a second kingdom."[42]

While some Neolithic artefacts and remains of the ancient Minoan civilisation have been found at Amorgos, perhaps what interested Le Corbusier more was the location of a well-known Neolithic marble Idol from Amorgos that he would have known from the Ancient Sculpture Collections at the Louvre Museum in Paris.[43] Carola Giedion-Welcker subsequently included the idol in her 1937 publication *Modern Plastic Art: Elements of Reality, Volume and Disintegration.*[44] Furthermore, the 1955 revised and enlarged edition of her book, now renamed *Contemporary Sculpture: An Evolution in Volume and Space*, would feature two full pages dedicated to the plastic qualities of Le Corbusier's works exhibited in his *Ozon 2* (a painted carved wood sculpture), his design for his *Open Hand Monument* (a sculptural work at Chandigarh, India) and at his 1955 Unité d'Habitation located at Marseille, the port city where 19 years earlier they had boarded the SS *Patris II.*[45]

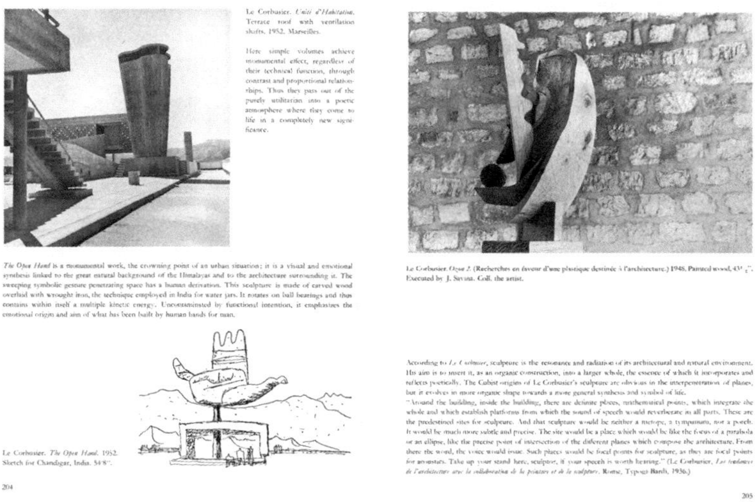
Le Corbusier. *Unité d'Habitation*. Terrace roof with ventilation shafts. 1952. Marseilles.

Here simple volumes achieve monumental effect, regardless of their technical function, through contrast and proportional relationships. Thus they pass out of the purely utilitarian into a poetic atmosphere where they come to life in a completely new significance.

The Open Hand is a monumental work, the crowning point of an urban situation; it is a visual and emotional synthesis linked to the great natural background of the Himalayas and to the architecture surrounding it. The sweeping symbolic gesture penetrating space has a human derivation. This sculpture is made of carved wood overlaid with wrought iron, the technique employed in India for water jars. It rotates on ball bearings and thus contains within itself a multiple kinetic energy. Uncontaminated by functional intention, it emphasizes the emotional origin and aim of what has been built by human hands for man.

Le Corbusier. *The Open Hand*. 1952. Sketch for Chandigar, India. 34⅛".

204

Le Corbusier. *Ozon 2*. (Recherches en faveur d'une plastique destinée à l'architecture.) 1948. Painted wood, 43½". Executed by J. Savina. Coll. the artist.

According to *Le Corbusier*, sculpture is the resonance and radiation of its architectural and natural environment. His aim is to insert it, as an organic construction, into a larger whole, the essence of which it incorporates and reflects poetically. The Cubist origins of Le Corbusier's sculpture are obvious in the interpenetration of planes, but it evolves in more organic shape towards a more general synthesis and symbol of life.

"Around the building, inside the building, there are definite places, mathematical points, which integrate the whole and which establish platforms from which the sound of speech would reverberate in all parts. These are the predestined sites for sculpture. And that sculpture would be neither a metope, a tympanum, nor a porch. It would be much more subtle and precise. The site would be a place which would be like the focus of a parabola or an ellipse, like the precise point of intersection of the different planes which compose the architecture. From there the word, the voice would issue. Such places would be focal points for sculpture, as they are focal points for acoustics. Take up your stand here, sculptor, if your speech is worth hearing." (Le Corbusier, *Les tendances de l'architecture avec la collaboration de la peinture et de la sculpture*. Rome, Typogr. Bardi, 1936.)

205

Carola Giedion-Welcker, *Contemporary Sculpture: An Evolution in Volume and Space*, New York: G Wittenborn, 1955, p. 204 (left) and p. 205 (right).

As has been shown, the CIAM sponsored voyage on the SS *Patris II* afforded rich exchanges between the passengers and especially between the Giedions and Le Corbusier. Their observations of ancient art and architecture, the two art historians' and the architect's subsequent reinterpretation and reinvention of them, allowed them to connect to the ancient past. Part of Le Corbusier's search for a Modern aesthetic that would claim his place in the present and for the future while simultaneously claiming a connection with the deep Neolithic past can be traced back to this historic voyage.

Additionally, these exchanges between the Giedions and Le Corbusier during the summer of 1933 would eventually find sculptural expression in the Swiss architect's future architectural projects such as his Jaoul Houses, 1952–1954, in

Paris and at Notre Dame du Haut, 1950–1955, at Ronchamp. At Jaoul Le Corbusier would recover and employ such devices as the Catalan arch, and plant-covered roofs like "the ancient Etruscans", evoking a "Mediterranean vernacular" a seemingly provincial architecture that would invite criticism by the younger generation of modernists such as James Stirling who remarked, "If Garches [Villa Stein, 1927] appears urban, sophisticated and essentially in keeping with '*l'esprit parisien*' then the Jaoul houses seem primitive in character, recalling their Provençal farmhouse community; they seem out of tune with their Parisian environment."[46]

The prismatic clarity of Le Corbusier's earlier domestic dwellings still resides at the Jaoul Houses. The difference between these houses and the earlier ones lies in his expressive use of exposed bricks, tiles, and the rough texture impressions left in the concrete by the wooden shuttering. Le Corbusier intended that the direct exposure of these materials would highlight their means of construction. Furthermore he felt that, "... the simplicity of seaside living, with its minimal furniture requirements, should be adhered to as far as possible".[47] While the Jaoul Houses were under construction Le Corbusier was busy giving shape to another building, one at Ronchamp that would bring him world-wide admiration, an acclaim voiced by professionals and the general public alike.

In his design for Notre-Dame-du-Haut at Ronchamp, Le Corbusier's interest in eliciting a primal response through his use of curvilinear shapes and sculpted rough surface textures struck a chord throughout the global architectural community. Again, James Stirling responded by saying that,

> ... the chapel by Le Corbusier may possibly be the most plastic building ever erected in the name of Modern architecture.... The immediate impression is of a sudden encounter with an unnatural configuration of natural elements such as the granite rings at Stonehenge or the dolmens in Brittany. The sensational impact of the chapel on the visitor is significantly not sustained for any great length of time and when the emotions subside there is little to appeal to the intellect and nothing to analyse or stimulate curiosity.[48]

Even Le Corbusier's professional colleagues, one of the calibre of James Stirling, could not immediately take in the profundity of Le Corbusier's search for a primal resonance in architecture, and in fact Stirling later recanted his original opinion on Ronchamp. Both Jaoul and Ronchamp can be understood as the fulfilment of Le Corbusier's search for the origins of architecture, a "patient search" that intersects the modern technological world. Those that had worked in Le Corbusier's atelier knew that the chapel at Ronchamp was perhaps the most challenging engineering feat of his career up to this date. The highly strategised rusticity and the equally calculated geometry of Ronchamp are testaments to Le Corbusier's skills and ingenuity in balancing the old and the new without compromising either one, but instead merging the two into a synthetic whole. It is exactly Le Corbusier's talent for creating this convincing mixture that echoes the *gravitas* of the Neolithic past of the Mediterranean and the buoyancy of his *l'esprit nouveau* expressed in his late works.[49] In July 1935, exactly two years after Le Corbusier's voyage on the SS *Patris II*, he could say with renewed confidence that,

> Architecture alone is an instance of total plasticity. Architecture alone represents the medium for total lyricism. A total thought can be expressed

top/ Le Corbusier, *Sapin stylisé*, c. 1905. Dessin FLC 2208. © FLC/ADAGP; **centre/** Le Corbusier, *Notre Dame du Haut* (1950–1955), Ronchamp. Image courtesy of the author; **bottom/** Le Corbusier, *Maisons Jaoul* (1952–1954), Neuilly sur Seine. Image courtesy of the author.

> through architecture. Architecture is self-sufficient. It is a genre that was created for expressing both through and in itself a whole cycle of emotions, the most intense of which stems from the influence of mathematics, where the play of plastic forms is symphonic.[50]

The prophetic sentiment of these words could easily describe his chapel at Ronchamp in the mid-1950s and projects Le Corbusier would still produce in the last decade of his career.[51] Standing in front of his chapel at Ronchamp, near the Swiss border of his homeland, Le Corbusier may have recognised that he had never abandoned his "patient search". This exploration had begun in the snowy mountains of his childhood in La Chaux-de-Fonds, taken him to Paris, and farther afield to the sun-baked Mediterranean, on a search to define the intersection between man, nature and the resultant origins of architecture.

/ **1.** See Le Corbusier, *L'Atelier de la recherche patiente*, Paris: Vincent et Fréal, 1960, trans into English as *Creation is a Patient Search*, New York: Praeger, 1960.

/ **2.** It seems significant that among Le Corbusier's favourite books was Miguel de Cervantès' *L'Admirable Don Quixote de la Mancha*. Later in life, he would have the 1847 edition that he probably possessed as a boy bound in the hide of his dog, Pinceau. See C De Smet, *Le Corbusier, Architect of Books*, Baden, Switzerland: Lars Müller, 2005, pp. 86–87. Another book of quests that likely belonged to the Jeanneret family library is the 1847 French edition of Ludovico Arisoto's *Orlando Furioso*, the sixteenth century epic poem of chivalric deeds and adventures in many lands. See P Venable Turner, *The Education of Le Corbusier. A Study of the Development of Le Corbusier's Thought, 1900–1920*, New York: Garland, 1977, p. 240.

/ **3.** The fourth meeting of the CIAM at Athens, 1933, resulted in Le Corbusier's 1943 publication, *La Charte d'Athènes*, see Le Corbusier, *The Athens Charter*, trans into English by A Eardley, New York: Grossman, 1973. In addition, José Luis Sert prepared a volume from the proceedings of this meeting of the CIAM, see JL Sert, *Can our cities survive? An ABC of urban problems, their analysis, their solutions; based on the proposals formulated by the CIAM, International Congresses for Modern Architecture, Congrès internationaux d'architecture moderne*, Cambridge, MA: Harvard University Press, and Oxford: Oxford University Press, 1942. For a description of the Congrès Internationaux d'Architecture Moderne, founded on 28 June 1928, see EP Mumford, *The CIAM Discourse on Urbanism, 1928–1960*, Cambridge, MA: MIT Press, 2000.

/ **4.** Le Corbusier, *The Athens Charter*, p. 25.

/ **5.** Sigfried Giedion (1883–1968) was born in Prague. His father co-owned a spinning mill on Lake Lorze at Baar, Canton Zug, Switzerland. See EP Mumford, *The CIAM Discourse on Urbanism, 1928–1960*, p. 278, n. 5.

/ **6.** For a list of other cruise participants, see EP Mumford, *The CIAM Discourse on Urbanism, 1928–1960*, n. 64, p. 293. The cruise from Marseille to the Piraeus and back to Marseille on the SS *Patris II*, leased from the Greek shipping company Neptos, began at Marseille on 29 July 1933, and returned to Marseille on 13 August. On board and at other locations such as Aegina, Seriphos, Santori, Ios, Lazlo Maholy-Nagy produced a film of the voyage which features Alvar Aalto, Ferdinand Leger, Sigfried Gideon, Le Corbusier, and Jose Luis Sert, see L Maholy-Nagy, *A film diary of the architects' congress*, originally produced as a 16mm film, 1933. See also S Giedion, "CIAM at Sea, the Background of the Fourth (Athens) Congress," *Architect's Year Book*, 3, trans P Morton Shand, 1949, Le Groupe CIAM-France, pp. 36–39 and Jos Bosman, "Sur le Patris II de Marseille à Athènes" in *Le Corbusier et la Méditerranée*, Marseille: Editions Parenthèses, 1987, pp. 73–79.

/ **7.** Le Corbusier, *The Athens Charter*, p. 25.

/ **8.** This anecdote and others cited in this text were recounted during a seminar meeting in February 2004 at the Carpenter Center at Harvard University, by Jerzy Soltan, who had worked in Le Corbusier's office from 1945–1949 on several projects, including the Unité d'Habitation, Marseille, and the development of the 'Modulor', the proportioning system that Le Corbusier used in his later work. Soltan was a guest speaker in support of this author's course, *Le Corbusier and Paris*, taught for the Rhode Island School of Design. The "heat of the summer of 1933", mentioned by Le Corbusier, is also cited in one of the captions in Maholy-Nagy's film, "The weather is hot enough for many to spend the night on deck." While the debate regarding the real scene of Homer's *Iliad and the Odyssey* suggests it took place in the north of Europe and not in the Mediterranean Sea, Le Corbusier was clearly referencing the locus recognised in popular belief, see F Vinci, *Omero nel Baltico*, with introduction by R Calzecchi Onesti and F Cuomo, Rome: Fratelli Palombi Editori, 1998. Paul Venable Turner has pointed out that Jeanneret's edition of Homer's *Odyssey*, Homère, *L'Odyssée*, Paris, n.d., was inscribed with his name and dated, "Ch E. Jenneret Paris 1909," see P Venable Turner, 1977, p. 251.

/ **9.** Turner, PV, *The Education of Le Corbusier*, p. 9.

/ **10.** See M Collignon, *Mythologie figurée de la Grèce*, Paris: A Quantin, 1883.

/ **11.** Turner, PV, *The Education of Le Corbusier*, p. 9; figs. 9 and 10.

/ **12.** Charles-Edouard Jeanneret Gris, also known later as Le Corbusier, was born on 6 October 1887 in La Chaux-de-Fonds, a world-renowned watch-making center located in the Swiss Jura Mountains, see H Allen Brooks, *Le Corbusier's Formative Years, Charles-Edouard Jeanneret at La Chaux-de-Fonds*, Chicago and London: University of Chicago Press, 1997.

/ **13.** See PV Turner, *The Education of Le Corbusier*, MP May Sekler, *The Early Drawings of Le Corbusier*, New York: Garland, 1977 and S Von Moos, *Le Corbusier. Elements of a Synthesis*, Cambridge, MA: MIT Press, 1979, pp. 1–35.

/ **14.** See J Jenger, et al, *Le Corbusier et la Nature*, Paris: Editions de La Villette, 2004.

/ **15.** For a descriptive history and interpretation of Jeanerret's watch design, see PV Turner, "The Beginnings of Le Corbusier's Education, 1902–1907" in *The Art Bulletin*, vol. LIII, number 2, June 1971, pp. 214–224 and HA Brooks, *Le Corbusier's Formative Years*, pp. 64–68.

/ **16.** Von Moos, S, *Le Corbusier*, p. 3.

/ **17.** This phrase, "sun-drenched Mediterranean," was often used by Le Corbusier, see meeting with Soltan, 2004, note 8.

/ **18.** Turner, PV, *The Education of Le Corbusier*, p. 31.

/ **19.** Jeanneret documented the trip in numerous sketchbooks, photographs, letters, and articles for his local La Chaux-de Fonds newspaper, *La Feuille d'Avis de La Chaux-de Fonds*, which he had persuaded to pay him for his dispatches, see Le Corbusier (Ch-E Jeanneret), *Voyage d'Orient, Carnets*, English edition, trans M Munson and M Shore, Milan: Electa spa., 2002, p. 12. See also, AM Vogt, "How Danube and Bosphorus Made a European out of Le Corbusier" in H Horat, ed, *1000 Years of Swiss Art*, New York: Hudson Hills Press, 1992, pp. 335–347 and G Gresleri, "The Balkans," in S Von Moos and A Rüegg, eds, *Le Corbusier before Le Corbusier*, New Haven: Yale University Press, 2002, p. 172.

/ **20.** Zaknic, I, ed, *Journey to the East. Le Corbusier (Charles-Edouard Jeanneret)*, trans I Zaknic with N Pertuiset, Cambridge, MA: MIT Press, 1987, p. 240.

/ **21.** For photographs and sketches of their trip to the East, see G Gresleri, *Le Corbusier Viaggio in Oriente*, Venice: Marsilio Editori, 1984. Also, see I Zaknic, *Journey to the East.*

/ **22.** Among the cities Jeanneret visited during his trip in 1907 were Florence, Vienna, Paris, Munich, see HA Brooks, *Le Corbusier's Formative Years*, pp. 95–116.

/ **23.** For a sectional view of the Scala Cinema in La Chaux-de-Fonds see G Baker and J Gubler, *Le Corbusier. Early Works by Charles-Edouard Jeanneret-Gris*, Academy Editions, London, St Martin's Press, New York, 1987, pp. 106–110.

/ **24.** For a description of the many design schemes for the Villa Savoye at Poissy see T Benton, *The Villas of Le Corbusier 1920–1930*, New Haven and London: Yale University Press, 1987, pp. 190–207.

/ **25.** Le Corbusier and Pierre Jeanneret, *Le Corbusier Œuvre Complète, Volume 1 : 1910–1929*, Zürich: Girsberger, 1930, p. 11.

/ **26.** These ideas paraphrase Soltan's recollection of Le Corbusier musing about this turning point in his career, see Soltan 2004, n. 7. Also, see W JR Curtis, *Modern Architecture, Mythical Landscapes & Ancient Ruins*, London: Sir John Soane's Museum, 1997.

/ **27.** Jeanneret moved to Paris in 1917, where, having met Amédée Ozenfant, he co-authored *Après Le Cubisme*, the catalogue of a joint exhibition of their paintings at the Galerie Thomas in Paris. Towards the end of 1919 Jeanneret and Ozenfant along with writer Paul Dermée formed an arts magazine, *L'Esprit Nouveau*, the first issue of which was published on 15 October 1920, with 28 issues to follow, up to 1925. The pseudonyms Le Corbusier and Saugnier were used for the first time for a series of articles in the first issue of their periodical. Le Corbusier represents Jeanneret and Saugnier represents Ozenfant. *Le Purisme* (Purism) appeared in the fourth issue of *L'Esprit Nouveau*, 1920, pp. 369–386.

/ **28.** These observations of the Parthenon would appear in his chapter, "Architecture. III, Pure Création de l'Esprit" in Le Corbusier—Saugnier, *Vers Une Architecture*, Paris: G Cres et Cie, 1923, pp. 161–182.

/ **29.** See V Magnago Lampugnani, "A History of Architecture of the Twentieth Century" in *Rassegna* 25, March 1986, pp. 18–29.

/ **30.** This review is one among her early writings when she was researching topics that included the plastic arts in Prehistory, Constantin Brancusi and James Joyce, see C Giedion-Welcker, "Ozenfant und Jeanneret, "Moderne Malerei", 1926 in R Hohl, ed, *Carola Giedion-Welcker, Scriften 1926–1971*, Köln: M DuMont Schauberg, 1973. James Joyce, another topic of conversation on the SS *Patris II*, was inspired by Homer's "Odyssey" (ninth to eighth century BC) to write what is considered by many to be the greatest epic of the twentieth century: "Ulysses". Later in 1965, Giedion-Welcker would publish a brief article that comments on a dialogue between Joyce and Le Corbusier, in particular the way that each artist was forging a new path in their respective disciplines, see C Giedion-Welcker, "Ein beflügelter Dialog im Jahr 1938 zwischen Le Corbusier und James Joyce", see R Hohl, *Carola Giedion-Welcker*, pp. 52–53.

/ **31.** Laugier's *Essai sur l'architecture* first appeared anonymously in 1753. The library at Jeanneret's Art School at La Chaux-de-Fonds contained a copy of the second edition, 1755, of Marc-Antoine Laugier's *Essai sur l'architecture*, that included the famous engraving depicting a "primitive hut". Also, from this early period it is clear that Jeanneret was at least familiar with Rousseau, since he owned an edition of Jean-Jacques Rousseau's *Les Confessions*, first published in 1781. The title page of Jeanneret's late nineteenth century edition was inscribed, Ch-E Jeanneret Paris août 1909, see PV Turner, *The Education of Le Corbusier*, p. 251.

/ **32.** See S Giedion, 1949, *CIAM at Sea*.

/ **33.** For Giedion's views on the Maltese Temples see S Giedion, *Architecture and the Phenomena of Transition*, Cambridge, MA: Harvard University Press, 1971, pp. 21–43.

/ **34.** See J Soltan, 2004, recalling this moment in one of his many discussions with Le Corbusier about the origins of architecture, n. 7.

/ **35.** See S Richards, *Le Corbusier and the Concept of Self*, New Haven and London: Yale University Press, 2003.

/ **36.** For Le Corbusier's commentary and drawings of these Neolithic examples see Le Corbusier, *Une Maison—Un Palais, "A la recherche d'une unité architecturale"*, Paris: Cres & Cie, 1928, pp. 38–40 and G Gresleri, *L'Esprit Nouveau: Parigi-Bologna: costruzione e ricostruzione di un prototipo dell'architettura moderna*, Milan: Electa, 1979, p. 28. For a measured plan of of the northern and southern temples of Ggantija on the island of Gozo, see S Giedion, *Architecture and the Phenomena of Transition*, Cambridge, MA: Harvard University Press, 1971, p. 30, fig. 15.

/ **37.** Le Corbusier, *Une Maison—Un Palais*, pp. 38–40. The indentations are transcribed as they appear in his original text.Translation of the author.

/ **38.** According to Jerzy Soltan, in the 1920s Le Corbusier, when working in his studio, stooped over to pick up a paintbrush and accidentally poked one of his eyes. His near blindness in one eye may have contributed to a self-image as Polyphemus, an idea expressed in his literary allusions and his design of a single-headlight automobile, the 1928 "maximum-car", see note 8. For the "maximum-car," see Le Corbusier, *L'Atelier de la recherche patiente*, p. 94.

/ **39.** Jerzy Soltan has suggested that only a small party from the conference group visited the island of Cyprus, which was not on the official CIAM itinerary. S Giedion, *The Eternal Present, Volume II: the Beginnings of Architecture*, New York: Bollingen Foundation (Pantheon Books), 1964, pp. 182–183. For measured surveys and photographs of the Khirokitia site, see P Dikaios, *Khirokitia; final report on the excavation of a neolithic settlement in Cyprus on behalf of the Department of Antiquities, 1936–1946*, London: Oxford University Press, 1953 and A Le Brun, *Khirokitia: a Neolithic site*, Nicosia: Bank of Cyprus Cultural Foundation, 1997.

/ **40.** Giedion, S, *The Eternal Present*, p. 183.

/ **41.** For comments by Le Corbusier that cite Jerzy Soltan and André Wogensky as key participants in the development of the Modular system and Soltan as the fabricator of the first Modular strip in 1945, see Le Corbusier, *Le Modulor, Essai sur une mesure harmonique à l'échelle humane applicable universellement à l'architecture et à la mécanique*, Boulogne: Editions de l'Architecture d'Aujourd'hui, 1950, pp. 47–49, 56 and Jola Gola, ed, *Jerzy Soltan: a Monograph*, Cambridge, MA: Harvard University Graduates School of Design, 1995, pp. 106–115. Six years later, while traveling in India in 1951, Le Corbusier commented on how he had lost the first Modular strip made by Soltan, "When you are riding in a jeep, you pull up your knees; things are liable to fall out of your pockets. Being careful is all very well.

This time the Modular had really gone from me", see Le Corbusier, *Modular 2 (Let the user speak next) Continuation of 'The Modular' 1948*, English language edition, Cambridge, MA: Harvard University Press, 1958, p. 34.

/ **42.** This anecdote describing this part of the CIAM voyage of 1933 was recounted by Soltan, see J Soltan, 2004, n. 8.

/ **43.** This Head of an Idol from the Island of Amorgos, would later be illustrated in Carola Giedion-Welcker's *Modern Plastic Art: Elements of Reality, Volume and Disintegration*, English language version by P Morton Shand, Zürich: H Girsberger, 1937, p. 85. Siegfried Giedion would later illustrate a violin-shaped female idol (c. 2500 BC), in marble, from Amorgos (Cyclades), see S Giedion, *The Eternal Present: The Beginnings of Art*, New York: Pantheon Books, 1962, p. 451, fig. 301. See also R Dussaud, "Les civilisations préhelléniques dans les Cyclades" in *Revue de l'École d'anthropologie*, XVI, 1906.

/ **44.** See C Giedion-Welcker, *Modern Plastic Art*, p. 85.

/ **45.** See C Giedion-Welcker, *Contemporary Sculpture: An Evolution in Volume and Space*, New York: George Wittenborn Inc, 1955, pp. 204–205.

/ **46.** Stirling, J, "Garches to Jaoul: Le Corbusier as Domestic Architect in 1927 and 1953" in *The Architectural Review*, 118, September 1955, pp. 145–151.

/ **47.** Boesiger, W, ed, *Le Corbusier*, New York: Praeger, 1972, p. 101. See also C Maniaque, *Le Corbusier et les maisons Jaoul. Projets et fabrique*, Paris: Picard, 2005.

/ **48.** Stirling, J, "Ronchamp: Le Corbusier's Chapel and the Crisis of Rationalism" in *The Architectural Review*, 119, March 1956, pp. 155–161.

/ **49.** Similar issues are explored by V Scully, "Le Corbusier, 1922–1965" in V Scully, *Modern Architecture and Other Essays*, with introduction by N Levine, Princeton: Princeton University Press, 2003, p. 247.

/ **50.** See Le Corbusier, "Sainte alliance des arts majeurs ou le grand art en gésine" in *Architecture d'Aujourd'hui*, number 7, July 1935, p. 86.

/ **51.** Pauly, D, *Le Corbusier: The Chapel at Ronchamp*, Paris: Fondation Le Corbusier, 1997, p. 8.

THE COSMIC ELEMENT IN MODERN ARCHITECTURE

NOTES OF A PRACTITIONER

Walter Hunziker

Mythology and cosmic elements are commonly attributed to archaic architecture, but they are omnipresent in all the significant works of architecture, irrespective of the period. Myth and the cosmic dimension are at the root of every deeper understanding of the art of building. They are probably the main generators in the development of architectural schemes and a driving force in the *vitae* of many architects. Throughout the history of Man, stone cutters, carpenters and craftsmen have been aware that what they were about to create would last much longer than their lifespan. Human beings are able to belabour a material, but they cannot reproduce the world from which the material is extracted. In spite of this, every artist aims to create something that goes beyond his existence. Therefore I believe very much that every significant work of art and architecture carries in itself a cosmic and mythical dimension. As a supplement to a scientific or academic approach, I would like to bring into the discussion more of the battlefield vision of a practising architect and artist.

Louis Kahn in *Silence and Light*, the memorable lecture he gave at the ETH in Zürich in 1969:

> Knowledge is very specifically something that belongs to each individual in his own way. The book of knowledge has never been written, nor will it ever be written for man. Certainly Nature doesn't need it. It's already written for Nature.

As a practitioner I would like to take a very pragmatic view. I will reduce the complexity of the theme to four significant principles, which act as indicators of the existence of myth and the 'cosmic element' in architecture. I will distinguish between:

/ The measurable versus the infinite and the eternal
/ Path and place—the ritual walk
/ Cosmic language—mystic sign and ornament
/ Light, time and space—the unique cosmic event

These four principles will be followed through selected time segments in the history of architecture:

/ a very special contemporary architect: Charles Correa
/ archaic cultures, e.g. Maltese megalithic cultures
/ baroque principles, in particular the work of Borromini and Le Nôtre
/ the so-called Modern Movement
/ current tendencies in architecture

CHARLES CORREA

Attempts to define the principles that can be called "cosmic" will invariably lead to Charles Correa, a guiding master figure in contemporary architecture. Charles Correa is of Indian origin. He studied in Michigan and at MIT, worked with Doshi and Le Corbusier. Since 1996 he is Pritzker Prize Juror. One of his famous essays is entitled *Blessings of the Sky*, 2000.

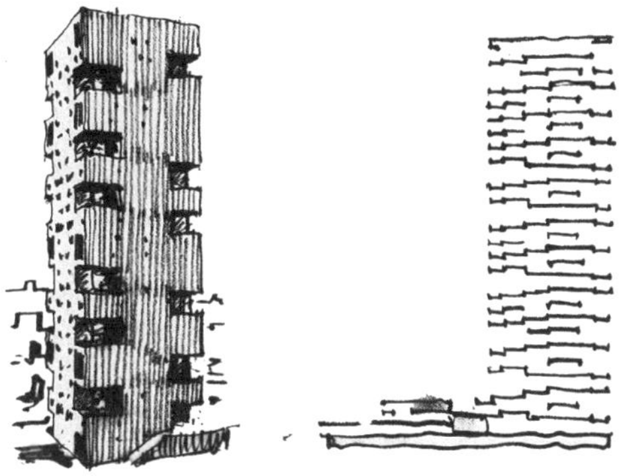

Charles Correa, *Kanchanjunga Apartments*, Bombay 1970–1983.

At first glance a typical boxy-rationalist and functionalist piece of architecture, but a second look reveals qualities that must derive from beyond the so-called rational/functional, in brief:

/ the notion of ornament beyond the significance of decoration
/ a sense of infinite growth upwards in a spiral movement
/ a deep concern with the penetration of light into a building
/ presence of the sky in the apartments

A work of architecture in which the functional on the one hand and the measurable and the infinite/eternal on the other are combined.

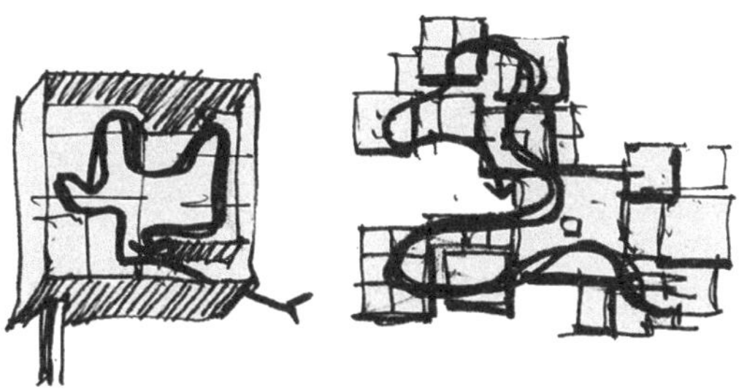

Charles Correa, *Handloom Pavilion*, Delhi 1958 and *Archaeological Museum* project, 1985.

At first sight an Arts and Crafts Museum, but also a very popular place to be and to meet. The building creates an architectural landscape embedded in the natural landscape. The inner world consists of a series of cellular spaces connected by stairs and passages. The similarity with megalithic temple sites is striking.

All these plan schemes with their refined, pure abstract geometry represent fine examples of plan figures based on the idea of path and place. The visitors' path becomes a ritual walk. The visitor decides when to walk and when to stop for an intimate interface with the works of art and craft. This idea has been all but lost in today's *ego-object-museum* architecture.

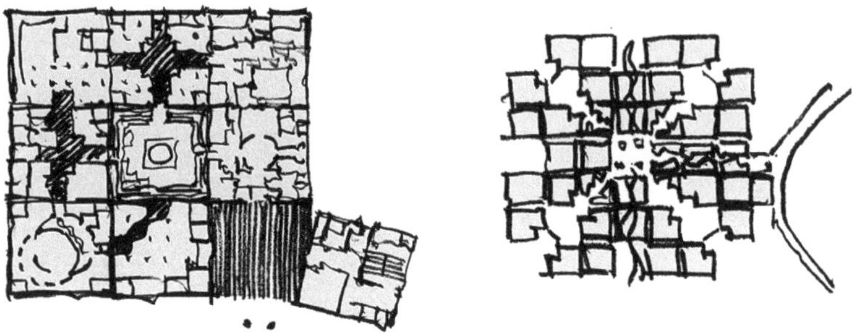

Charles Correa, *Jawahar Kala Kendra Cultural Centre*, Jaipur 1996–1992
and master plan New Bagalkot.

When we look for signs of cosmic language, myth and ornament in modern architecture, two works of Charles Correa come to mind. Both seem to be transfigurations of a *mandala*, creating a strong constitutional order and directing all the functional activities into a new cosmic order. Architecture cannot exist without light. But in the following examples the presence of light goes far beyond the play of light and shadow. The building acts as a sun dial. The light is almost materialised and reflects the daily, monthly and annual cycles of architecture as a unique cosmic event.

Charles Correa, *Villas at Verem*, Goa 1982–1989, window.

Here we are faced with a new definition of inside-outside, the creation of an almost spiritual relationship between inner world and outer world. Very much like in some of Louis Kahn's early houses, these openings represent something between a door, a window, a moulding and a stencil.

MALTESE MEGALITHIC CULTURES

The same four principles can be found in early Maltese megalithic cultures dating back thousands of years.

Maltese Megalithic culture.

The front wall seems to be set up in order to receive something from very far away or radiate out something beyond the limits of our world. Apart from the direct cosmic axes it is this emitter/receiver aspect that we might call cosmic, in the sense of the infinite and the eternal.

Bas relief of Tarxien altar piece.

Tarxien temple complex and Ronchamp site plan by Le Corbusier..

Abstract ornaments are like a universal language, they do not need translation; they function like a type of Esperanto in the world of the figural/figurative. Behind ornaments such as these we sense the quality of the waves on the sea, a never ending movement which comes and goes, an endless two-dimensional figure, a code that stands for the eternal, an example of a mystic sign and ornament.

Mnajdra temple.

The handling of natural light in architecture is the best indicator of a society's approach towards nature. Early cultures had to work with nature and natural cycles. Nowadays we try to control nature, and by doing this, we work against nature. The light and the unique cosmic event are exemplified by the equinox of the Mnajdra temple.

BAROQUE PRINCIPLES

As we work our way forward towards modern architecture we stop in the first part of the seventeenth century: Rome of the Popes, the beginning of the Baroque. In many ways this period is characterised by an almost pre-modern approach, the acceptance of the world as a sphere, Newton's new recognition of relativity in mathematical equations (analysis). The previously stable and systematic Renaissance order becomes a dynamic interface between spaces. The notions of perimeter, precinct, inside-outside, and of black and white becomes relative. Clear perimeters can simultaneously become part of two entities: a particular construction site, but also part of a global cosmic space, as if the building grounds extend beyond the specific site to become part of a greater entity. This fundamentally changes the notion of space and the notion of place.

Here are some sketches from my years at the Swiss Academy in Rome. The study shows the geometry of a major horizontal cut at ground floor level. Were one to 'slice' the building body further up, the plan would change dramatically. Concave and convex surfaces correlate diagonally to create a highly intricate spatial system. The view bounces from wall to wall in an endless movement with no beginning and no end.

Borromini, Study of the base of a pilaster of *San Giovanni in Laterano*.

During my stay at the Swiss Academy, and influenced by Paolo Portoghesi, I became interested in *chiaroscuro*. What does it ultimately mean, and what has it got to do with the cosmic element?

Black, white and the scale of shades between them appear in a new light. Grey is not just a shade between two extremes, black and white. Grey becomes the reference from where shade can develop towards the infinite black—*oscuro*, or the infinite white—*chiaro*. Behind the blackest black and the whitest white exists an open scale. This open-ended definition is the new and radical contribution of the Baroque.

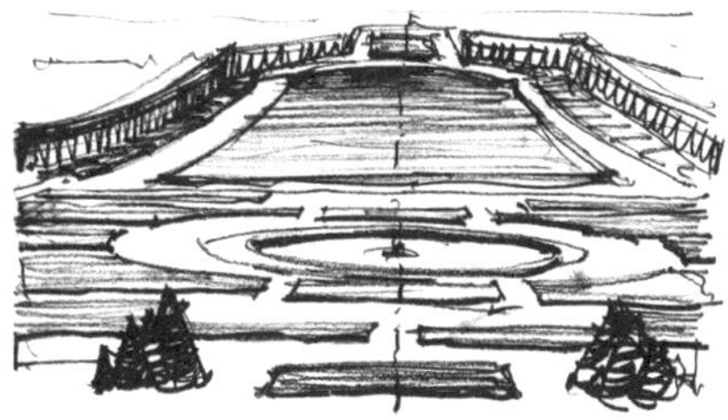

Le Nôtre, *La plaine des Quatre Statues de Sceaux.*

This is not just an academic essay on perspective, open space and theatrical illusion as commonly attributed to Baroque garden architecture. Just looking at the refined shaping of the terrain, one is overwhelmed by the feeling that these artificial landscapes in fact address supernatural dimensions, reflecting virtual landing strips that communicate with the cosmos or something between past and future.

Le Nôtre, *Sceau-Taille sévère.*

When visiting a French Baroque garden I am always intrigued by the strange combination of the organic growth of the plants and the attempt to shape them into pure, abstract geometric forms. What might be the reason behind all this? It is probably the endeavour to reach the absolute on earth, symbolising the extreme contradiction between the now and here and the eternal.

The formerly clear boundary between spaces/places and the notion of the linking figure of the path between them changed into a new dynamic entity, a new synthesis where place and path become intermingled and compressed in a new spatial body, a hybrid body, which at the same time fulfils the qualities of path and the qualities of place. The new space is in constant vibration and in constant fluctuation between the two formerly very clear elements which constituted architecture.

Le Nôtre, Saint-Germain-en-Laye.

This marks the end of the dogma of *frontality* and the birth of an interactive game between man and architecture. All in one, it is a new and dynamic version of the principle of path and place in architecture. The notion of the two-dimensional field. There is a clear rational geometric base structure which produces a multitude of unexpected views when one moves diagonally through it. The typical French park chairs can be grouped to form small gatherings which can be altered from day to day. This type of highly organised landscape offers a simultaneous and constantly changing pattern of paths and places, layered views and alleys in different directions. One of the mysteries of French garden culture has to do with how these absolute symmetrical and hierarchical plans allow an almost unlimited, unexpected and un-hierarchical freedom of movement, combined with a very human, playful and highly functional occupation.

Almost every detail in Borromini's work can be decoded as Christian symbols. But Borromini was also a master of abstract geometry. One of the finest examples is the orthogonal 90/45 degrees floor pattern, combined with a hexagonal plan. Can there be an explanation for the co-existence of two incompatible geometries in this plan? A deeper analysis reveals a very sophisticated interplay between these two geometries: only one apse is allowed to coincide with one of the floor axes, thus indicating a sublime emphasis on the 'main' axes of the Della Porta courtyard of the Sapienza. In my view, it is a combination of symbolism, myth and pure geometry.

MODERN MOVEMENT

Let us now finally move to the twentieth century and the Modernist Movement. What kind of approach is actually hidden behind the key slogans we all know very well?

/ Adolf Loos: "Ornament is a crime"
/ Louis Sullivan: "Form follows function"
/ Frank Lloyd Wright: "The rational plan is the master"
/ Le Corbusier: "Architecture as a machine for living"
/ Alvar Aalto: "Function as organic form"

As a matter of fact these important protagonists of the Modern Movement are only offering a new mixture of the principles described earlier. The new 'modern' synthesis relies at first glance very much on the measurable. Thus Le Corbusier creates his famous Modulor, which he presented as a universal instrument to control proportion and beauty. There was never proof, however, of its efficiency.

Almost all architects of the Modern Movement make it a major issue to redefine a new interface between inside-outside by means of glass technology.

Path and place—the former ritual walk—gets transformed into a system of fluctuating layered spaces, and defines a new correlation between space and time like simultaneous views in Cubist paintings.

A new approach towards nature is discovered by Scandinavian architects. Alvar Aalto and Gunnar Asplund are looking for the "landscape within the house", and take an almost radical anti-intellectualistic position, proclaiming a "symbolist interpretation with nature as the designer of form".

In the following examples, the four principles reappear in a new mixture. Le Corbusier designed the book jacket of the first publication on Ronchamp, Gerd Hatje edition, 1957, where we find the following statement:

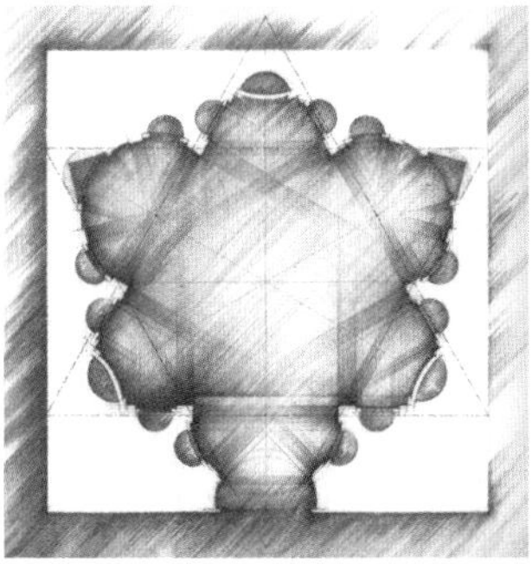

top/ Borromini, *Sant Ivo*; **centre/** Borromini, Second study of *San Giovanni in Laterano*;
bottom/ Borromini, *Santa Agnese* in Piazza Navona—Bernini fountain.

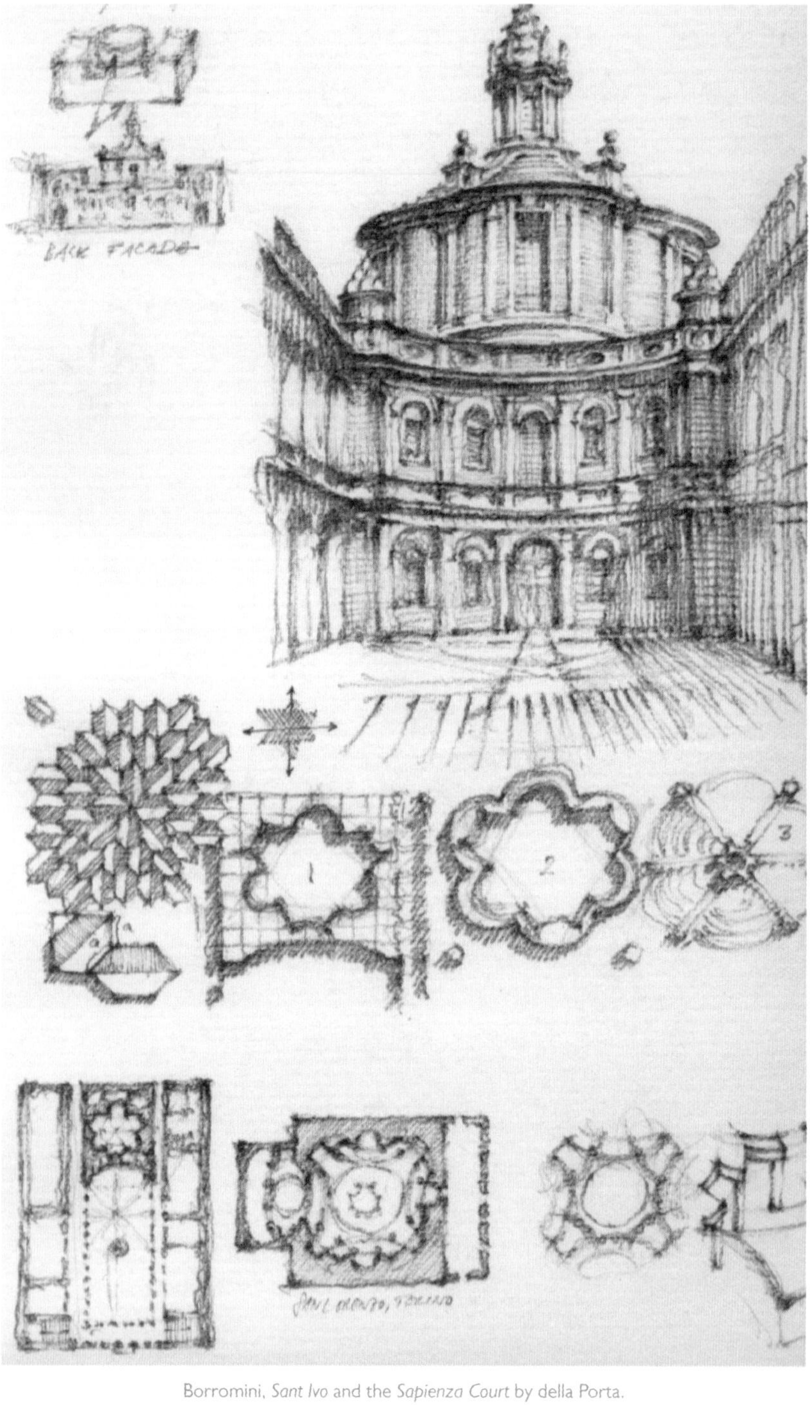

Borromini, *Sant Ivo* and the *Sapienza Court* by della Porta.

"... anachronic, in the meaning of being contemporary with the only Light". Daughter of the Spirit of which we neither know whence it comes nor whither it goes.[1]

In his inauguration speech Le Corbusier stated:

"Le sentiment du sacré anima notre effort. Des choses sont sacrées, d'autres ne le sont pas, qu'elles soient religieuses ou non."[2]

Louis Kahn, *Esherick House*, Philadelphia 1959–1961, and Dacca, *Assembly* 1962–1983, detail.

We continue on the subject of light.

Louis Kahn, *Silence and Light*

"light gives a feeling of inspiration [...], besides inspiration there is a place, the sanctuary of art" or "structure is the maker of light. When you decide on the structure, you're deciding on light [...]"

Louis Kahn, *Unitarian Church*, Rochester 1959–1961.

Louis Kahn distinguished very clearly form and design. While form was for him something absolute (cosmic), design was something that belonged to the individual creator. In his spoon example, he claims there is only one form for a spoon, but thousands of designs. Kahn again in *Silence and Light*: "I only wish that the first really worthwhile discovery of science would be that it recognises that the un-measurable, you see, is what they're really fighting to understand. And the measurable is only a servant of the un-measurable; everything that man makes must be fundamentally un-measurable."

Louis Kahn, Dacca, *Assembly* 1962–1983, front and back view.

Frank Lloyd Wright, *Falling Water*, Kaufmann, Mill Run, Penn. 1936.

CURRENT TENDENCIES IN ARCHITECTURE

Here are some examples of competition results and recently built architecture taken from the press release of the 2004 Venice Biennale. Even the present day avant-garde architecture cannot deny reference to cosmic elements.

The *Musée des Confluences*, in Lyon, France, 2001–2007, by Coop-Himmelb(l)au, could be seen as an example of the infinite and the eternal, insofar as its aestheticism alludes to fragmentation/de-fragmentation, space ships, explosion, the big bang....

The recently built Mur Island, in Graz, Austria, 2003, by Acconci Studio is a contemporary version of path and place, common for exchanger and transformer spaces such as complex bridges, train stations, airports. Instead of a functionalist direct link between two points, the project recalls a place which acts as a knot in the middle of the passage.

In the *Design School Zollverein*, in Essen, Germany, 2003, by Leeser Architecture, the building itself becomes a mystic sign and geometric emblem symbolising an endless loop and reflecting very much the current meaning of architecture as creator of artificial corporate identities, logos and urban landmarks.

Michele Saee's *Publicis Drugstore* in Paris, France, 2004, offers an intriguing contemporary use of light, transparency and mirror-effects, evoking spatial illusions, disco- and event-architecture.

The current tendencies could ultimately lead to an architectural non-culture, the results of which we already suffer from and know very well.

"Traveling, you realise that differences are lost: each city takes to resembling all cities, places exchange their form, order, distances, a shapeless dust cloud invades the continents. Your atlas preserves the differences intact: that assortment of qualities which are like letters in a name."[3]

But much more than these examples of 'serious' contemporary architecture, the so-called cosmic element becomes an important asset in tourist marketing. The recently opened Mystery Park in Interlaken, Switzerland is a perfect example of artificially created mysteries. The 'cosmic' element exists in the form of cheap plastic replicas. There is no sense of place making, since the park sits on top of a former military airfield, in full sight of a real mystery, the famous gigantic mountain chain of *Eiger, Mönch und Nonne* and *Jungfrau*, the true representation of a 'sacred place'. Once more, two quotes from Charles Correa.

> Throughout human history, the sky has carried a profound and sacred meaning. Man intuitively perceived it as the abode of the Supernatural. Hence to climb a path to the top of the hill, where the gods dwell, is a paradigm of such mythic power that it has been central to the beliefs of almost every society, since the beginning of time.

> Architecture is never born out of the vacuum. Architecture imperatively has to be an expression of what we believe in—implicitly or explicitly—and of what makes the centre of our life.

During his visit to Switzerland some time ago, Charles Correa spoke to me about the different 'volumes' of the book of history. If I understood him correctly, he said that creating architecture has to begin with 'volume zero', the volume that was never written and will never be written, but still comes before all the other volumes. This volume zero is all about the founding myths in architecture.

Eiger; Mönch, Nonne und Jungfrau.

/ **1.** Le Corbusier, *Ronchamp*, trans J Cullen, Stuttgart: Verlag Gerd Hatje, 1957 (reprint 1975); quote taken from the book jacket.

/ **2.** Le Corbusier, *Notre-Dame-du-Haut, Ronchamp; Inauguration speech, 25 June 1955*: "A sense of the sacred animated our effort. Some things are sacred, others are not, whether they be religious or not."

/ **3.** Calvino, I, *Invisible Cities*, trans W Weaver, San Diego, New York, London, HBJ 1974; p. 137.

All illustrations courtesy of Walter Hunziker.

INDEX

B

C

D

E

F

G

H

I

M

O

P

Q

R

S

T

U

V

W

X

Y

Z

EUROPEAN REGIONAL DEVELOPMENT FUND
MALTA2007-2013

Artifice Press, 298 Regents Park Road, London N3 2SZ, United Kingdom

+44 (0) 20 8371 4047
office@artificeonline.com
www.artificeonline.com

Design: Rachel Pfleger
Editorial Direction: AP Valletta Ltd
Editors: Konrad Buhagiar, Guillaume Dreyfuss, Jens Bruenslow
Translations: Vanessa Eggert, Kristine Eggert

British Library Cataloguing-in-Publication Data.
A CIP record for this book is available from the British Library.

ISBN 978 1 907317 17 0

cover image/ Charles Frederick de Brocktorff, *Ruins of the Principal Altar, in the Little Temple*, National Museum of Archaeology, courtesy of Heritage Malta.

This is an AP Valletta project.

Operational Programme I—Cohesion Policy 2007–2013
Investing in Competitiveness for a Better Quality of Life
Project part-financed by the European Union
European Regional Development Fund (ERDF)
Co-financing rate: 42.5% EU Funds, 7.5% National Funds,
50% Private Funds

Investing in your Future

Artifice